Secret Cinema

Secret Cinema

The Rise and Fall of the Blue Movie

John Baxter

Sticking Place Books
New York

© Sticking Place Books 2024

Designed by Goran Tovilovic

www.stickingplacebooks.com

All rights reserved.
No part of this book may be reproduced, stored in or introduced into a retrieval system, or transmitted, in any form or by any means (electronic, mechanical, photocopying, recording or otherwise) without the written permission of the publishers, except in the case of brief quotations embodied in critical articles or reviews.

ISBN 978-1-942782-79-7

Contents

Introduction	1
1. In the Playpen of the Damned	9
2. Whores and Cinematographers	21
3. From Paris, Under Plain Wrappers	29
4. On the House	41
5. Stags and Smokers	53
6. A Little Bit of What You Fancy	61
7. The Girls Next Door	71
8. The Dark, and Strangers	89
9. Danish Blue	103
10. Mary, Mary, Not Quite…	109
11. Naked Lady Movies	115
12. Behind *Behind the Green Door*	127
13. The Sound of One Hand…	141
14. Cutting *Throat*	155
15. 99^{44}/$_{100}$% Sexy	169
16. Evil	189
17. *Sophistiqué soft*	203
18. Dirty Business	227
19. Media Woman, Media Man	237
20. New Kids on the Block	255
21. Candid Ginger	265

Introduction

> All great things must first wear terrifying and monstrous masks in order to inscribe themselves on the hearts of humanity.
>
> Friedrich Nietzsche

Secret Cinema would not exist had someone in charge of the final banquet at the 45th World Science Fiction Convention not thought it amusing to seat at the same table three authors of novels about meteorites striking the Earth. That's how John (*The Hermes Fall*) Baxter met Jerry (*Lucifer's Hammer*) Pournelle and William (*Shiva Descending*) Rotsler. (With slightly more effort, he could have added Harry "*Skyfall*" Harrison, just a stone's throw away.)

Genial, bearded Bill Rotsler was a regular at these events, admired for his witty science fiction novels and for the illustrations and cartoons he furnished free for fanzine editors. Fewer people, however, knew of the activity that occupied most of his time: adult cinema, or what, back in my native Australia, were called "dirty movies."

Not that we saw many of them. On islands such as Australia where points of entry are few, censorship flourishes out of simple geography; it's easy to do, so it's done. Some cuts to films showed the niggling precision of those physicists who assay cigarette ash and compute the weight of the smoke. A couple of frames trimmed from *Darling* saved us from a subliminal flash of Julie Christie's nipples as she fell forward onto a bed, and *BUtterfield 8*, while retaining Elizabeth Taylor's confession to Eddie Fisher that she'd been molested as a child, omitted her admission that she enjoyed it.

And yet... occasionally, a censor, drowsing at his desk, admitted a glimpse of the sensual world outside. I was fourteen when I saw a British film called *The Seekers*, in

Elizabeth Taylor in *BUtterfield 8*.

which Jack Hawkins and Glynis Johns struggle to settle New Zealand and confer on the Maoris the dubious benefits of Christianity. There was blood galore, but no sex – until, that is, Hawkins encountered Moana, wife of the local chief, fishing with a spear by torchlight.

We first saw Laya Raki, who played Moana, up to her neck in water. As she waded, smiling, towards Hawkins, the level descended to her shoulders, then her chest… We waited for the cut, but it never came. Hardly believing our good fortune, we gaped as her magnificent breasts emerged, beaded with water, from the Pinewood Pacific.

In retrospect, the reason for this lapse was obvious. Moana was a Maori. And, as we could see from the *National Geographic* and other magazines, the taboo against nudity appeared to apply only to white women. Had the censor known that Laya was born Brunhilde Marie Jörns in Hamburg, Germany, and possessed only a dash of Asian blood, this golden moment in my sexual development would never have taken place.

Years later, I met Ms. Raki at the opening of the Sydney Film Festival. True to form, she had dressed for maximum effect. As columnist Earl Wilson said of her gowns, "she looks like she only wears the zipper and has forgotten the material."

Our guest of honour that year was the director Josef von Sternberg.

"If I had known you would be here," Laya told him, flustered at meeting the director who made Marlene Dietrich a legend, "I would have worn something more..." She fluttered her fingers apologetically over her breasts, barely less exposed than in *The Seekers*. "...Sternbergian."

Sternberg's face was level with Laya's nipples, but he rose to the occasion.

"Not at all, madam" he said. "I have seen naked women before."

And, taking a chiffon scarf that dangled from the shoulder strap of the dress, he draped it across her cleavage, as one might hide something unpleasant brought in by the cat.

Bill Rotsler and I chuckled over such stories once I relocated in California. By then, a back injury had confined him to his bungalow in the sun-blasted sprawl of the San Fernando Valley. Strewn around him was the detritus of his careers as glamour photographer, magazine publisher, fan artist, science fiction author – and producer, writer and occasional performer in erotic films. Framed nude photographs decorated the walls, and filing cabinets held decades of cartoons and designs. Many of the pictures, however, hung crooked, and the cabinets overflowed. Drifts of his magazine *Adam Film World* sagged across the floor, piling up against cartons of video cassettes. Nobody had vacuumed for a decade; one walked on cartoons, photographs, unanswered letters.

Even more dispiriting than his incapacity was his failing potency. Surrounded by images of naked women ecstatically embracing trees or exposing themselves to the desert sun, he embodied – to me anyway – Dylan Thomas's "old ramrod, dying of women." The Sixties had been his golden era. "Sex was so easy and so common and so free! There were so many women. And I was in the business of naked ladies! Y'know, photographing them in movies and in stills." Runaway teenagers or frustrated young wives arrived by dozens at his studio and those of other makers of sex films, the trademark of their rebellion the "midnight haircut," evidence of a hated hairstyle hacked off in front of the mirror before they packed a bag and took the first Greyhound to LA.

Laya Raki in *The Seekers*.

Bill condensed his intimate knowledge of sex films into a scholarly but witty study, *Contemporary Erotic Cinema*. The fact that he had thought seriously about the medium set him apart from most people in the X-rated film community, few of them noted for insight.

To Bill, the variety and complexity of erotic films, as reflected in which of them people chose to watch, appeared limitless, particularly since their appeal changed according to the person viewing them, each bringing to a film his or her own unexpressed desires.

"You see a man and a woman balling," he said. "You know nothing about them except, say, they're brother and sister. No, no. I made a terrible mistake. They're not. He's blind and she's being nice to him. Uh, no, that's another film. Sorry about that. They're really long-lost lovers. Oh, no, that's another movie too...

"You can go on like that, with the same couple, but just switching their characters. Each time, the context in which you put them alters your feelings. If it was brother and sister, or son and daughter, or father and mother – none of those may excite you. But it's a hell of a lot different if it's, say, a student and his teacher." Or, for that matter, husband and wife. British journalist Simon Hoggart was startled by an X-rated film in which actors indulged in steamy sex while playing a married couple, something so uncommon it almost seemed like a perversion. He imagined a customer murmuring furtively to the video store clerk, "Do you have something... er, *matrimonial*?"

To eke out his pension, Bill odd-jobbed round the edges of the sex business. For the 1-900 phone sex industry, he applied his knowledge of erotic genres to inventing personalities for the women taking the calls, assigning them biographies and sexual preferences that personalised the experience for each client – and kept him talking longer.

He also designed and created the Heart-Ons. These heart-shaped wooden plaques were presented each Valentine's Day by the X-Rated Film Critics' Organisation for excellence in what was then fashionable to call "Adult Movies." The awards were only given for a few years during

William Rotsler.

the late Eighties, and the 1989 ceremony, which I attended, would be the last. I covered it for *Playboy,* my article too limited a canvas to incorporate everything I'd learned from Bill and others. Hence *Secret Cinema,* which explored the history of film erotica from the earliest days to that time. But the juggernaut of video porn was already starting to efface the very concept of adult films. The title change imposed by *Playboy* on my article about the Heart-On ceremony should have warned me. What I called *In the Playpen of the Damned* appeared as *Night of a Thousand Orifices.*

I had no sense that I would be writing an obituary, or that the period between 1969 and 1990, when I did my research, would come to be known as The Golden Age of erotic film. I put the book aside, meaning to finish it when the effects of the VHS revolution were clearer, but instead left the United States to live in France, and moved on to writing about less controversial topics, including biographies of Federico Fellini and Luis Buñuel; subjects of such significance, wiser heads suggested, that publishing *Secret Cinema* could only impair my credibility. (As I learned later, Fellini and Buñuel, as well as Woody Allen, Stanley Kubrick and others about whom I wrote, knew and often appreciated film porn; some even flirted with the idea of creating it.)

Each new project pushed this one further back on the shelf, until it became little more than a pleasant memory. So why publish now? Partly it's the encouragement of such productions as HBO's 2017 series *The Deuce,* produced by and starring Maggie Gyllenhaal as a street sex worker who becomes a star and eventual director/producer of X-rated films. For the first time, the commercial cinema seems ready to acknowledge the parenthood of its bastard child.

Also, at times of seismic shifts in society, it can be instructive to look back. Vaudeville lasted for seventy years, to be replaced by the cinema, which, seventy years later, was supplanted by television. It's now seventy years since the emergence of television, and we face a new world of streaming, with its promise of near-infinite visual stimulation, under the ambiguous management of artificial intelligence. A suitable time, one might think, to consider one of the oldest of all movie genres and where it belongs in this nervous new world.

1
In the Playpen of the Damned

Valentine's Day, 1989. From the offices along Sunset Boulevard, the picture windows offered a classic LA view. No palms, no lawns, no vivid cerise cascades of bougainvillaea: leave those to the residential suburbs closer to the Pacific. Here, in the DMZ between Beverly Hills and Hollywood, the landscape was architectural. Both inside their air-conditioned office suites and on the advertising their façades thrust before us, the monuments were all to bad taste and the hard sell. Movies interfaced with the music industry, mass-market paperbacks with the trashy end of fashion. On The Rox disco, Tower Records' sprawling warehouse store, Bill Gazzarri's Rock Club, with its giant self-aggrandising portrait of its pouchy proprietor, and his boast of the groups launched here... all gone now, and nothing to show they ever existed...

...because in Hollywood each season brings a gaudier image, a louder voice. In 1989, it hovered above the Strip. Higher, brighter, more strident than anything else in sight, a billboard trumpeted the one-woman junk-lit industry of Jackie Collins, author of *Hollywood Husbands* and *Once is Not Enough*. She stared out over her domain, ten times larger than life. Underneath her image was the rubric of her reign. *More Than a Hundred Million Sold.*

As the sun sank, Sunset came alive with black leather, spandex, studs. At Hollywood's smartest restaurants, Le Dôme and Spago, black stretch limos queued decorously to drop off their clients. Downhill, closer to Tower Records, Harleys and Porsches growled and purred as, twittering like parakeets, valley girls from Sherman Oaks and Encino, asses and tits compressed into tank tops and jeans tight and hard as lacquer, jostled for attention as they gathered for a night of disco. Manes of moussed hair – male and female – shimmered in the streetlights, and down the gutters rolled dusty skeins of tape from gutted cassettes: Sunset

Tumbleweed. As if at a signal, Jackie's billboard ignited, neon outlining the imperious Collins silhouette. Showtime.

"And now, for your entertainment pleasure, Barbii!"

The star of *Barbii Unleashed* and *Back Door to Hollywood* threw her leg over the wooden bannister of the staircase leading to the stage at Gazzarri's and slithered towards us.

Light shimmered from her sequined G-string. Sweat glittered in the pores of her breasts as she prowled the fug of smoke, breath and gossip, and the roar from the bar muted to a whisper. Even the pros recognised a class act when they saw one. And that was just what, by the not-terribly-elevated standards of the movie business, we were here to view – a class act. For we'd gathered to witness the fifth annual – and, as it would turn out, the final presentation by America's X-Rated Film Critics of their awards for erotic excellence, a moment that represented, better than any other, the high-water mark of popular and critical acceptance of pornographic films.

Half the industry had turned out that night. Among those beaming their approval of Barbii as she strutted her stuff were actors known around the world under the *noms de porn* of John Leslie, Joey Silvera, Randy West, Randy Spears and Ray Victory. All were gold medallists of contemporary bedroom athletics. Every face wore the look of smug confidence unique to men with penises the size of cucumbers.

They and their female co-stars were here to acknowledge that the Heart Ons, unlike the rival prizes of the Association of Adult Film Producers, didn't simply reflect which company spent most on promotion or handed out more jobs. "The XRCO honours the heat and the meat," veteran porn performer Nina Hartley told me succinctly at the bar before the event. "They vote on sex scenes rather than set decoration." Tom Byron, winner of the night's award for Best Sex Scene, agreed. "It's the only honest award show in town."

Barbii loped off stage, to be replaced by mistress of ceremonies Nina Hartley. Demure in a green harem costume, she incongruously cradled a teddy bear. A prime mover behind the female porn performers' sororal group The Pink Ladies, Hartley enjoyed a privileged role in the business, and a reputation for good sense and high principles. A registered nurse and famous proselytiser for the extended sexual family, she shared her life with a man and a woman, both of whom she called her "wives." Another adult movie star, Jerry Butler, called her "the earth mother of erotica."

When Artie Mitchell, one of the producers of the pioneering *Behind the Green Door*, was murdered by the other producer, his brother, it was Hartley who stepped in as headline stripper at their O'Farrell Street theatre in San Francisco, and showed that the business stood solid behind its colleagues. One inspiration for the porn star Amber Waves, played by Julianne Moore in Paul Thomas Anderson's *Boogie Nights*, Hartley has a small role in the film as the promiscuous wife of cameraman William H. Macy, ready to spread her legs for anyone anywhere.

Introducing Hartley, XRCO spokesman Bill Margold, producer of, writer of and occasional performer in hardcore, identified the bear she carried. "Mr. Stubbs," he explained, was "the mascot of the X-rated industry; the emblem of the playpen of the damned where recess is 24 hours a day and the bell never rings." After that, he announced the night's first presenter – "our Heart-On girl, the star of *Dreams in the Forbidden Zone*, Champagne."

For the next hour, it was the usual game of celebrity musical chairs as the prize winners were announced. Champagne handed over to Aja and Aja to Laurel Canyon and Laurel Canyon to Ariel Knight and Ariel Knight to Randy West (Best Sizzling Support Male) who thanked "all the men in this business who've made it easy for me – and all the women, who've made it hard for me."

Awards went to films whose titles, as was traditional, traded on Hollywood successes. There was an X-rated *Beauty and the Beast*, a *Very Dirty Dancing*, even a *Last Temptations of Kristi*. Tried and true come-ons, however, weren't totally abandoned: also nominated were *Loose Ends IV* and *Talk Dirty To Me VI*.

Bill Gazzarri's Rock Club, Sunset Boulevard.

One soon noticed a division in style between male and female stars. For the guys, it was just another business evening, with no nonsense expected or countenanced. Collecting the Best Sizzling Support Female award on behalf of a friend, one sullen stud even used the platform to pass on a personal message. "I owe Tracy Adams $900 and Joey Silvera $600 from when I was busted a year ago," he announced in a surly tone. "You'll get it. I don't want to hear any more comments about that."

Reflecting the mood, the men had dressed way down, with hardly a tie or suit in sight. In suede jacket and open-necked shirt, John Leslie, winner of best director and best film for *The Cat Woman*, might have just stopped by on his way to the supermarket for a bag of bagels.

By contrast, the women, bedizened in red and blue leather minis from Long Beach Leather, just up the road on Sunset, with black lace bras revealed by slit-to-the-navel jackets, scampered on stage, hugged and hopped and squealed their appreciation.

As brave and bright as they might appear under the lights, the ladies betrayed, especially around the eyes, a desperate fatigue. Yet they giggled and embraced and, pressing the heart-shaped awards to their tight tummies, grinned until their lips slid off their teeth. It was showtime, and if they didn't play their part, someone out there in the smoke and shadows might lean over to a friend and say "Christ, she looks like shit. Doesn't she look like shit?"

Arriving at Gazzarri's, one expected a protest at the door; pickets perhaps from AIDS activists or radical feminists. The only impediment to our entry, however, was self-appointed guardian Jim Holliday, historian of the XRCO, who levied an impromptu $20 from every member of the press.

To their chagrin, anti-AIDS campaigners found little to attack in the porn industry. A February 1992 article in *Premiere* magazine which listed hundreds of film industry victims identified only four from the porn world: John Holmes, actor/director Joseph Yale, and performers Beau Matthews and Larry White. Even adding contested cases, the incidence of AIDS in adult film was minimal. (Herpes, on the other hand, was almost epidemic. Jerry Butler estimated 70% of porn performers were infected.)

Feminists had been equally disarmed by a female enthusiasm for video porn. Editor and author Nancy Friday, doyenne of erotica since the success of *My Secret Garden* and *Forbidden Flowers*, put the point succinctly in her collection of fantasies *Women On Top*:

> What is generally overlooked is that the great majority of women in burlesque houses and in the pages of *Playboy* and *Penthouse* have chosen to be there. These women like to take their clothes off and spread their legs in front of an audience. You don't see big-breasted women with great legs picketing burlesque houses or joining their petition-waving sisters on the street corners, crying "They made me do it!" No one made them do it. That is probably what is driving the angry feminists crazy – not rage at the entrepreneurs but at the naked women who dared to break

> The Rules against exhibitionism on which
> all girls are raised. How dare they! How
> dare they get into that power all little girls
> swore at mother's knee never to use, the
> power of their naked breasts, the hint of
> what lies beneath the dirndl skirt, between
> the carefully crossed legs!

This simplistic statement of a complex situation had, nevertheless, its elements of truth. Tales of women coerced into porn films were laughably wide of the mark, a throwback to Twenties fantasies of white slavery where convent girls, shot full of dope in the local Bijou, awoke in a brothel in Valparaiso. In the real world, women competed vigorously to crash porn films. Only the handful who showed a facility for the life made the grade. They worked hard but were paid well; more than $1000 a day at that time, plus, in the case of the better-organised, a percentage of the gross. Women in porn – an indigestible fact for feminists – earned triple the salary of their male counterparts. "Women in porn sell their bodies," argued the feminists. "They're ours to sell," responded groups such as The Pink Ladies, "and we make a big profit."

On the downside, porn was run largely by men you would not want to date your daughter. Some had connections to organised crime. Drugs were common. But this was true of the film industry in general, and of music, advertising, professional sports. Nobody said porn was a nice business. But nobody *forced* anyone to participate.

An hour into the presentations, it was time for another break. "Hyapatia Lee loves to dance," cooed Nina Hartley, "and she's going to dance for us tonight."

One of the most strikingly beautiful women in the business, Lee, real name Vicki Lynch, and wife of porn director Bud Lee, attributed her mass of black hair and dusky skin to a Cherokee princess somewhere in her genome. She danced, as she did everything, with a stern authority, breasts swinging, haunches working. Yet even nude except for sling-back sandals and a G-string, she was oddly un-erotic. I couldn't shake off the fact that, half an hour before, I was chatting to her and her husband, all business, at the bar.

"The money is definitely still there," Bud Lee agreed when I asked him about that week's forecast of slumping porn profits in *Variety*. He was casually knowledgeable on foreign sales, cable TV and the growing rental market.

What about the moral backlash? Despite constitutional safeguards for freedom of speech, some states were contemplating legislation to curb erotic film. Britain had banned it totally. Unmoved by a well-publicised visit Down Under in 1981 by porn star Ginger Lynn to promote the anti-censorship cause, Australia too followed suit, though due to an ironic technicality, porn was still legal in one state – the tiny Australian Capital Territory that surrounds Canberra. As a result, the fourth largest manufacturing industry of the national capital was the copying of erotic videos, ten thousand of which were shipped every week.

Lee was unconcerned at threats of restriction. "The most money was made in this business when it was pushed underground," he said. "Some of these people..." He looked around the room, coldly surveying his colleagues, "they might be sitting here saying, 'Yeah, go ahead. Do it. That's when we made all our money. 'Cause we can charge a lot for it.'" He was articulating a truism of porn. Twenty years before, a porn distributor told British film censor John Trevelyan that he feared the anti-porn crusade then being led by the Catholic peer Lord Longford because of its inevitable pro-porn backlash. "I have an uneasy feeling that the end result will be to make this stuff legal," said the producer, "and that wouldn't suit me at all."

Hyapatia brought her act to a climax and the audience rose to its feet in appreciation. But despite the atmosphere of genial self-congratulation, there were silent presences here tonight whom nobody cared to acknowledge.

One was serial murderer Ted Bundy, electrocuted in Florida the month before for the murder of innumerable women. On the night before his execution, Bundy blamed pornography for his crimes; every sex killer, he claimed, shared his addiction. With its force as a near-deathbed confession, the statement won new support for the anti-erotic film movement.

So did the apostasy of porn's most famous actresses. People who once knew and employed her preferred to not even speak her name, but Jim Holliday invoked it now from the Gazzarri stage in announcing the year's inductees to the organisation's Hall of Fame. "There are always four factors that determine a person's entrance qualifications," he said

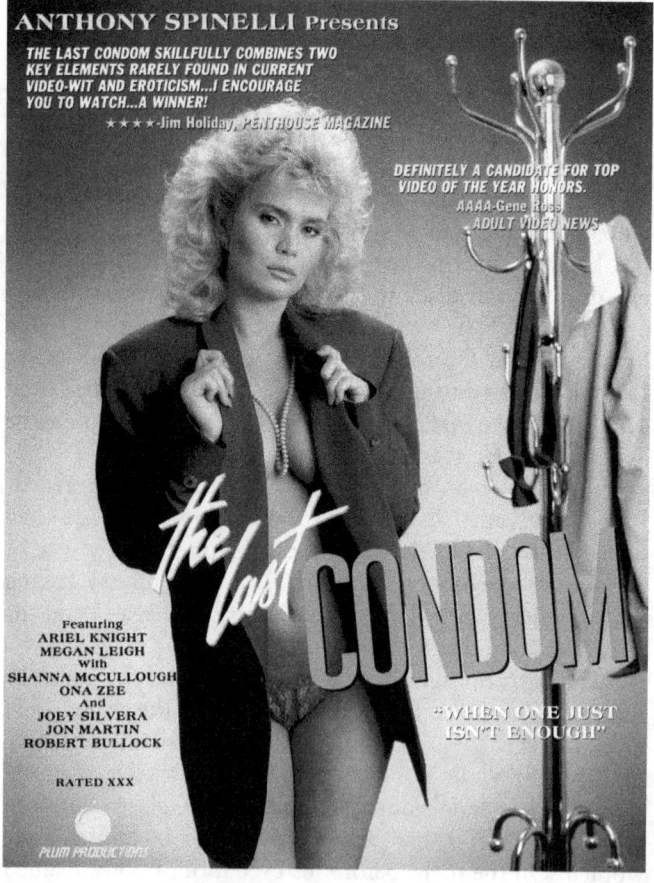

Ariel Knight in *The Last Condom*.

belligerently. "The quantity of films, the quality of films, the impact on the industry – and the attitude of the performer. Linda Lovelace is better known than any porn performer in the history of the business, but with her attitude she ain't *ever* gettin' in."

There was general applause. This wasn't the night to contemplate *Ordeal* and *Out of Bondage*, the ghosted memoirs in which porn's most famous star claimed she had been terrorised, sometimes at gunpoint, into performing in *Deep Throat* and scores of other porn films. It was a night instead for solidarity, and the affirmation of what the X-rated cinema liked to think it stood for – health, beauty, sexual freedom. And the first recipient of a Hall of Fame Award for the night provided it.

Holliday was ecstatic in introducing him. "The first hard dick in the entire history of this business! He made 54 films from 1969 to *Sodom and Gomorrah* in '74. But everybody will forever know him as the guy from *Green Door*. Ladies and gentlemen, wearing the same *Green Door* outfit, Mr. George S. McDonald!"

McDonald diffidently descended the stairs, a tall, balding man, dressed – as advertised by Holliday – in a double-breasted blue blazer and grey slacks that shrieked "Sixties." He took his plaque and stood in the spotlight, apparently overawed by the crowd, the smoke and heat, the roar from the bar.

"It may not seem like a big deal to all of you," he said almost inaudibly, then paused. There was a moment of embarrassment – until, silently, his authority began to dominate the crowd. A few hisses for silence turned into a sustained appeal for quiet. "You don't know what it's like unless you've been under 50,000 watts of light,' he continued. "It's the hardest thing you can do on the planet."

At this, there was heartfelt applause from the room, with no hoots or whistles of mock derision. Almost everyone here knew *exactly* what he meant. As the uproar faded, McDonald looked down at his plaque. "Whatever it is to the rest of you this evening," he said, "it's a big deal to me. I appreciate it."

A roar of approval accompanied McDonald as he left the stage, followed by a perceptible lull in the level of conversation. The element of seriousness he had introduced was hard to dispel. Making films about sex was not much different to sex itself. To do it well, one must enter a private world. And anyone who opens the door admits a blast of cold reality.

Everyone in Gazzarri's tonight knew they had only a brief hold on their notoriety. Porn fame was fickle and porn money famous for slipping through one's fingers, frittered away on good coke or bad boyfriends. Few X-rated stars could act well enough to find work in the mainstream industry. Those who tried, such as Marilyn Chambers, Ginger Lynn and Traci Lords, soon ran out of roles. Others returned to stripping, or slipped back into prostitution. Some married. A few looked for work outside showbusiness – with dire results. The gossip writer for that week's issue of the trade magazine *Hot Times* noted, "While stopped at a light the other night, I saw ex-porn queen Nikki Charm waiting for the bus. The girl was dressed like the last secretary going to work!" What put a true chill on the item was the thought of anyone in LA except maids and pool men using public transport. (In 2002, Charm, real name Shannon Eaves, was sentenced to five years in prison on charges of burglary and car theft.)

The presentations continued on stage, but most of the action was at the bar. There was some talk about the use of condoms. Nobody was enthusiastic, at least not among the men. "They shoot for shit," someone said. And it's true that a penis cloaked in the white caul of a Trojan was no pretty sight. Female stars, however, were bitter about the general refusal to employ them. Annette Haven, with long, straight hair, porcelain white skin and a look of well-bred disdain, was one of the most beautiful of the Seventies porn actresses. She came closest to having a feature movie career when Brian De Palma considered casting her as the star of *Body Double*. "I will not put my life on the line for a porno film," she said. "Yet, for some reason the producers will not, with few exceptions, protect their actors. What is so frightening about the sight of a rubber? I personally will fuck the brains out of any guy in a movie wearing one."

That double standard was on display in the night's big winner, *The Cat Woman*, John Leslie's stylish rip-off of *Cat People*. The producers inserted an announcement before the film. "We highly recommend that individuals follow the Surgeon General's accepted guidelines for 'safe sex,' which are monogamy, and/or abstinence or, at a minimum, the use of a condom combined with a selective choice of sexual partners." Almost everyone in *The Cat Woman* shared sexual partners. Nobody wore a condom.

Towards midnight, the crowd was thinning. Those revellers who remained looked as weary as the repertoire of the band, which didn't run much beyond *Tequila* and the *Peter Gunn* theme.

All over the United States, with the children and, in some but not all cases, their wives in bed, men were slipping X-rated cassettes into VCRs and settling back to watch Jerry Butler and Ginger Lynn, Barbii and Champagne and John Leslie display their undoubted skills. In New York (but not in California, except on the softcore *Playboy Channel*) one could get the same material on broadcast TV. Late-night hardcore screenings and shows such as Al Goldstein's Channel J *Midnight Blue* were an easy target for the Moral Majority, though its dislike wasn't shared by the mass audience they claimed to represent. In 1985, Manhattan Cable, owned by Time Inc. offered its 228,000 subscribers the option of a "lock box" which would prevent kids from watching Channel J. Only nineteen were installed.

Back at Gazzarri's, things on stage were getting a little riotous. A stream of people climbed to the backstage dressing rooms, to descend shortly after, visibly more cheerful. Two well-known starlets came on stage, hand in hand, obviously gay and even more obviously stoned, to present an award. A Hall of Fame inductee announced that, as a committed homosexual, she was now producing female gay erotica using only lesbian talent. As if to affirm solidarity with her, three women playfully clustered at the edge of the stage and started to fool around, plucking at one another's clothes and giggling. The photographers homed on them like sharks.

Guests were already drifting into the chill of Sunset Boulevard. Hyapatia and Bud Lee had to work. At 6 a.m. she, like many of these people, would be submitting to full body make-up and the first grinding encounter of the day – though only after all her co-performers had produced a current AIDS test certificate. After three days, the Lees, having completed the film, would fly back to their Indiana horse ranch for a well-deserved rest.

But behind us, in the playpen of the damned, a few tots were still partying. Richard Pacheco, accepting a Hall of Fame award for his role in the classic *Easy*, thanked co-star Jessie St James, "who gave me a blow job in the parking lot the night before our scene because I was so afraid I wouldn't be able to get my little *schwantz* to work."

Dirt. It's an arty job. But someone has to do it.

2
Whores and Cinematographers

"Not many people I know carry their end of the conversation when I want to talk about water deliveries," wrote Joan Didion in *Holy Water*, a reflection on the mystical significance to her of the network of canals and dams that irrigate the gardens of Los Angeles.

It was the same talking about film pornography, even to other people in the film business. Everyone had seen at least one porn film, of course. Their defence, however, was Guilty, But With an Explanation. They were drunk. Friends persuaded them. They did it on a bet. They couldn't think of an excuse to leave. As for the experience, they insisted that it offered little stimulation. The actresses – nobody could ever remember names – looked like whores and drug addicts; the men kept their socks on and had pimply arses. The experience, if it wasn't squalid, was tedious. They were, they'll tell you, bored.

Others, more honest, admitted their fascination. Federico Fellini amassed a large collection after being introduced by another aficionado, Groucho Marx. Michel Simon, star of Jean Renoir's *Boudu Saved From Drowning* and Jean Vigo's *L'Atalante*, had one of the world's largest collections of erotica. Stanley Kubrick discussed at length with author Terry Southern, himself a devotee of X-rated movies and a friend of *Hustler* publisher Larry Flynt, the possibility of directing a big budget porn feature. Though the film never got made, it inspired Southern to write his novel *Blue Movie* in which a world famous director, based on Kubrick, accepts the challenge.

The French Surrealists, who respected spontaneity, relished the innocence of what their makers called *radiants*. René Crevel wrote a script for a porn comedy, Paul Éluard regularly attended screenings, and urged his wife Gala (later to become the partner of Salvador Dalí) to accompany him. Luis Buñuel discussed with Marcel Duchamp and Fernand

Léger the idea of making a porn film, and contemplated, as an act of Surrealist mischief, stealing an innocuous documentary being shown at a Parisian cinema to an audience of children and substituting the porn short *Sister Vaseline*.

Plenty of stars rubbed shoulders, and much else, in softcore films. Willem Dafoe, no stranger to the wild life, has a small scene in an S&M club (fully clothed) in the 1983 softcore *New York Nights*. Kevin Costner did his best to keep his first film appearance in the 1974 *Sizzle Beach* off the screen, only to see it resurrected in 1986 after he had begun to get starring roles. In the 1970 *A Party at Kitty and Studs*, for which he was reputedly paid $200, a bare-arsed Sylvester Stallone thrashed an equally undressed girl, then flung himself on her. The film was exhumed in 1978 and reissued as *The Italian Stallion*, with much footage missing and a commentary added. Told that complete copies traded for tens of thousands of dollars, Stallone offered, for that kind of money, to visit the buyers and re-enact his role in person.

Struggling to make a name as a singer in New York in the Seventies, Madonna posed for nude shots and starred in the softcore feature *A Certain Sacrifice*, directed on a $20,000 shoestring by Stephen Jon Lewicki. The singer played a tough Manhattanite living in a ménage with three "sex slaves." When she is raped in a restaurant toilet, they take revenge. Madonna tried strenuously to keep the film out of circulation, even taking Lewicki to court to overturn the release she had signed in 1980. The judge declined to intervene, and Lewicki made a fortune selling copies at $59.95 each.

Early in the 1990s, the industry at large began to show a serious interest in porn. In May 1989, at Cannes, Palmes d'Or were won by director Steven Soderbergh and his star James Spader for *sex, lies and videotape*, in which Spader played a man who records the sexual confessions of women, then masturbates to them. The following summer, the film succeeded massively on its United States release. In February 1990, in Hollywood, director John Waters announced his new film *Cry Baby* would feature former porn star Traci Lords.

Some stars were more intimately involved. In June 1990 in Wentzville, Mississippi, the Drug Enforcement Agency raided the estate of rock pioneer Chuck Berry and seized drugs, cash and homemade porn videos. In March 1990, Rod Lowe, Brat Pack star of *St Elmo's Fire* and *About Last Night*, was convicted of videotaping sex acts in an Atlanta, Georgia hotel room with two under-aged girls. (In August 1990, *Bad Influence*, a new feature by Curtis Hanson, featured an unprincipled character who secretly tapes his friend with a woman and plays the tape at his engagement party. The victim was James Spader, of *sex, lies and videotape*. The joker was Rob Lowe.) In April 1991, comedian Paul Reubens – aka Pee Wee Herman – was arrested in a Miami porn cinema and charged with masturbating while watching a hardcore film. In 1995, Disney Studios was embarrassed when the director of its new film *Powder*, Victor Salva, was revealed to be a convicted child molester, when a video he had made of himself performing oral sex on a twelve-year old boy came to light.

In December 1990, under the headline "She Can Sleep With Any Woman She Wants," trash tabloid *The Globe* published a report on actor Charlie Sheen and his new girlfriend, porn star Ginger Lynn. The report did neither Sheen nor Lynn much harm, Even the revelation a few years later that Sheen was one of the best clients of Hollywood madame Heidi Fleiss merely added to his box office appeal. As for Lynn, when Spanish director Pedro Almodóvar's film *Tie Me Up Tie Me Down* featured Victoria Abril as a softcore sex film actress, the film magazine *Premiere* commissioned a review from an expert – Ginger herself.

Did any star or personality appear in hardcore? Linda Lovelace claimed that the extensive porn film collection of *Playboy* entrepreneur Hugh Hefner contained films featuring people who would later become famous, but names no names. Marilyn Monroe was optimistically identified in some Fifties porn films, including one known as *The Apple-Knockers and the Coke*, in which a young blonde tickles her

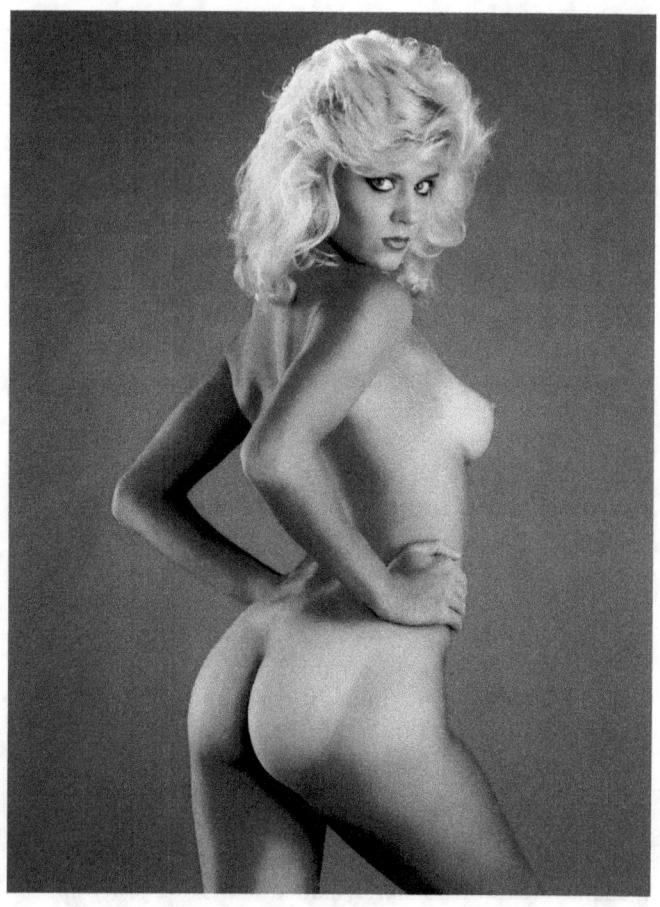

Ginger Lynn.

breasts with the leaves of a plant and then masturbates with an apple and a Coke bottle. The actress was, however, not Monroe but her lookalike, 1954 *Playboy* Playmate Arlene Hunter. Other films rumoured to contain MM actually featured stripper Candy Barr. While it was common knowledge that, in her early days, Monroe circulated promiscuously among Hollywood executives, most people dismissed the possibility of any Monroe sex film, only to be confounded in 2011 by the discovery of a few minutes of her demonstrating her fellating skills.

The low technical quality of most porn prints encouraged misidentification. Among the flickering footage in underground circulation is a scene of a man who may be silent star Jack Pickford, brother of Mary Pickford, being fellated by a cow. In another, homosexual acts in a Hollywood park purport to feature Chuck Connors, star of Fifties TV Westerns who graduated to action roles in movie thrillers.

The star most confidently identified as having played in porn was Joan Crawford. A plump and freckled teenager working as a $20 a week burlesque dancer in Chicago in 1924, she was said to have eked out her wages by posing nude and acting in such stag films as *Velvet Lips*, *Coming Home*, *She Shows Him How* and, most famous of all, *The Casting Couch*.

In *The Casting Couch*, Crawford (or her lookalike) plays a starlet auditioning for a producer. He asks her to model in a bathing suit, then peeks at her through the keyhole as she changes. When he bursts in and tries to rape her, she throws him out. Her attitude changes, however, after she reads a book called *How To Become A Movie Star*. When the producer reappears, she's more than obliging; as the final title puts it, after lively exhibitions of fellatio, and of sex both standing up and then recumbent on the couch of the title, "The only way to become a star is to get under a good director and work your way up."

Crawford never admitted having made these films, a line to which her biographers have staunchly clung. Film authority Arthur J. Knight, who wrote *Playboy*'s history of sex movies and advised Hugh Hefner on purchases for his library, insists that Hefner, obviously any vendor's first stop, was never offered verifiable Crawford porn. He also dates *The Casting Couch* to around 1919, when the actress would still have been in pigtails. Nevertheless, persistent rumours of a porn past haunted Crawford. Nude stills from her pre-film career were widely circulated. For twenty years, she and her studios bought up copies of the films until it became evident that, given a good internegative and an obliging laboratory, the supply was infinite.

A handful of porn stars made it to the big screen. During the Eighties, Ginger Lynn and Traci Lords migrated from porn to mainstream movies, in both cases without conspicuous success. Marilyn Chambers had a small role in *The Owl and the Pussycat* before her porn career, and afterwards as the star of David Cronenberg's *Rabid*. Sybil Danning, the busty Valkyrie of *Battle Beyond the Stars*, Roger Corman's 1980 science fiction version of *The Magnificent Seven*, also played in softcore, both in her native Denmark and in West Germany – appearances she later tried vigorously to deny. Georgina Spelvin, star of *The Devil in Miss Jones* and scores of other porn films, has a cameo in *Police Academy* administering a blow job to George Gaynes under the podium while he addresses some visiting dignitaries.

For most, however, their excursions outside porn ended in failure. When a performer chose a porn career, it was generally an acknowledgment that every other route to fame was blocked by a lack of talent. The majority, however, didn't look for careers elsewhere. Celebrities in their own right, they were more than happy to make their lives, and their fortunes, within it. And why not, when the world seemed to be embracing erotic cinema and its protagonists?

In June 1987, Italian porn star Ilona Staller, aka La Cicciolina – The Dumpling – was elected a member of the Italian Parliament for the Radical Party. In August 1991, American NeoPop artist Jeff Koons, invited to exhibit at the Venice Biennale, presented a series of tableaux showing him naked and erotically entwined with his new wife: Ilona Staller. In September, among the celebrity performers on the catwalk in Paris displaying the autumn collection of Jean-Paul Gaultier, next to Ivana Trump and Madonna, was American star of bi-sexual porn, Jeff Stryker.

If porn made news, the reverse was also the case. On June 23, 1993, Lorena, the wife of John Wayne Bobbitt, severed his penis after an argument, drove off and threw the organ out the window at a nearby intersection. Recovered, it was successfully reattached. Ex-porn stud and sometime filmmaker Ron Jeremy approached Bobbitt, until then a nightclub bouncer, to star in *John Wayne Bobbitt Uncut*, in which the victim proved his total recovery by making desultory love to eight women. Premiered, with notable *chutzpah*, in a hired theatrette at the Academy of Motion Picture Arts and Sciences in Los Angeles, home of the Oscars, Jeremy's film became a major success in video.

The same year, Nicholson Baker, highly regarded author of *The Mezzanine* and *U and I*, published *Vox*, a book taken up entirely with a phone-sex conversation and the masturbatory activities of the two people involved. He followed it in 1994 with *The Fermata*, about a man who uses his ability to freeze time to satisfy his sexual fantasies. Both books were widely, if not always approvingly reviewed by the serious literary press. Madonna's 1994 video *Erotica* featured images drawn from porn film. Some of them appeared in Steven Meisel's album of erotic photographs of the star, called simply *Sex,* one of the most sought-after titles among rare book collectors. In 1995 two new films, *Amateur* by Hal Hartley and Woody Allen's *Mighty Aphrodite*, featured porn performers as major characters without subjecting them to any particular censure, and the acclaimed 1998 *Boogie Nights* celebrated the life and death of a male porn star based on the ill-fated John Holmes. Brian De Palma tried to recruit Annette Haven for *Body Double* and Philip Kaufman, seeking a credible performance in a sexual exhibition at a Parisian brothel in *Henry and June*, coaxed Brigitte Lahaie, France's premiere porn actress, out of retirement.

Belatedly, critics caught up with porn. In February 1995, London's National Film Theatre devoted a season to softcore porn director Russ Meyer, who was interviewed on stage as part of a personal-appearance series that had included Bette Davis, Laurence Olivier and Graham Greene. Shortly after, the Cinematheque Française in Paris, cradle of the *nouvelle vague*, offered a brief season of films on *La Orgie*, including a screening of *Behind the Green Door* and *Deep Throat*.

At the height of their popularity, when the conventional American cinema produced fewer than two hundred films a year, the X-rated industry put out three hundred new titles and circulated anything from ten thousand to fifty thousand copies of each. Sixty percent of American video stores carried porn. For them, it provided more than twenty percent of their total income. In 1995, sex videos in the US alone were a $3 billion a year business.

Who watched? A lot of us, though we didn't always admit it. A third of porn cassettes were borrowed by male/female couples, only a quarter by men alone. Why did we watch? Theories proliferated. In the AIDS generation, some asserted, the safest sex was the sex that needs no partners. "Don't knock masturbation," quipped Woody Allen. "It's sex with someone I love." Maybe, rival authorities remarked, the risk of infection made us all voyeurs. Or were we, others question, voyeurs already, and AIDS simply provided a pretext?

For someone seriously interested in cinema, pornographic movies posed a problem, simply because they failed to satisfy almost every definition of a "good" film. Except in the Seventies, when director Gerard Damiano was indulged by an industry still dizzy at the success of his *Deep Throat*, there were no porn tragedies, few porn dramas, only a handful of porn thrillers. Laboured parodies and domestic comedy/romance were the norm. Adult film aspired to, but only intermittently achieved, the bland visual style and undemanding parade of incident characteristic of American daytime soap opera.

Yet the pedigree of film pornography is as long as that of serious cinema – in fact, longer. And it was at one time the single most popular genre of motion picture entertainment in the world. Porn clearly merits attention. Might it also even deserve respect?

3
From Paris, Under Plain Wrapper

For once, the standard criticisms of a porn film are justified. These women are indeed ill-favoured. They are, in fact, two of the least attractive women ever to be seen performing a sexual act naked on film.

They're first seen chatting at the shuttered second-storey windows of a modest country house. Shortly after, they reappear in the garden, wearing unbelted housecoats, high heels and chemises that barely conceal meaty thighs. Flopping into garden chairs, they fall to fondling. Spying on them is a gardener of villainous appearance, improbably dressed for the country in suit pants, collarless white long-sleeved shirt with sleeve garters, and mask-like sunglasses. Before long he joins in their game. We're treated to a succession of sexual acts, after which the girls skip away into the garden, pausing to wave at the audience.

A French porn film called *À l'Ecu d'Or ou la Bonne Auberge* was circulating in 1908. Actually meaning "At the Piece of Gold, or The Good Inn," the title was the inevitable pun, in this case on *ecu* and (pronounced almost the same) *cul* – ass. This film of high jinks in a country garden may well be *À l'Ecu d'Or*, but it lacks titles. It dates recognisably, however, from the same period and was made in France, already acknowledged around the world as the *fons et origo* of porn. In 1908, the Russian government outlawed what were already known as films of "the Paris genre." The Mephistopheles Kino in Moscow tested the law and was speedily closed down.

Cinema was only a decade old when it discovered porn, but few technological advances have not been adapted to trigger the sexual imagination. Mediaeval printers scarcely got through using movable type to reproduce the Bible before they turned to porn. Almost as soon as clockwork was invented, the rich could buy tick-tock sex scenes. Photography was speedily co-opted. From 1849,

Daguerreotype porn was widely circulated. The French photographers such as Auguste Belloc, Louis Duboscq-Soleil and Félix Moulin, whom Queen Victoria praised at the Great Exhibition of 1851, all produced erotica as a sideline, evading the strict legal penalties by registering their innocuous 'art studies' with the Bibliotheque Nationale while reserving porn shots taken with the same models for private distribution.

In Paris brothels of the late nineteenth century, clients could browse through albums of licentious images, some from Japan. Other *maisons de tolérance* featured tableaux of group sex or scenes that often depicted couples disguised as monks or nuns having sex. In 1895, hearing of Roentgen's discovery of X-rays, American legislators made a daring intuitive link with photography and rushed through a law making it illegal to employ this new technology in the manufacture of binoculars and opera glasses, lest voyeurs use X-rays to penetrate women's clothes. Their scientific knowledge was deficient but, as proved by countless subsequent fantasies of invisible men invading dressing rooms and X-ray eyesight breaching dormitory walls, their sexual imagination was absolutely up to date.

The earliest porn films were designed to be seen by one person standing alone at what was known as a Mutoscope, though most people spoke of it, using the name of a popular title, as a *What The Butler Saw* machine. From 1897, one could see 60-second Mutoscopes such as *Pajama Girl* and *Pajama Statue Girls*, in which women in baggy male pajamas dance and do calisthenics; the sight of women exercising, like that of girls swimming, was a potent stimulant at a time when a lady never moved faster than a languid stroll. *Girls Swinging* from 1897 shows a girl on a swing pushed by two others. As yet, nobody had transgressed one of the most potent taboos, that of showing women in male trousers, still a crime even in liberal France.

The earliest reputed erotic film was Henri Joly's *Bain de la Modaine*, a simple striptease shot in 1895, a year after Louis and Auguste Lumiére projected their first documentary images of workers leaving the family factory

at La Ciotat. Two years later, Georges Méliès included Jahanne D'Arcy (his mistress, later his wife) in a film known variously as *After the Ball*, *The Tub* and *The Bridegroom's Dilemma*. A woman stands up naked after a bath and her maid accidentally mistakes a bucket of water with one of soot and douses her with it. Méliès is mostly remembered for jolly fantasies such as the 1902 *Voyage dans la Lune*, but it's clear from the appearance in that early interplanetary film of a chorus line in tights and high heels at the space vehicle's launching that he was not above turning to erotica when money was short.

Méliès' major and more successful competitor was Eugene Pirou, whose 1897 *Le Coucher de la Mariée* put on film a routine performed by Louise Willy at the Olympia the previous year. According to the catalogue description, "the film showed a newly-wed couple preparing for bed. The girl's husband removes her satin slipper and presses it ecstatically to his lips, then she disrobes and puts on her night attire while her husband watches with evident desire. Finally Mlle Willy does a provocative little dance." US and British catalogues featured the films shortly after they were made. *Le Coucher de la mariée* became *A Parisiennes Bedtime*. Méliès' *L'Indiscret aux Bains de Mer* turned into *Peeping Tom in the Dressing Room*. The Warwick Trading Co. which distributed them in Britain, described all the films as "welcome at any smoking concert or stag party."

Some early films are optimistically co-opted into histories of erotic cinema on the basis of their titles. *How Bridget Served the Salad Undressed*, a Biograph film of 22 feet, which appears in catalogues of the mid-1890s, at least comes with a short synopsis. Bridget the maid misunderstands an order for an "undressed" salad and serves the meal "in a state of dishabille hardly allowable in polite society." The film has disappeared but we know how undressed Bridget would have been from surviving stereo photo cards, which, along with vaudeville burlesque routines, were the primary source material of such films. Around 1898, at least eight companies produced photo series of *How Bridget* (or *Biddy*) *Served the Salad* (or

How Bridget served the Potatoes „undressed".
I'll not take off another stitch if I loose my place.

Potatoes Undressed), all of which ended with the servant stripped only to her petticoat. Bridget "undressed" still wore enough cloth to wrap a Jersey cow.

Other photo series included *Love's Young Dream* (1904), showing a girl in her petticoat, stockings and shoes reclining on a couch, with a mirror displaying her back view. In the same year *Jolly Mr. Jack* takes a man backstage at a burlesque show to peek at the girls in tights. *The Living Picture Model* shows a reclining nude draped in a sheet. In a series of pictures by William H. Rau, also from 1904, two chorus girls relaxing in a bedroom, sharing chicken salad and oysters after the show, read a note from a lover. One bestows a kiss on her mirror. Neither undresses beyond camisoles and black stockings with garters, but for America in 1904 this was salacious enough.

One Way of Taking a Girl's Picture, *As Seen on the Screen*, *Behind Her Screen* and *Waiting for Santa* all offered glimpses of girls walking about in voluminous underwear. Occasionally a film went a little further. *The Pouting Model* from June 1901 shows two women pulling back a stage curtain to reveal a nude girl with her back to the camera while a bearded artist paints her. Tableaux such as this were common at men's "smoking concerts," which was probably where the filmmaker got his cast and setting. The same was true of the more elaborate *The Trapeze Disrobing Act*. This was produced by Edison as part of its output of films for "smokers." It uses a painted backdrop, with the addition of a fake stage box in which two yokels in long beards and wigs (standard disguise for male porn performers until well into the Twenties) watch a girl strip to her knickers and camisole while swinging on a trapeze.

Who produced *À L'Ecu d'Or* and other early porn films? The classic answer was given by Peter Boyle in Paul Schrader's 1979 film *Hardcore*. He's a sleazy private detective hired by George C. Scott to find his daughter, who has drifted into the business. Scott asks Boyle who made the 16mm "loop" in which she appears. "Nobody made it," explains Boyle wearily. "Nobody sold it. Nobody sees it. It doesn't exist."

We can, however, infer a few things. This film and others like it from before World War I share the technique of all primitive cinema. They are shot in the open, because insensitive orthochromatic film stock demanded sunlight. Film language was still primitive, so they lacked the emphasis of close-ups and the dynamics of creative editing. Since nobody yet knows how to perform for the camera, actions and expressions are exaggerated. But they *are* well shot. The image quality is acceptable. They're edited correctly. People enter and leave the shot according to the rules of cinema. The films are, in fact, professionally done.

The Lumiéres were not only manufacturers of the Cinématographe, but producers and distributors of its products. By 1900, Lumiére-licensed cinematographers were reaching the furthest corners of the world and sending back coverage of such exotic events as a bandit's beheading in China and Australia's 1896 Melbourne Cup. The Cinématographe was ingenious. Designed to make these travelling filmmakers totally self-sufficient, it doubled as both a camera and, with the addition of a light source, a projector. The factory supplied reels of raw film stock as well, along with directions for processing them. Anyone with access to a Cinématographe could make a porn film.

From 1901, American Biograph turned out scores of Mutoscope films designed to be shown as flip card series. By day, the company shot one-reel comedies on its rooftop Manhattan studio. After hours, it made *A Scene in a Dressing Room* and *The Merry Widow at a Supper Party* for the Mutoscope. Some could have been shot by Biograph's most prolific director, D.W. Griffith, and featured up-and-coming young comic Mack Sennett.

As for "Who sold it?" and "Who saw it?" the answer was still easier. From the enthusiasm, energy and game-for-anything manner of the ladies in our film, one assumes they were sex workers, and not too fussed about performing for the camera. Which makes sense, since for the first twenty years of their existence, porn films were shown almost exclusively in brothels.

Le Coucher de la Mariée.

There were few countries where brothels had become more thoroughly assimilated into the culture than France. Until 1946, when they were made illegal, any French city of 20,000 people would have boasted at least three *maisons closes* or *maisons de tolerance*, each catering to a different social level and each employing between five and fifteen women.

Anyone who visualises the brothel of the early twentieth century on the pattern of later low-rent establishments would be astonished by the reality. For both women and men, and especially women and men with money, the European brothel experience was exotic and elaborate.

Some Parisian bordellos had bars, musicians, even restaurants. For The Sphinx, the most modern – it opened in 1931 – artist Kees van Dongen created gilded Egyptian figures ten feet high that would have done credit to a Cecil B. DeMille film. Most large brothels had musicians and "American Bars," which encouraged patrons to make a night of it. At Le Chabanais, conveniently close to the Bibliothèque nationale, one could fornicate amidst furniture and fittings from the Japanese pavilion at the 1889 World Exposition. After it won a prize, one of the brothel's owners bought the whole room and had it installed intact. Another added a suite in the style of Louis XVI, with porcelain medallions painted with plump pink nudes *à la* François Boucher. American expatriate Harry Crosby, nephew of financier J.P. Morgan, praised "the Persian and the Russian and the Turkish and the Japanese and the Spanish rooms, and the bathroom with mirrored walls and mirrored ceilings, and the thirty harlots waiting in the salon."

The itinerary of every dignitary and crowned head visiting Paris included "a night with the president of the Senate" which was actually spent at Le Chabanais. The same house created an "armchair of love" for a valued client, the Prince of Wales, later Edward VII. Fitted with rollers and kneeling pads, it allowed his majesty, who was somewhat overweight, to enjoy the services of the staff without excessive exertion. When Salvador Dalí, then an unknown young Spanish painter, shy and sexually under-endowed,

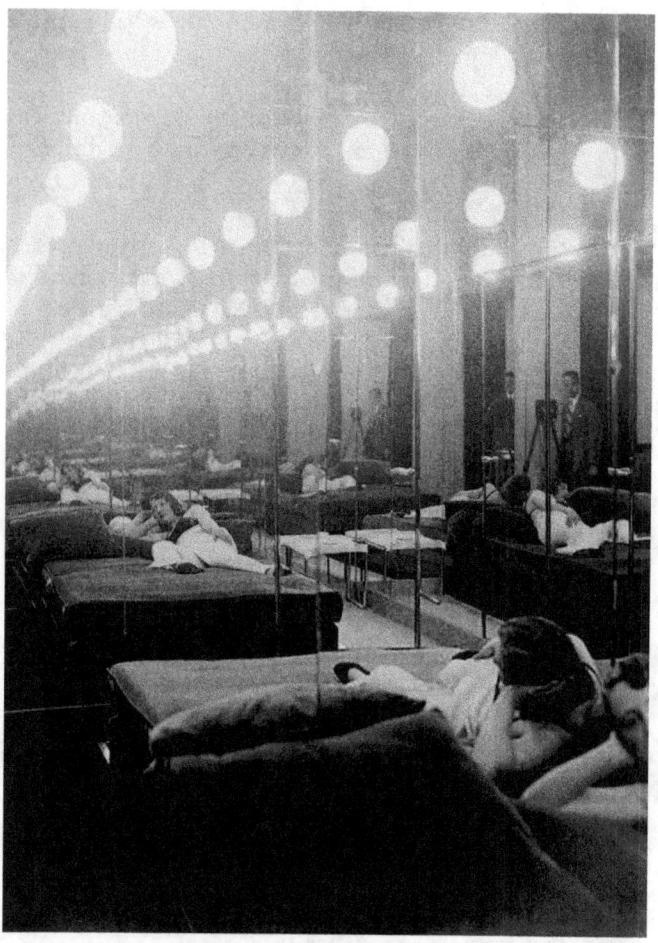

The mirrored bedrooms upstairs at Le Sphinx.

arrived in Paris in 1929, he asked a cab driver at the railway station to take him to a brothel. The cabby delivered him automatically to Le Chabanais, where they quickly assessed him as a voyeur and let him watch for an hour through the house's system of peepholes. He left, he said, "with enough to last me for the rest of my life in the way of accessories to furnish, in less than a minute, no matter what erotic reverie, even the most exacting."

Other rooms offered the exotic ambiance that clients had learned to expect in trips to North Africa and the East. Rooms were decorated in Moorish style, with plants and even a swimming pool, black sheets on the beds and heavy red and gold hangings around them. In some, a canvas panorama of desert scenes unrolled discreetly in the background. Some used Japanese screens, and one even provided a mock igloo in which a girl could strip the chilled explorer and rub his limbs to restore circulation. Discreetly expert lighting effects were an essential part of the experience. So were mirrors. Rooms were lined with them. In 1876, at a brothel near the Opera Comique in Paris, a bevelled glass ceiling fell on a girl and her client, injuring both.

Early porn films show a degree of sophistication in setting and performance impossible outside the brothel culture. Their fetishistic costumes and props and the expert sexual choreography were honed in those houses where play-acting was a part of the job. Girls were used to acting out the clients' fantasies, pretending to be wives caught *in flagrante*, or virgins fending off half-feared advances. They routinely dressed as nuns, brides, eighteenth-century ladies in crinolines, and harem girls – or boys.

There was nothing antique about the appointments of these places. Electric vibrators were in use half a century before the bedside torpedo of the Seventies. Clients also had access to "Doctor Mondat's Suction Pump" to revive failing erections, and electrical equipment for administering selective sexual shocks. In the brothels' exhibitions, nudes often appeared on electrically operated turntables. As soon as movies began to attract an audience, the larger houses bought or gained access to Cinématographs and used them, as they had co-opted most other theatrical and technical devices of the nineteenth century, to entertain a clientele greedy for sensation.

4
On the House

Though it flourished in Paris, pornography on film wasn't exclusively a French preserve. Both Germany and Italy were early producers, and there are descriptions of an Argentinean film from between 1907 and 1912 in which women bathing in a river are attacked by a devil, complete with horns, tail and false whiskers – a brothel show transplanted outdoors, where the light was better.

It was the French, however, who pushed the envelope in the years immediately after World War I, when Paris became the world centre of erotic gratification. Porn films were known as *radiants* because they were in a sense radioactive, suggested one authority, or maybe because of the bomb-flash effect they were designed to have on an audience. Most were made for those brothels which advertised *la projection* as one of their attractions. Those that survive are often impressively elaborate. They include one-reelers featuring the *commedia dell'arte* characters Pierrot, Pierrette and Harlequin, and a satire of Puccini's opera (and David Belasco's play) *Madama Butterfly*. Another was set in a dungeon during the Revolution, complete with painted backdrop, men in full eighteenth century costumes and girls dressed in crinolines and wigs – for a while anyway.

Madama Butterfly dates from around 1920. It's the first of countless porn films to travesty a classic, though the connection hardly runs beyond the title. Later, more ambitious subjects for porn satire would include the Old Testament (*Sodom and Gomorrah: The Last Days*, Mitchell Brothers, 1979), Shaw's *Pygmalion* (*The Opening of Misty Beethoven*, Radley Metzger, 1975), *Snow White and the Seven Dwarfs* (*Seven Into Snowy*, Anthony Shepherd, 1977) and a Nineties French version of *Cyrano de Bergerac* in which the great swordsman's nose is eight inches long, and shaped like a phallus.

For its time, *Madama Butterfly* is ambitious. It even includes a few metres of Asian street footage, an extravagance which visibly attempts to free the film from the state-less society-less world in which porn cinema had existed since the first days, and where it would remain until Marilyn Chambers took the audience on a Rolls-Royce tour of London in *Insatiable* (1980).

Unfortunately, *Madama Butterfly*, for all its pretence, is dismally un-erotic. Arriving at his Asian home (transparently nothing but an arrangement of Chinese screens), Pinkerton, pausing only to sodomise his manservant Binh-Lap and be fellated by him, surprises Butterfly consoling herself with her girlfriend Soussouki. He joins in – as does, eventually, Binh-Lap, companionably masturbating in concert with his betters. Both women are played by Occidentals in kimonos and eye make-up, and the action, aside from the homosexual episode, is standard for the time. Everything about the film suggests the involvement of an individual familiar to cinema in all its manifestations, not simply the pornographic – someone with more money than taste.

The Pierrot film contrasts strikingly with *Madama Butterfly*, even though its technical resources are almost identical. The action is played on a bench against a black backdrop. Pierrot, complete with traditional mandolin, meets Pierrette and they embrace. Harlequin arrives, strips Pierrot to find she's a girl, after which a three-way sex scene ensues, with the obligatory 'come' shot.

The girls, slim and young for a change, play on the eroticism of their costumes by retaining ruffs and skullcaps (as well as the rolled silk stockings and high heeled shoes) after discarding all else, and the film even runs to a title in verse, adapted from an old nursery rhyme: "*Au clair de la lune/Mon ami Pierrot/Prête-moi ta plume/Pour t'écrire un mot.*" ("By the light of the moon/My friend Pierrot/Lend me your quill/To write a word"). Here, in short, is a film made by someone who, within the restrictions of the one-reel porn form, might be called an artist. In a world with a different morality, might such films have led to a sex cinema as lively and creative as that other brothel-fostered art, jazz?

As it was, sex film became trapped in an artistic dead end it wasn't to leave for decades.

Graham Greene wrote his short story *The Blue Film* in 1954, one of those typical Greenian vignettes of lost hope and defiant desire. Carter, an ageing world traveller, is in Hong Kong on a rare holiday with his wife. When his wife taunts him about the tameness of their visit, Carter takes her to a pornographic film show.

> The first film was peculiarly unattractive and showed the rejuvenation of an elderly man at the hands of two blonde masseuses. From the style of the women's hairdressing the film must have been made in the late twenties. Carter and his wife sat in mutual embarrassment as the film whirled and clicked to a stop. "Not a very good one," Carter said, as though he were a connoisseur.

In a second film a girl picks up a young man in the street and takes him back to her room. Carter recognises the girl, the room – "a doll over a telephone; a pin-up girl of the period over the double bed" – and, finally, the man. It's himself, thirty years before. This being Greeneland, Carter is filled with loneliness, guilt and a sense of loss. But his wife, after professing to be bored by the first film and disgusted by the appearance of her husband in the second, is so aroused that, when they return to their hotel and make love, she has her first orgasm in years.

Shame, ennui, a sometimes unexpected lust; the reactions are exactly right. Greene knew porn. The environment is accurate as well. A furtive, foreign setting, the sense of illegality that adds the essential guilty thrill. We can be sure Greene had his facts right because one of the films he describes actually exists. French, silent, running eight minutes, it's generally called *Massages*. Though it has been dated as late as 1937, Greene was probably right to place it in the late Twenties.

Introduction card for a Paris brothel, c.1923.

Massages opens with a close-up of Monsieur, in a smoking jacket and artificially greyed hair, reading, with exaggerated amusement, the small advertisements in the Parisian daily *Le Matin* which promise cures for impotence. He turns to another paper, probably *La Vie Parisienne*, a weekly of genteel titillation that survived for almost a century on a ration of discreet nudes, naughty cartoons and page after page of *petites annonces*. Via its pages, Norma Dixie sold *Livres Erotiques*, either from her premises at 34 rue Godot de Mauroy, or by mail *"direct et rapide sous enveloppe fermée."* You could buy *preservatifs* (condoms) by post from Maison Bellard in Montmartre (forbidden under American law, and in fact technically illegal even in France.) There were also numerous ads for *Sages femmes* – Midwives, though actually abortionists, in the grisly argot of the time *Faiseuses d'ange* – Angel-makers.

Among the ads for such products as *Erector* and *Vigorax*, Monsieur notices another for Madame Irma, who promises to *rend la jeunesse aux vieilles cloches* – literally to put youth into old bells. It ends with the promise *Qui est venu – reviendra* ("He who has come will return again"). Since the French don't talk of "coming," the English translation manages an extra pun with "If you come… you will come again." With an ill-acted expression of resolve, Monsieur, presumably having failed with Vigorax, decides "to try once more" with Madame Irma.

The scene changes to an apartment where two women wait expressionlessly, one reading a magazine, the other buffing her nails. They wear classic twenties nurse regalia, complete with white surgical coats, white stockings and long Red Cross headdresses, correctly pinned low on the forehead and reaching almost to their waists at the back. When Monsieur arrives, he is quickly stripped and laid naked on a table. Decrepitude ends at his powdered hair. In every other respect, he's young and healthy. A still photograph of his limp penis, however, with *Pendant* printed across it, reminds us of the nature of his problem, while also conferring a quasi-medical tone to the film, in case it needs to be defended in court.

The nurses set to work on Monsieur's back. After pummelling his spine, using the edges of their four hands in unison with all the expertise of duo pianists, they switch to an electric vibrator. When it's applied to Monsieur's genitals, he quickly responds and the women strip to their rolled white stockings and veils, revealing a single error in Greene's memory; only one is blonde. After a vigorous session of cunnilingus, fellatio and conventional sex, Monsieur ejaculates successfully. At this point there is a shot of the two women smiling towards the camera and mouthing *À vous*. This is amplified in a title as *À vous Messieurs, à vous Mesdames*. The film ends with the image of an erect penis poking from the flies of a dark suit with the title *Aprés*. No translation was felt to be necessary.

In a long-established tradition, the film would have been used to promote the attractions of the brothel in which it was shown. From the erotic murals on the walls of Roman brothels to the pillow books of Japan and the photo albums of the 1850s, sex workers have always used images as a form of advertising. Film simply carried on a tradition pioneered by peep shows. A series of drawings by Reznicker from around 1908 shows a gentleman in a top hat brushing aside a woman who accosts him in the street. He goes into a peep show arcade, drops a coin into a machine and watches the one-minute film, then changes his mind about the girl and walks off with her.

The second movie in *The Blue Film*, the one in which Carter took part, has presumably been invented by Greene, since it breaks some of the laws which audience expectation and technical restriction had, by the Twenties, imposed on pornographic film. First, a young man picks up a girl in the street when no porn filmmaker of the period would have drawn attention to himself by shooting in a public place. Second, it's implied that the girl's own room was used for filming, when most such films employed mocked-up interiors, initially built in the open air to exploit natural light, then on brothel premises. To set up cameras and lights in a Parisian bedroom poses considerable technical problems even today. Moreover, most porn films of the Twenties and Thirties weren't so much stories as compendia of erotic elements which had proved their effectiveness over decades, perhaps centuries; distillations of what the filmmaker knew would turn his audience on. By those standards, what sounds like the conventional sex of Greene's film would have been weak stuff.

The idea of the cast or the filmmaker addressing, appealing to or exhorting the audience as the women do in *Massages* was common in early porn films, which would normally have been shown to brothel patrons, either to keep them occupied on busy nights or as a form of on-site advertising. Such films transgressed the "fourth wall" rule of cinema, that the audience shouldn't be openly acknowledged. In *Le Telegraphiste* (ca. 1921-26), a telegram boy tries to seduce the maid, but is himself seduced in turn by the wife and then, in a scene of sodomy and voyeurism, the husband. He leaves behind a telegram which, when the husband opens it, reads "After seeing this picture, rush over to some nice girl and get taken care of." Such suspension of disbelief is more common in porn than in conventional cinema, and audiences got used to being reminded that they are, in some sense, conspirators. In its most obvious form of merchandising, porn films have always been used to promote the sale of sequels. The one-reel striptease and bondage films made in New York in the Forties and Fifties with Bettie Page bear the title "If you liked this film, you can get more like it from Irving Klaw."

There was a more complex relationship between erotic films and stars who were also sex workers. The rivalry between up-market sex services and men's magazines such as *Playboy* and *Penthouse*, in which call girl agencies tried to place newly recruited girls as centrefolds in order to increase their price, carried through into adult films. Bill Rotsler, historian of porn cinema and a producer of softcore films during the Sixties, comments, "There are a few women who – I think – got into this as a way to get publicity perhaps for their prostitution efforts. When you've got a woman who's fucking all kinds of people, I mean, it's not all that different to pick up a quick $100 or $200. And if she's a porn star it might be $500."

The practice was international. In an obituary for Mary Millington, Britain's top porn actress of the Seventies, her last co-star, John M. East, acknowledged that she had sex with many men – "some famous, some not" – during her brief career. "She always put a charge on these friendships," he continued solemnly, in what he probably saw as a tribute to Millington's professionalism, "but I can tell you she always gave value for money." Among her clients was the Shah of Iran. He flew her to Switzerland for their tryst, and afterwards presented her with a diamond bracelet, which she immediately sold.

After the early Lumiére and Edison films, usually nothing more than moving snapshots of exotic corners of the earth or bizarre events, film learned to tell stories. It developed narrative, character, and a style in which eroticism took its minor place. Pornographic films, however, didn't change. In the simple five- or ten-minute film of cinema's earliest years, without sound, without elaborate visual effects – with, in fact, the barest possible narrative – it had found its ideal form. It wasn't to alter in any important respect for fifty years.

The technology that brought porn film into being also limited its early growth. To process 35mm film, the stock must be passed at a continuous speed in darkness through chemical baths, then dried on large frames. Multiple copies demand, in addition, an optical printer. There were few film laboratories in the early days of film and, if later experience was any indication, most would have shunned pornography.

Backyard lab work accounts for the poor technical quality of many early porn films. They survive today mostly in murky, badly copied prints, produced, at their worst, simply by pointing a camera at a screen. What transformed porn film, turning it from an aspect of the brothel experience to something like mass entertainment, was the introduction of narrow-gauge film. 16mm came first, followed by 9.5mm, then 8mm. 9.5mm film stock first appeared in 1922, turning the hand-wound Pathé Baby camera with its easy-load system into a popular favourite. 16mm followed in 1923 and 8mm in 1932.

The porn business, as usual, was not slow to exploit technological innovation. Around 1932, a new line of advertisements appeared in *La Vie Parisienne*. Those for the Curious Bookshop of Mademoiselle Claude at 7, Rue de la Lune, are typical. They echo in their breathless enthusiasm, sketchy syntax and notional punctuation the eagerness of their customers:

> Realistic films… Best model of MONT-PARNASSE and MONTMARTRE. All films with two or four persons SOMETHING YOU HAVE NEVER SEEN BEFORE. Films for the Pathé Baby, Kodaks and other systems. Price from 1 pound and upwards. Beautiful collection of 6 REALISTIC-LOVE-ACTION FILMS for only six pounds. Rapid and VERY DISCREET SERVICE, letters sent out in ordinary plain envelops, parcels in plain wrappers. SEND YOUR ORDER TODAY….

More intriguing still were the ads of Ginette for her bookstore at 4, rue du Ponceau. She offered:

FILMS CINEMA avec des personnages jeunes et beaux, filmes dans notre studio SECRET, donnant l'illusion de la VIE. Voici quelques series uniques:
  1. *Vierges et Demi-Vierges.*
  2. *Brutalities Feminines.*
  3. *Melanges Savants.*
  4. *Etreintes Passionées.*
  5. *Les 32 Caresses.*
  6. *Scenes d'Orgie....*

A film in 9.5mm cost 100 FF and the 16mm version 300 FF. You could have all six in 9.5mm for 500 francs or in 16mm for 1500 francs – not cheap, at a time when 200 francs would buy a man's overcoat or a suit.

Films could now be shot with light cameras. Shohei Imamura's 1966 film *The Pornographers* shows filmmakers shooting with four 8mm cameras taped together, producing instant multiple prints, a technique European porn producers of the Thirties almost certainly used. The resulting prints could be processed in a bathroom, carried in a pocket and, most important of all, sent through the mail. As the bilingual advertising suggests, many films found their way to England. A few ended up in the United States, though America could be more readily serviced from within, or from Mexico, which became a major supplier to the American "stag" market. With the arrival of 8mm, pornography had been presented with a mass audience.

Parts of the same audience, however, were also discriminating. Graham Greene was far from the only intellectual to find porn film diverting. The Surrealists in particular were drawn to its directness. Committed to the primacy of the unconscious, they saw in porn film an acceptable spontaneous alternative to professional cinema. André Breton, founder of the movement (and the son of a gendarme), disapproved of both porn and brothels, so Paul Éluard, Luis Buñuel, Louis Aragon, René Crével and the others hid their enthusiasm for both.

Louis Aragon, Elsa Triolet, André Breton,
Paul Éluard and his second wife Nusch.

Crével roughed out a brief treatment for a porn film called *The Geography Lesson*, in which a map of the world, particularly phallic Italy, comes to life and wreaks havoc in a girl's classroom. Éluard was then sharing a *ménage à trois* with his wife Gala and painter Max Ernst, but Gala was recovering from tuberculosis in a Swiss clinic, so Éluard wrote her in April 1929 with news of the porn he had seen on a trip to the south with his friend Andre Gaillard.

> Obscene cinema, what a marvel! It's exhilarating; a discovery. The incredible life of enormous and magnificent organs on the screen. The sperm that leaps. And the

life of loving flesh, all the contortions. It's glorious. And very well made, a tremendous eroticism. How much I would like you to see it. And if you come to Marseilles, you will go – with Gaillard, who is an incarnation (truly) of decency, and who has already taken many very "bourgeois" ladies.

The movies turned me on in an exasperating way for an hour. It was a near thing that I didn't come simply from the show. If you had been here, I couldn't have stopped myself. It's a very pure show without theatrical effect. The actors don't move their lips, at least not to speak, it's a "silent" art, a "primitive" art; passion vs. death and stupidity. They should show this in every theatre and in schools. It would result in workable marriages – the first; sacred unions, multi-faceted. Alas, poetry is not born yet.

Brothels would continue to be the primary market for French porn makers until World War II. Many filmmakers later to become well known dabbled, and spent a lifetime trying to deny it. They included Henri Dominique, who was famous for a saucy backstage short of 1923 called *Pendant d'Entracte* (*During the Interval*) which traded on the fame of Sarah Bernhardt by calling the actress "Sara Barnum." The Divine Sarah was not amused. Natan Tananzapf, also known as Bernard Natan, became a producer with the large Pathé company after having made one of the most famous examples of S&M porn, *Massage Hindou*, around 1930. In 1933, one of the more prolific producer/directors, who cheekily adopted the *nom de film* of "Griffith" and claimed to have made plenty of "straight" films under his own name, let a journalist watch a day's shooting. He paid his performers about 250 francs a day, he explained, and routinely realised 12,000 Francs for a film – an imbalance that porn performers of all countries and eras will recognise.

5
Stags and Smokers

"Everything about sex was secretive," social historian William Manchester writes of the United States in the Thirties. "The closest thing to a girlie magazine was *The Stocking Parade*, which published photographs of fully clothed young women whose skirts were hoisted five or six inches above the knee. Pornographers were midgets in those days."

Manchester was right about the secrecy, but wrong about everything else. Porn was ubiquitous; it simply wasn't acknowledged. Albums showing naked women, their pudenda discreetly shaded, were offered "For Art Students." "Health and efficiency" magazines featured pages of statuesque air-brushed nudes, interspersed with articles about the Bran Diet and the joys of a harsh purgative. Pulp magazines such as *Spicy Detective* and *Spicy Western* bore covers which routinely featured busty girls in tableaux of rape, torture and bestiality.

Then, as now, every level of American culture had pornographers. The smallest community supported its quantum of vice: a sex worker, an abortionist, a bookie and a town barber who sold condoms and acted as informal distributor of French "novelty booklets" and postcards. A few wide-open communities supported a semi-public sex industry of burlesque theatres, brothels and a cinema that showed semi-porn movies. Local morality could be subtly modified by a complaisant sheriff, a powerful local political machine, a nearby port or military base, a fact that would justify the appeal to "local community standards" enshrined in the Supreme Court decisions of the Fifties that legalised porn in the United States.

Minorities had the liveliest sexual subcultures. Dashiell Hammett, a former private detective, accurately sketched the world of San Francisco's Chinese brothels in his story *Dead Yellow Women*. African American Pullman staff, barred from white hotels, set up communal "buffet flats" in the ghettos of most northern cities. Run like the best brothels, buffet flats (pronounced with a hard "t") offered to these travelling men, a relatively prosperous elite of the black working class, not only good food and a bed but music, sexual exhibitions and pornographic films.

If the Twenties was the era of the brothel film, it's the "stag" label that most indelibly marks the Thirties. There is no consensus on the source of "stag," though it probably derives from the term for a young male deer, an image of sexual potency: a pair of horns, implying another mate, has long been the symbol for a deceived husband or cuckold. Any private event involving young men could be termed stag, and "going stag," i.e. attending an event without a female partner, also entered the language.

Between the two world wars, the private porn screening insinuated itself so deeply into the American sexual experience that by 1970 the Presidential Commission on Obscenity and Pornography would frankly acknowledge that "stag films are a familiar and firmly established part of the American scene [...] shown privately, not only by individual citizens, but also by civic, social, fraternal and veterans' organisations. The National Survey conducted by the Commission (Abelson, 1970) revealed that 44% of male adults acknowledged having seen one or more stag films in their lifetimes." (By 1986, a *Time* magazine survey raised that figure to 77%.)

Many of these Thirties American porn films show impressive effort, if not much art. The cameramen were competent, the directors and performers workmanlike. With the exception of cartoons, clearly made by professional animators treating themselves to a little joke, there is no evidence that any major director ever tangled with porn, except as a member of the audience. The most likely candidate among Hollywood directors was Erich von Stroheim. He certainly enjoyed the company of sex workers, and, needing a carriage full of them for *The Wedding March*, approached Hollywood's best brothel, that of Lee Francis, and hired the real thing.

Bypassing the mails, porn film distributors of the Thirties sent their films out on the road with a projectionist who often, in imitation of the striptease and burlesque tent shows which followed the county fair circuit, travelled the same route each year, presenting his programme at anything from $25 to $100 a night. Audiences of 200 were not unknown, with the local law paid off and, in all probability, attending the show. In Bloomington, Indiana, the local branch of the American Legion even advertised its next stag screening in the local paper.

Stag parties, the male equivalent of the bridal shower, where men ritually mourned the end of a friend's bachelorhood with gorging, boozing and sex, were another standard setting for the screening of filmed pornography. Their milieu has often since been exploited by writers and filmmakers. The 1957 *Bachelor Party*, from Paddy Chayefsky's TV play, evokes the seedy atmosphere typical of secret cinema before its Seventies liberation. Generally the setting was a games room or cellar, the door locked against women and children. A grainy image jitters on a wall or a crooked screen, almost all detail in the print bleached and blurred by countless duplications.

Secrecy, privacy, comradeship typify the experience, as they typify those other shared rituals of maleness, the first drunk, the first whorehouse visit, the first tattoo. Purists of porn have argued that readily accessible video porn, in eradicating the intensely male communal experience of the stag screening – with its camaraderie and ribald commentary – robbed society of a valuable social institution, just as sleekly produced modern striptease shows have superseded the burlesque with its bellowed exhortations to "Take 'em off!" Others respond that one might as well deplore the tubeless tire because it deprives us of the experience of changing a flat at 2 a.m. in the rain.

In the United States, films shown in private to consenting adults without payment of admission conveniently fell through a crack between the laws against pornography and those protecting free speech and the right to privacy. The bill passed by Congress in 1873 at the urging of moral crusader Anthony Comstock used as its pretext and weapon the sanctity of the mails. It banned from postage "every obscene, lewd, lascivious or filthy book, pamphlet, picture, paper, letter, writing, print or other publication of an indecent character." Had the law wished to stamp out stag movies, a further provision, to ban "any article or thing intended or adapted for any indecent or immoral use or nature" gave them the power, but it was one they used infrequently, knowing that few prosecutors would take the case to court, and fewer judges convict.

In the Thirties, as now, the laws against running a brothel offered the best chance of convicting a filmmaker, since recruiting performers could be considered as pandering, and a number of producers and distributors were put out of business in this way. Such laws, however, were seldom used against audiences watching such films, least of all at lodges and fraternal societies, where the audience might not belong to the arrestable class. "Three shots of corn likker," wrote Nelson Algren of lodges in his novel *A Walk On the Wild Side*, "and the whole stuffed zoo – Moose, Elks, Woodmen, Lions, Thirty-Third Degree Owls and Forty-Fourth Degree Field Mice begin to conspire against the very laws they themselves have written."

What might one have seen at a stag evening in the United States between the wars? Given the scarcity of material, most films would have been old, some dating back twenty years. They would range from venerable French and German productions through professional strip films, down to a stratum of semi-amateur porn created as much for the pleasure of the filmmaker as for profit.

Some of the American films would have been almost legal. At the 1933/34 Chicago World's Fair, cadet entrepreneur Mike Todd, later the husband of Elizabeth Taylor, made his name with an attraction called *The Streets of Paris*. Visitors braved a fake flea market and caricaturists (eerily dressed like the actors in French porn films, with false moustaches, striped jerseys and berets) to reach the cafe where stripper Sally Rand performed her famous Fan Dance, nude but for sheaves of ostrich feathers and high-

Sally Rand.

heeled pumps. Filming the show, Todd sold hundreds of prints as souvenirs.

Porn films were often doctored or "doubled up" to extend their life. The collection held by the Kinsey Institute for Research in Sex, Gender and Reproduction contains many of these. Their print of *A Free Ride,* also known as *A Grass Sandwich,* an ambitious American stag film (reputedly the first made in the US to survive, and variously dated from 1915 to 1919), begins with scenes of two female hitchhikers having sex with the driver after he stops on a country road to urinate, but abruptly cuts to a different couple indoors, a sequence excerpted from the much later *The Casting Couch*. "How the end of a 1924 film came to replace that of a film produced in the teens I cannot say," historian Linda Williams has commented, though the explanation – an exhibitor or collector simply joined two incomplete or worn prints – seems obvious enough.

A similar impulse motivated another well-documented stag film, *The Virgin in Hot Pants*, which begins with a cartoon sequence of a woman pursued round a room by an ambulant set of male genitals, which penetrate her as she hangs from a chandelier. A cartoon mouse with a giant penis penetrates a cat. Following this, the film switches to live action. Naked women dance, kiss and penetrate one another with a dildo. Following the style set by *Massages* and other brothel films, a title card addresses the audience directly: "You there in the front row, spread those lips apart for us." In close-up, a man's hands spread the labia of one of the women. The title continues, "Turn over honey so we can see how it looks from behind." The woman obliges. Another title "How about you two getting into your favourite dish?", and a man was seen performing cunnilingus on one of the women. Again a title card: "Just a minute girls, this is an art picture!" In another close-up a beer bottle was inserted into a vagina, a daunting evocation of fragility and vulnerability which was to reappear constantly in porn film.

The brief animated sequence probably began as one of the Climax Fables, a technically proficient series of pornographic cartoons made in America during the late Twenties. Most large animation studios made porn, for their own amusement and that of other animators. On a famous occasion, animators at Disney Studios in the Thirties created a porn version of Mickey Mouse. Walt Disney's taste in humour ran to the farmyard (in trying to find a word to cover his taste for outhouses, fat-uddered cows, and plump pigs with human-looking haunches, Jack Cutting, one of his animators, came up with "rural"), so the makers assumed he would enjoy the joke. Disney laughed as loudly as everyone else – then fired them all. They had transgressed Disney Law #1: "Don't Fuck With The Mouse."

Once attributed to Pat Sullivan and Gregory La Cava, the Climax Fables were probably the work of Walter Lantz, later to create the *Woody Woodpecker* series. Lantz, a former newspaper cartoonist who worked during the early Twenties at the New York studios of John Randolph Bray on animated adaptations of popular comic strips such as *The Katzenjammer Kids*, *Krazy Kat*, *Mutt and Jeff* and *Happy Hooligan*, could well have been involved. The main character, Eveready Harton, resembles Colonel Heeza Liar, the parody of Theodore Roosevelt who appears in an animated series on which Lantz worked for Bray in 1922 and 1923.

The hero of *Buried Treasure*, "big-hearted" Eveready Harton, is a small moustachioed figure with gigantic and near-autonomous genitals. Stranded naked on an island where birds, dogs and snakes all boast large penises, Harton glimpses a naked girl masturbating on a rock and, bearing his giant dick before him on a small trolley, offers to satisfy her. She squirts him with milk from her breast while her vagina, exhibiting a life of its own, sucks greedily at Eveready's erect penis. Trying to enter her, Eveready encounters bits of debris, then a huge crab which pinches him so painfully that his genitals detach themselves and run away. He coaxes them back, treating them like a nervous puppy.

For the rest of the film, Eveready's dick is subjected to various indignities. It is employed as a sabre to fence with another well-hung local, then plunged into a cactus. Thrust for safety into a pile of sand, it penetrates an irate man who drags it out to enormous length as he flees, leaving it bent out of shape. Eveready hammers it straight with a rock and finally finds satisfaction when he pushes the abused organ through a knothole in a fence, on the other side of which a cow is waiting to lick it.

Following World War I, stag films began to show the influence of Hollywood. Combat cameramen who served in the US Signal Corps and found jobs in Hollywood moonlighted in porn. Until then, stag films had been mostly rural in setting, with a few obviously shot in hotel rooms, but from around 1919, the settings and the technique changed. *Strictly Union* of 1919, which bears some resemblance to Chaplin's 1916 Mutual short *Behind the Screen*, depicted a series of high jinks in the Fuckem Right studios, while *The Casting Couch* of 1924 told the cautionary tale of a girl prepared to do whatever it takes to get on in the film business. The use of camera fades and irises shows a professional skill, as do the well-drawn titles. Porn would never truly be a part of the cinema, but it was catching up.

6
A Little Bit of What You Fancy

"Stag films," the 1970 Presidential Commission noted,

> seem to represent the preferences of the middle-class American male. Thus, male homosexuality and bestiality are relatively rare, while lesbianism is rather common. In recent years, there has been an increased emphasis on group sex, usually three or four individuals, but as many as seven have been noted in a single film. Many stag films attack certain forbidden social and sexual themes; for example, taboos against miscegenation, cunnilingus, and fellatio are constantly assaulted in American stag films, while foreign countries with a strong religious base have a significant anti-clerical strain in their stag films. The taboo against pedophilia, however, has remained almost inviolate. The use of pre-pubescent children in stag films is almost nonexistent.

The claim of anti-clerical content in stag films from Catholic countries was hard to justify (though Italian and Spanish softcore producers in the Seventies, following the lead of Pier Paolo Pasolini's *The Decameron*, more than made up for the omission with regiments of randy monks and complaisant nuns), but the remaining assertions are irrefutable. The pattern established by American porn films before World War I remained in place for generations, as distinctly national in orientation as the Western.

Occasionally a film would feature animals, in particular dogs or, more rarely, a donkey, trained to have sex with women. These were rare, not because they were especially difficult to produce – such sex shows were common along the Mexican border, and in Cuba – but because the American male had no taste for them, any more than he relished sadomasochism or male homosexual films.

Gay Talese, who spent most of the Seventies investigating the American sex business and incorporating his findings into his book *Thy Neighbor's Wife*, concludes that porn films "catered to the wish-fulfilment fantasies of middle-aged male customers who frequented most X-rated cinemas in large cities and small towns. The porno starlets in the films, unlike women in real life, made their bodies quickly available, rejected no man's advances, required a minimum of foreplay, seemed multi-orgasmic, and sought no romantic promises." Kenneth Tynan agreed that American men were nervous of their women, but without reason, since most, he suggested, were secretly eager for a man who could crack their shell. They "often seemed to come in a capsule, as highly polished as vinyl. They had a marvellous, hard-plastic surface, weatherproof, bombproof, waterproof, sexproof, but if you pierced that, then underneath there was a warm wet marshmallow that would cling with an unbelievable tenacity."

Rotsler's *Contemporary Erotic Cinema* lists six basic stag film plots:

1. A woman alone at home becomes aroused by reading or by handling some phallic-shaped object. Masturbation follows. A man arrives, is invited inside, and sexual play begins.
2. A farm girl gets excited watching animals copulate. She then runs into a farmhand or a travelling salesman, and sexual play begins.
3. A doctor begins examining a woman and sexual play begins.
4. A burglar finds a girl in bed and rapes her or vice-versa.
5. A sunbather or skinny-dipper gets caught and seduced.

The first three themes also occur in European sex films, the last two almost never. American films such as the 1927 *Rape in a Warehouse*, *Slow Fire Dentist* (c.1920), where a dentist puts his pretty patient under ether, then rapes her, or *Masked Rape* (c.1932) which shows a burglar overcoming his sleeping victim, have no European equivalents. The heroine of Europe's most popular bondage/S&M film of the eighties, *Histoire d'O*, endures imprisonment, torture and mutilation, but does so first to please her lover, then in an existential affirmation of free will.

Since pursuit, rape and seduction have little place in the brothel tradition that nurtured Europe's *cinema clandestin*, their absence from porn films is understandable. American porn, however, exists in the real world, where women must be competed for, wooed and satisfied, and where men risk rejection, even contempt, if they fail. How much more attractive to imagine a magic ring that renders bathroom walls transparent, or a drug that makes all women complaisant and passionate. A drugged, sleeping or bewitched girl was that most potent of aphrodisiacs, the "sure thing."

Buried Treasure marks an early appearance of male performers chosen for the size of their penis. Men in porn films of the Teens and Twenties were almost uniformly of normal proportions, but over the next forty years, the size of the male organ would preoccupy filmed pornography, as big breasts would dominate the "glamour photography" and pin-ups of the time.

The mythology of huge penises would develop through the Havana performer "Superman" and his protégé "Superboy" (celebrated in Coppola's *The Godfather*, where John Cazale's Fredo takes Michael Corleone and friends to a sex show featuring this legendary freak), to the suspect enormity of Eighties black porn star Long Dong Silver, laudatory references to whom in conversation with a female colleague almost prevented Justice Clarence Thomas in 1991 from taking his place on the Supreme Court Bench. By the Nineties, penises with an erect length of more than ten inches were as much a requirement of any porn stud as a highly visible ejaculation.

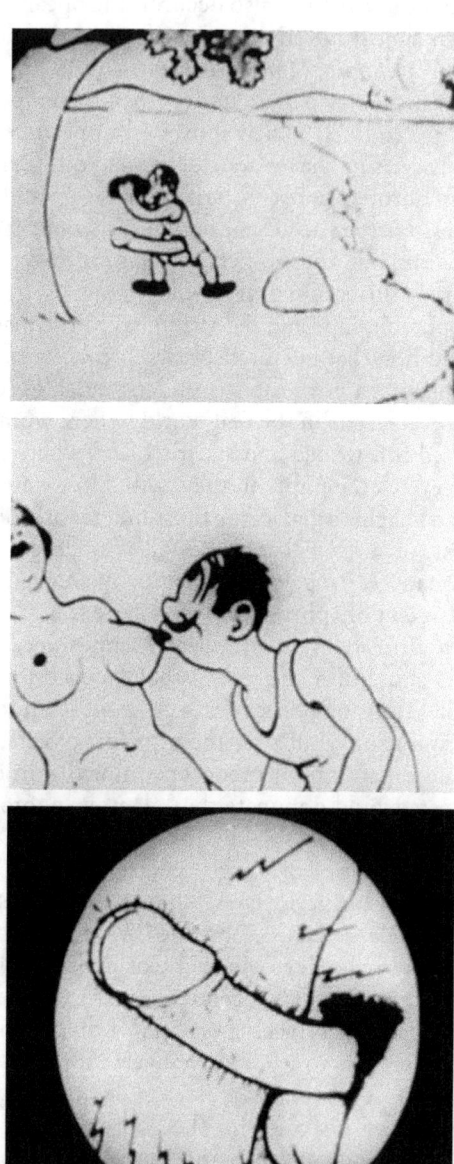

Buried Treasure.

Content to satisfy the *homme moyen sensual*, porn films seldom strayed into the jungle of fetishism, ignoring the often bewildering range of objects, situations and odours that offer sexual arousal. Rubber and leather clothing, underwear, high heels and shoes in general have armies of adherents. So do voyeurism, colonic irrigation and animals. Most of the fetishes catered for in brothels of the nineteenth century are as popular as ever, with a few exceptions. Every *maison close* with a kitchen once offered a specialty in which an omelette was slid, still sizzling, onto the naked body. There's little call for it today.

Paying money for sex can itself be a powerful stimulus, an idea with which Luchino Visconti flirted in his episode of the omnibus film *Boccaccio '70*, where heiress Romy Schneider finds she can keep the interest of her playboy husband only by forcing him to pay her the same rate as his call girls. The corollary, that Schneider herself might be excited by the arrangement, was too risqué for those pre-*Deep Throat* days. In a related scene, Anouk Aimée as the jaded socialite in Fellini's *La Dolce Vita* lures Marcello Mastroianni to the home of a sex worker in order to have sex in her bed.

Women in uniforms, especially nurses, maids and other menials, have almost universal erotic appeal, and frequently appear in porn. Women retaining their shoes and stockings while otherwise nude is another common turn-on, and today a bedroom – and cinema – commonplace. *Hot Times*, a porn film trade journal, published a letter asking "Why do all the women (in porn films) wear high heels in bed?" The editor, rationalising furiously, suggests "photographers think that a woman's leg is sexier-looking in heels; also, the bottom of the foot is not the most photogenic part of the body." "The only thing I ever got out of it," he ends on a *cri du coeur*, "was holes in my sheets."

Both the animated *Buried Treasure* and live-action *The Goat* – an American film dated between 1920 and 1926, in which a man, extorting sex as the price of returning the clothes of three girls he has surprised swimming nude, is tricked into fucking a goat through a hole in a fence – show sex with animals, not an especially popular fetish, nor one featured a great deal in movie porn, if only because of the logistical problems.

The concept of sexual contact through a fence or other barrier, however, became a staple of porn, and remains so today. Anyone acquainted with porn peep-shows or public lavatories frequented by gays will be familiar with so-called Glory Holes. A New York club in the early Eighties called The Glory Hole offered little more than two stories of corridors and holes. Around the same time, a SoHo gallery presented *Glory Hallelujah*, a photographic exhibition of such holes in public toilets. Their popularity was international. Gael Knepper described their appearance in an Australian sex shop.

> The video booths are small spaces where 25c in the slot will buy one and a half minutes of video porn. In this particular place there is a row of ten brown cubicles, like confessionals. I locked the door behind me and in the unfamiliar blackness was assailed with the strong smell of semen. My eyes adjusted to the light. I put the coin in the slot and the space filled with flickering electric colour. In one of the cubicle walls, at about hip level, there was a roughly scratched hole in the plywood, straight into the next cubicle. My feet were sticking to the floor. The space was filled with a blur of groans as the horny, naked stud started coming into the rear of one of the accommodating models. Then it went black, needing more coins. In the quiet I heard a door bang in the next cubicle. Someone shuffled and unzipped and a coin clonked into place.

Fiction has variously glorified the practice or deplored it. The marijuana farmers in T. Coraghessan Boyle's 1984 novel *Budding Prospects*, horny after months cultivating their weed in the wilderness, scour San Francisco for sex on their one night off. They end up in a back-street garage. It's empty except for a Cerberus with a nightstick and a copy of *The Wall Street Journal*, and a wall of plasterboard pierced by holes.

"I was stunned," says the narrator. "This was crude, this was obscene, the ultimate in depravity, moral turpitude and plain bad taste. Talk about the zipless fuck, this was real anonymity, cold and soulless as an execution. I was repelled. But as I watched Raul, Rudy and Gesh count out their money, I began to see the perverse allure of it too." *Dancer From the Dance* (1978) by (the pseudonymously punning?) "Dennis Holleran" was enthusiastic about the practice. But in Tony Fennelly's *The Glory Hole Murders* (1985), a New Orleans psychopath traps gays by skewering their penises on the other side of the hole, making it impossible for them to withdraw. He then nips round to administer a fatally corrosive enema.

Porn film enthusiastically embraced the glory hole, notably in *Liaisons Coupables*, an up-market French porn film made by Michel Ricaud in 1987. Chris Lerique and her equally beautiful companion, naked but for stockings and suspenders, take refuge from the denizens of a Paris sex club in the male urinal. Large holes have been drilled in the walls. A penis pokes through one of them, a 500FF note wrapped round it like a lettuce leaf on a hot dog. The girl starts to masturbate it. Two more holes, two more cocks, another 1000 FF. Lerique gets to work on both.

One fetish has shown surprising durability, to the extent of becoming essential to most modern porn films – the so-called "cum" or, in more modern terminology, "money shot." British critic Alexander Walker wrote in 1977 that recent X-rated films had in common "the explicitness of sexual ejaculation, now visibly portrayed and indeed regarded as an earnest of authenticity [...] Where pelvis thrusts and erect members were deemed sufficient only a few years ago, visceral evidence is now wanted as a guarantee that the act is not being simulated."

In this, as in much else, Walker was mistaken. Far from being a phenomenon of the Seventies, the money shot features in the earliest porn films. Its justification wasn't as "an earnest of authenticity" – the actors' erections supply that – but simply a need to satisfy those viewers excited by seeing the emission of semen, It provided a joke in Terry Gilliam's 1991 *The Fisher King*. The proprietress of a video rental store (Mercedes Ruehl) quizzes the potential borrower of an X-rated video: "Whatcha looking for? A story? What?" When he mumbles "Something with semen," she thrusts a tape into his hand. "Here y'are," she says. "*Creamer vs. Creamer*. It won a prize." The fetish soared in popularity with the emergence of Japanese *bukake*, in which multiple masturbators ejaculate onto a woman's naked body.

Producers have occasionally attempted to discard the "money shot," always without success. San Francisco producer/director Lowell Pickett, a contemporary of the Mitchell brothers, producers of *Behind the Green Door*, tried in films such as the 1973 *Rendezvous with Anne* to show sex more realistically. Despite the quality of his work, audiences refused to accept a film that lacked visible ejaculation. It was like a Western without a gunfight, a romance without the clinch.

So crucial is the money shot that films go to extraordinary lengths to include it. If an actor can't produce a sufficiently photogenic emission, a grip will fake one with dishwashing detergent or shampoo. When, in the Seventies documentary *Making the Blue Movie*, an actress was shown spitting out a wad of ejaculate onto a man's thigh after fellatio, the effect to anyone who has seen many porn films was startling. Such shots never make it into a complete film. Semen in porn films may be gulped, licked, savoured, rubbed onto the skin and otherwise treated with respect, but expectorated? Never. It became far more common for the man to ejaculate onto the woman's face, and for her to visibly relish theexperience, an act known as a *facial*, while a shot of a vagina oozing semen was dignified with the label *cream pie*. Given hidden agendas of such complexity, inventing the action for a pornographic film can have all the restrictions of setting a chess problem. It's no trade for amateurs, not even those as well-informed as Graham Greene.

Paris remained the international capital for sex throughout the Thirties. Even during World War II, Parisian brothels flourished under a German occupation that encouraged business as usual. Le Chabanais and five other famous establishments were requisitioned for the exclusive use of officers, and a further sixteen set aside for enlisted men. Interestingly, condoms were compulsory everywhere. The *laissez-faire* attitude of Parisians to the German presence was summed up by Arletty, star of *Les Enfants du Paradis* and *Les Visiteurs de Soir*. She shrugged off accusations of sexual liaisons with the invaders with a wisecrack: "My heart is French but my ass is international." The post-war administration was not so understanding. She was briefly arrested, and, to re-record her dialogue for *Les Enfants du Paradis*, brought to the studio in handcuffs.

In 1946, however, reformer Marthe Richard, a heroine of World War I, when she had spied for France, was funded by the Catholic church to run for municipal office in Paris. She campaigned so vigorously against brothels that, while prostitution remained legal, officially sanctioned *maisons de tolerance* and *maisons closes* were forced out of business. In a subtle protest, some auctioned off their furniture, pointedly supplying a scandalous provenance for the more important pieces. Filmed pornography almost disappeared, even in Paris, the city that had been its capital. It was, however, a hardy weed, and had already cropped up elsewhere, flourishing in foreign soil.

7
The Girls Next Door

Anonymity, for decades a tradition of public sex, began to erode in the late Forties as American stag cinema moved tentatively closer to the limelight. The process was gradual, however, and nobody in the porn world would ever abandon their incognito without a struggle. There was a tradition of heavily facetious pseudonyms. *A Free Ride* credits its direction to "A. Wise Guy," photography to "Will B. Hard" and the titles to "Will She." (After his fall from grace in 1922 with the Virginia Rappé scandal, comic Roscoe 'Fatty' Arbuckle directed a few shorts under the rueful alias "Will B. Good.") Other participants include "R.U. Hard" and "Ima Cunt."

The tradition can be seen flourishing in Europe after World War II in an ambitious one-reeler called *La Femme au Portrait*, starring, according to the credits, "Clio Clitoris," "Colette Cholera" and *Queue de Beton*; i.e. "Tail (penis) of Concrete." Relentlessly pursuing the joke, the "Director of pollutions" was given as *Bandeur* (hard dick), the "Technical Supervoyeur" as *Lebigleur* (cross-eyed) and the "Director of pornography" as *Lefrustre*. The practice continues today, without much improvement in humour. Strippers called "Stormy Tempest" and (more subtly) "Sha Landres" i.e. Shall Undress, have been joined by contemporary porn stars and technicians called "Candy Samples," "Laurel Canyon," "John Dough," "Vari Knotty," "April Rayne" and "Penny Arcade." The costumes on *Insatiable II* are by a "Raynor Shine."

Post-World War II, however, many dropped their pseudonyms. With film and radio appearances, strippers such as Lily St Cyr and Gypsy Rose Lee revealed that living people hid behind the sexual images. Both made brief (and sanitised) Hollywood movie appearances. In particular Lee, born Rose Louise Hovick, skilfully merchandised her image, in part under the guidance of director Otto Preminger, with

Rita Hayworth in *Gilda*.

whom she enjoyed a long liaison, and by whom she had a child. In 1941, Lee, like a number of Hollywood stars, let her name be put on a novel, in her case a detective story, *The G-String Murders*, ghosted by crime writer Craig Rice, alias Georgiana Craig.

No porn star enjoyed this degree of acceptance, but audiences, for whom the intellectual disrobing of strip stars had been almost as interesting as their physical *deshabillé*, improvised by inventing a reality or attaching one already in existence. Pocket-sized pornographic comic booklets, the "Tijuana Bibles" that were the comic strip equivalent of porn film, had already experimented with the same thing. Some invented original characters. Others parodied such familiar strips as *Barney Google* or cartoon character Mickey Mouse. More common than either, however, were crudely drawn strips featuring real-life characters; Mae West screwing her way through Hollywood's stud farm, Fred Astaire and Ginger Rogers locked in improbable coitus, or a nymphomaniac Bonnie Parker taking time off from banditry to be serviced by a well-hung yokel who's honed his skill on his mule.

From celebrities caught *in flagrante delicto,* it was a short step to imagining one's own love objects similarly exposed. Julian Symons, analysing the plots of Sixties' crime novels in his study of detective fiction *Bloody Murder*, notes that "blackmail by means of pornographic films or photographs is commonplace [in crime fiction], with the pictures sometimes described." Occasionally there is an elegant variation. The psychopathology of the serial murderer in Thomas Harris' *The Silence of the Lambs* feeds on a conviction that a woman in a nudie film is the mother who abandoned him. More

A "Tijuana bible" version of comic strip *Barney Google*.

popular, however, was Graham Greene's theme in *The Blue Film* (employed by writers from Raymond Chandler in *The Big Sleep* to Robert Parker in *Immortal Stakes*) that early porn appearances by a movie star, socialite or politician's wife may come back to haunt them.

During the early Forties, an image of the American male's sexual ideal began to emerge. She did so, as most such images do, by consensus, swimming up from the collective unconscious of a population drawn to the sleek, plasticized women of movies and advertising, but yearning for a hometown girl who might accept their embraces without derision or resistance. This girl had the lush body, perfect legs and long, dark, carefully coiffed hair of a film star, combined with a farm girl look, humorous and unsophisticated.

She first appeared in the work of pin-up artists Hugh Petty and Alberto Vargas, who crossed pornographic imagery with glossy advertising layouts and sold the result to magazines such as *Esquire*, which featured their air-brush fantasies as the first centrefolds. Pirated, the figure decorated the sides of Flying Fortresses during World War II, was recycled in comic strips as the Dragon Lady of Milton Caniff's *Terry and the Pirates* and "Sand Serif" of Will Eisner's *The Spirit*.

By 1946, that image was already sufficiently familiar (and cleansed by that familiarity) for Hollywood to adapt it for Rita Hayworth in *Gilda*. Under her (discreetly baggy) strapless evening gown, the bumping, grinding, long-glove-waving Hayworth of *Put the Blame on Mama* was this ideal made flesh, though it was left to someone from the porn world to become its perfect incarnation.

Ads for Charles Vidor's film proclaimed "There Never Was a Woman Like Gilda," but Bettie Page came close. She became the best known of all forties photo models, and, long after she disappeared from the scene, still has millions of devoted admirers. British pop artist Allen Jones called her's "a phallic image, a male image of female parts." More important than the proportions of Page's body was the pleasure she obviously took in it. No matter what contortion or bizarre costume her job demanded, she retained her smile and naiveté. She was the pin-up made flesh, the personification of that American sexual ideal – "the girl next door," in the words of a later porn star, Ginger Lynn, "who did the things the girl next door would never do."

Bettie Page and Irving Klaw.

Born in 1923 in Kingsport, Tennessee, Page graduated with a BA from Peabody College for Teachers and became a schoolteacher. In 1942, she married her childhood sweetheart, Billy Neal, and moved to San Francisco when he enlisted in the Navy. Bettie took acting and dancing lessons in Los Angeles for the next three years, and caught the eye of Art Grayson, who ran a small talent agency. He sent some pictures of her to 20th Century Fox but they rejected her because of her strong southern accent and the uncategorizable exotic look she attributed to her mother's mixed Cherokee ancestry.

Bettie's marriage didn't survive the war, and by 1948 she was in New York, working as a secretary on Wall Street, supplementing her salary with modelling and some summer stock acting. According to legend, amateur photographer Jerry Tibbs spotted her at Jones Beach on Long Island in 1952 and sent his pictures to Robert Harrison, publisher at the time of *Wink*, *Titter* and *Eyeful*, but later of the notorious scandal magazine *Confidential*. Page's career as a sex symbol was decisively launched.

Page became, and remains, an erotic product of extraordinary potency and wide appeal. One of the best works about her was written by Bernardino Zapponi, screenwriter for Federico Fellini's *Satyricon*. Her image permeates the work of illustrator Frank Frazetta. Allen Jones incorporated her distinctive figure into his paintings after having seen it in a mail-order catalogue. Page herself was even a character in Dave Stevens' comic strip *The Rocketeer*, and the feature film based on it. Page so fascinated Stevens that he chose his wife Brinke for her resemblance, and made her over into her lookalike.

Page did most of her film work for New York entrepreneur Irving Klaw. The first American to turn the production of pornography into a business, Klaw, having identified the market during World War II, bombarded it for the next two decades, applying his considerable talents as producer and salesman. At a time when it was rare for a sex filmmaker to make more than half a dozen productions – the 1970 Presidential Commission found only 51 individuals or groups who had made more than five films – Irving Klaw was a one-man industry. Through his "Movie Star News," which sold movie stills to collectors, he distributed pin-up shots of Bettie Page and other models. As "Beautiful Productions Inc." he made two feature films, *Variatease* and *Teaserama* featuring stripper Tempest Storm, with Page taking second billing. As "Nutrix," he merchandised

16mm and 8mm strip and fetish films, as well as novels and magazines for the bondage market.

Klaw shrewdly cross-collateralized his many enterprises. Films included advertisements for other Klaw productions. Regular customers would be offered photos of models such as Page in fetishistic costumes being spanked, whipped or confined in elaborate systems of ropes or cages. The same pictures were used to illustrate his novels. Gillian Freeman, writing about Klaw's books in *The Undergrowth of Literature,* her pioneering 1967 survey of porn, noticed that Klaw fiction such as *Slave Mistress* contained "several plugs for the publishing house, Nutrix Books [...] Gerald is actually drawing a bondage pose for Nutrix when Portia pounces, and later on, "She bound Gerald into a kneeling position and then sat on his body in order to read a book put out by the Nutrix Company."

Short, plump and balding, Klaw needed only a cigar and three days' stubble to fit everyone's image of the pornographer. Nothing in the record, however, suggests he was anything but a conscientious employer. Photographs show him as an amiable presence on the set, sharing coffee and doughnuts with his smiling employees. His sister Paula acted as chaperone and studio manager, and designed the gadgets in which Page and her fellow models were trussed up.

Even hostile commentators have found it hard to discover anything especially vicious in Klaw's operation. Gillian Freeman too was more bemused than offended by Nutrix's books and magazines. "*Slave Mistress* is to be commended for its variation and style," she wrote. "*Bondage Enthusiasts Bound in Leather, Bondage Devotees Tied, Gagged and Disciplined, Initiated and Spanked by Satin-Clad Bondage Fans, Holiday in Fetterland* and numerous other works are less elegantly phrased and employ a smaller vocabulary, though some, such as *Dominating Tame-Azons Shame Men into Subjection*, employ novel devices." About Paula Klaw's "novel devices" of leather and rubber, her leg-irons, straitjackets and miscellaneous swings and roundabouts, Bernardino Zapponi's book on Page is positively avuncular. He fantasises about her conceiving "torture devices that even a child could duplicate, tying her little sister upside down from the swing, her little butt well exposed." Such images, he asserts, can have therapeutic value. "Looking at Bettie and her colleagues, even a Minnesota farmer come to town to buy some tools discovered he could buy a rope for his wife."

Collectors Cartoon Classics, published by Nutrix.

Bettie Page's career in the kinkier end of the Klaw operation is harder to research. She never appeared in outright pornographic films or even posed for photographs more outrageous than some so-called "split-beaver" shots. Though none of her bondage or "cat fight" (female wrestling) films have found their way onto the market, at least nineteen of her "exotic dances" are in circulation, all that remains from the fifty-odd films she made between 1951 and 1955. His five-minute reels sold for $12 each in 16mm and $8 in 8mm. At such low prices, they quickly found their way into thousands of surreptitious basement screenings and stag nights. The fact that they exist today almost entirely in prints so battered, scratched and re-copied as to be barely watchable is an index of her popularity. Yet through the grain and the flare, beyond their blankly utilitarian photography, and irrespective of the naive sets (couch, carpet, curtain and lamp, if that much), something was communicated by this girl in the black underwear, undulating and smiling through the debris of half a century – an innocence and sensual pleasure that is archetypally American.

Page's career was transformed when she met model and figure photographer Bunny Yaeger on a holiday in Florida. Yaeger, knowing nothing of her background, shot a series of pictures that revealed her essential innocence, the girl-next-door quality that made her particularly appealing. One of Yaeger's pictures, of Page dressed in a somewhat modified and abbreviated Santa Claus costume, became *Playboy*'s centrefold for January 1955.

Cutting herself off from porn, Page returned to acting class, even studying with one of New York's most respected teachers, Herbert Berghof. She failed to get into the Actors Studio but had small roles in *The US Steel Hour* and other TV shows, and auditioned for work on stage. Pressured to return to modelling, she compromised by hiring out to camera clubs for "glamour weekends," where she posed for scores of admirers, some of whom even had cameras. Among those who turned up, without a camera, for such a weekend was later screenwriter/actor Buck Henry, an unashamed Page admirer.

Hollywood in the Forties and Fifties was far from blind to the existence of porn. For a decade, smaller Poverty Row companies had been quietly turning out features intended solely for the exploitation market. Never registered for copyright nor given a general release, these films were distributed by a group of independents known in the business as "The Forty Thieves" who hauled them around the Midwest and the South in the trunks of their cars and took over local cinemas, paying off the manager and, usually, the law. Once the amenities had been observed and the police returned to the station, distributors supplied a "square-up reel" of more salacious material which could be added to the film for special screenings. Since projectionists were notorious for clipping out frames from interesting scenes, they also offered duplicate copies of erotic sequences, a practice that continued in porn until the Seventies.

This was the sleazy world celebrated by Tim Burton's *Ed Wood*, of starvation budgets, broken-down directors and performers, and above all of the gaudy poster and the hard sell. Wood's *Glen or Glenda*, supposedly a film about homosexuality and transvestism, was intended to tap the same market. The films often masqueraded as sex education documentaries or warnings against venereal disease, the "White Slave Traffic" (i.e., forced prostitution), or the use of marijuana. Screenings were preceded by a lecture from the stage by a presenter whose white lab coat implied medical credentials, while a similarly dressed "nurse" sold the explanatory booklets, more profitable than admissions. The 1936 *Tell Your Children*, directed by Louis Gasnier, which survived as a cult film under its later reissue title *Reefer Madness*, was better remembered than more successful films such as the sex education drama *Mom and Dad*, directed in 1944 by another veteran, William Beaudine, and featuring the first scenes of childbirth most of these audiences would ever have seen on screen.

Mom and Dad was conceived by showman Kroger Babb, who saw how the rural market could be exploited by a shrewd appeal to secrecy and guilt. David F. Friedman, an admirer of Babb who bought the rights to *Mom and Dad* in 1956 and re-released it to a whole new generation, described to Kenneth Turan and Stephen Zito how "this fucking *Mom and Dad* was everywhere. There ain't a theatre in America that didn't play this picture. They had a show for women at two o'clock in the afternoon, another show for women at

Collectors Cartoon Classics, published by Nutrix.

seven o'clock, and then a show for men at nine, and everybody had to listen to the lecture, and everybody bought the book – no, two books – how to do it, how not to do it, when to do it, why to do it, how not to get the clap, how to get the clap." Friedman estimated the film grossed more than $40 million for its various proprietors.

While the law routinely harassed producers and distributors of stag movies, only a unique combination of malice, bad judgement and ill fortune could bring a solid citizen into the courts for viewing them. In 1942, such a disaster befell Lionel Atwill, star of horror classics such as *Doctor X* and *The Mystery of the Wax Museum* and second lead of von Sternberg's *The Devil Is a Woman*. The actor's parties at his home on D'Este Drive in fashionable Pacific Palisades, like those of Cecil B. DeMille at his nearby Paradise Ranch, were famous for their exotic entertainments and complaisant women. Two of the latter denounced Atwill for pleasuring himself with them on a tiger skin rug at his 1940 Christmas party while running two porn films, *The Plumber and the Girl* and *The Daisy Chain*.

When the police arrested Atwill, friends rallied round, denouncing the claims as lies by a party girl/pimp and her friend who, already pregnant when she attended the party, had decided to shake down Atwill as another actress, Joan Barry, was about to accuse Charlie Chaplin in a false paternity suit. Under oath, Atwill admitted he did sometimes show films to his guests, but only "travelogues and short subjects dealing with home life in many lands." A man named Carpenter, a long-time Atwill friend, backed him up, and it was the girls who were punished, while Atwill was acquitted. A year later, Carpenter, in jail for writing worthless cheques, retracted his testimony. Atwill reluctantly acknowledged he had acquired some porn films, but only to be shown at a stag party for an old friend, a Canadian Mountie – a party, the actor insisted, he hadn't himself attended, being on the tennis court at the time. He lied in the first trial, his lawyer claimed, "like a gentleman," to protect a friend. The court reluctantly convicted him of perjury but gave him only a five-year probationary sentence, which was later quashed.

Fears of retribution kept most professional filmmakers leery of porn, but some flirted with it. Luis Buñuel, who fled to the United States from occupied France, was marooned in New York for months during the early Forties. He spent his time with André Breton, Marcel Duchamp, Fernand Léger and other émigrés, holding Surrealist *séances* in apartments lent by local sympathisers. The large, secluded and well-vegetated balcony of one of them suggested making a porn film among the potted palms and creepers with the skyline of Manhattan in the background. Buñuel's only experience of porn had been *Sister Vaseline*, a film involving a nun, a randy friar and the obligatory obliging gardener, shown to him in Paris by Jean Mauclaire, proprietor of Studio 28, the first cinema to screen his *Un Chien Andalou*. However he shared the Surrealist enthusiasm for the amateurism and subversion of porn, and had no trouble persuading the others to discuss the project. Plans were well advanced when someone explained the risk of fines or imprisonment under American law, stricter than that of France. After this, their enthusiasm dwindled, and they began talking about opening a bar instead.

Pornographers and the US Post Office continued to skirmish well into the Fifties, but this was guerrilla warfare with little hope of more than random victories for the forces of repression. Few porn film distributors had any existence beyond a post office box and a mailing list, and seldom demanded the special mail privileges that would have drawn attention to themselves.

In 1952, the Senate Special Committee to Investigate Crime in Interstate Commerce, led by Senator Estes Kefauver, acknowledged publicly for the first time that most vice in the United States was run by "a nationwide syndicate [...], a loosely organised but cohesive coalition of autonomous crime 'locals' which work together for mutual profit. Behind the local mobs [...] is a shadowy criminal organisation known as the Mafia." This was no news to the FBI, which had been struggling with the Mafia for decades without conspicuous success. Hurriedly, the Bureau's boss J. Edgar Hoover and his friends in the administration looked around for a distraction. In the Thirties, he had disguised an inability to destroy Capone and other crime bosses by targeting rural bandits such as John Dillinger, "Pretty Boy" Floyd and Bonnie Parker and Clive Barrow, all of whom were hunted down and killed in the glare of the newsreel lights. Now he turned to street gangs and stag films for his villains.

In 1955, a Senate sub-committee was set up to investigate Juvenile Delinquency. It specifically targeted pornography and its use of the mails. Police, from Hoover down, solemnly testified that "lewd photographs and magazines stimulated latent sexual desires among adolescents and tended to trigger serious sex crimes." One officer testified that he could not recall a single arrest in a juvenile sex case where quantities of pornography were not found in the offender's possession.

The committee probed the suggestive small ads (*Men! 500 Breezy Fotos!*) that clogged the back pages of pulp magazines. Men who bought baseball bats, stamps or penknives by mail testified that they sometimes received offers of stag films. A New York "Movie Club" would sell you "four tantalising movies on one big reel for $9.99," but what one got, complained a disgruntled buyer, was "three minutes and fifty seconds of children's magic shows, animal pictures and travelogues, with a concluding ten-second shot of an alluring dame."

"Stronger" material was being produced, but professional pornographers were too canny to bother with such scams. Most new productions were disguised as documentaries – one early porn film was called *Wonders of the Natural World* – or as remedial sex films. *Advice to the Lovelorn* and *Honeymoon Helpmeet*, for instance, turned out to be less – or more – educational than chance viewers expected. The latter were both "cat fight" films, "built," charged the committee, "on the same tawdry theme that constantly recurs in these stag productions – the fight between two half-clothed or wholly nude women. Presumably there is some special sexual bang that results from the sight of a dumb blonde, with her breasts flopping, clawing aimlessly at another dumb blonde with her breasts flopping. The acting is ludicrously poor. The girls are not attractive; their appeal is nudity alone."

Some of the porn in circulation was created in Mexico or Europe. From Amsterdam, a group operated as both Univers and Cosmopolite offered a varied catalogue at anything from $12.50 to $78 a film:

> No. 1. Suzy longing for love – still alone – can hardly wait for her boyfriend – how on earth can he resist such beauty?
> No. 2. Suzy could not possibly wait any longer and is now amusing herself.
> No.3. Yes, Suzy rides again and how. Life is too short to be alone, and therefore she rides again.
> No 4. Did you ever see two lovely girls massaging each other?

In 1957, the US Post Office obtained "unlawful" orders against Univers/Cosmpolite, barring them from the mails, but they were soon back in business. The busy post-war economy was expanding, and the stag film with it.

Porn dealers such as Irving Klaw, Burton Steiger, James Frew, Louis Tager, Daniel Loewinger, Harold Steiner and the principals of such companies as Nutrix, Camfield House, Saturn and ARA were, one campaigner acknowledged, anything but the intellectual midgets of William Manchester's description and certainly not "crude illiterates, speaking in dese-and-dose accents." The Post Office held in particular esteem Albert J. Amateau, who operated as ARA Productions Inc. from a Los Angeles address. For $10, Amateau offered to list punters in a Certified Buyers' Registry. Supposedly limited to only 350 members, this would entitle them to receive advance offers of "items of unusual personal interest." The application form demanded not only name, address and occupation but two references. No fool, Amateau specified letters on headed notepaper and did actually check references for authenticity.

Aware that the Post Office came down heavily on anything minors might read, Amateau, who was of Turkish ancestry, also scrambled the descriptions in his catalogues in a mixture of English and Turkish. A typical $115 film was described as *#33 Nugg uvoleotain "Bobuz Sattur." Uzieng, buotafel, brenuttu bobuz sattang fir babuzif ggadiggur; gghum fozzur luovoes, fumolu endressus ti bozzu serprasus zzu ggimon nokud an zu bozzu. Hu andecus hur ta uzauld. Ggimon has buoetafelluz farmud bizus, smoll farm bruosts and napplus. Fozzur till, uzieng, hendsim, hoaruz and mescelor; hu ruterns himu...* Subscribers with the codebook could translate this as "#33 New Evaluation 'Baby Sitter.' Young, beautiful, brunette baby sitter for baby of widower; when father leaves, female undresses to bathe. Father, tall, young, handsome, hairy and muscular; he returns home, surprises the woman naked in the bath. He induces her to yield. Woman has beautifully formed body, small firm breasts and nipples."

When the Post Office got on his trail, Amateau fell back on another cipher ("Please! Keep it safe and strictly confidential. New offers in this code will not be sent until acknowledgment is received in sealed envelope.") After prodigies of transposition, clients discovered that *18 st6r4 b8h7nd 18 st6r4 – J6 7* ch9rL84 9r8 b5s dr7v8r...* described a film in which Joe and Charley, bus drivers, take Betty and Genie from the dispatcher's office out into the woods and have an agreeable time. Police tracked Amateau's operation to a warehouse in Alameda, NM. He was arrested in October 1958 while trying to flee the country. Judge Harry C. Westover said he had seldom seen films as shocking as Amateau's, but, in deference to his sixty years and, one suspects, the ingenuity of his operation, he gave him three years, all but six months suspended.

The Kefauver committee also put Irving Klaw out of business, indicting him for mail fraud. His stock was seized, and an attempt to move his operation to New Jersey failed. Bettie Page was also called to testify and defended Klaw, but Kefauver, apparently incensed that America's most popular pin-up should be from his home state, responded by lecturing her on the evils of her life. Page left New York for Florida, where she remarried. After returning briefly to teaching, she gravitated to Hollywood where, in the most improbable of all career changes, she fell under the sway of evangelist Billy Graham and became a born-again Christian. Retired to Los Angeles, she refused even to acknowledge her life in porn.

Klaw and Amateau were unlucky to be charged at all. Two years later, in 1957, the US Supreme Court in *Roth vs. US* decreed that a work was obscene only if it "outraged local community standards." This took decisions on censorship out of the hands of the Post Office and returned them to the states and, in some cases, to individual cities. Given the elastic standards of some communities, distributing porn became no longer a matter of cunning and resource but of gauging what the market would bear.

8
The Dark, and Strangers

Mark Lewis spends his days as a cameraman in a London film studio. Nights, he shoots sex films or, driven by childhood horrors of a father who used him as his lab rat in psychological experiments, roams Soho's back streets, stalking women. He impales his victims on a blade attached to one leg of his tripod, filming their deaths in 16mm while they watch themselves die in a mirror attached to the lens.

A glimpse of London's well-repressed world of public sex, Michael Powell's 1960 film *Peeping Tom*, as written by Leo Marks, reveals as much about the erotic preoccupations of the country – and the director – as its exact US contemporary, *Psycho*. Pamela Green, then Britain's most popular nude photographic model, has a featured role. Venerable character actor Miles Malleson plays a punter circumspectly inquiring if a newsagent has any "views" for sale, and smacks his lips over the album produced. Upstairs, where Mark shoots his pictures, the models wear the "exotic" outfits – Spanish hats, net stockings, fringed shawls – typical of British pin-ups of the time, and pose against mocked-up Paris street backgrounds.

A complex covert sex industry flourished in Britain for decades, creating its own subculture and codes. Cards in tobacconists' windows advertised "French lessons" and "Correction" by "young models" or, more deviously, "rubber goods" or antique furniture ("40-inch chest for sale, in good condition"). Nude photographs were sold as "art studies" or appeared in magazines that documented nudism. The shows at Folies Bergère imitations such as London's Windmill Theatre, which, by defying the Blitz ("We Never Closed"), had been adopted as a national institution, remained acceptable only as long as its pasty nudes maintained goose-fleshed immobility.

In his 1962 play *Under Plain Cover*, John Osborne theorised about the kind of people who might enjoy a

fulfilling sexual life in this chill moral climate. Jenny and Tim, fortuitously both devoted to the same fetishes, flourish in the grey milieu of suburban England like a phosphorescent fungus under a rotting log.

> Jenny: Do you think there are many people like us?
> Tim: No. Probably none at all, I expect.
> Jenny: Oh, there must be some.
> Tim: Well, yes, but probably not two together.
> Jenny: You mean just one on their own?
> Tim: Yes.
> Jenny: How awful. We *are* lucky.

Perhaps Tim and Jenny only enjoy a little cross-dressing. As, however, real life later illustrated, they could just as easily be murdering children. Those not so fortunate as to have confederates had to find their fun where they could, either in tobacconists' windows, in the nudist magazines, or among the ammoniac "cottages" of the public parks.

If, on the other hand, you were rich, such problems didn't arise. The tradition enshrined in the Edwardian ballad *She Was Poor But She Was Honest* still applied into the Sixties. "It's the same the whole world over/It's the poor what gets the blame/It's the rich what gets the pleasure/Isn't it a bleeding shame?"

In his 1962 novel *Close of Play*, Simon Raven evokes the upper-class sexual milieu of the time as effectively as *Peeping Tom* does its middle-class equivalent. A young intellectual who lives by the rule "Never regret anything" becomes a caterer of gourmet sex to the aristocracy. An Oxford friend questions the fairness of serving only the rich: "It seems a pity so much talent should be wasted on decaying old men when there are so many young and beautiful people who must go without." He replies "The young and the beautiful make their own arrangements."

In Anglo-Saxon cultures, that which is foreign is also exotic, and therefore, in certain circumstances, sexually arousing. For the British, labelling something "French" – knickers, postcards, kisses – always implied an element of the forbidden. Such cultural shorthand was widely employed in discussing sex. Sodomy, in whatever country it turned up, was "Greek" or "Italian," but flagellation always the "English vice." Condoms were "French letters" in England, *Capotes Anglaise* in France. Syphilis was traditionally the "French disease" in England but the "Neapolitan disease" in France – which, in venerable Gallic tradition, shifted the blame south.

Britain has never been a major source of hardcore. Producers encountered the same problems as the UK film industry in general: domination by foreign product and a lukewarm local audience. Why Buy British when you could have German or Danish porn mailed direct to your home Under Plain Wrapper? So potent was the promise of "foreign" porn that British pornographers went to ridiculous lengths to acquire the right label. According to John Trevelyan, British film censor throughout the Sixties, a number of porn films made in Britain were exported to Denmark, then re-imported with the crucial "Danish" tag.

"There was an Obscene Publications Squad then," recalled softcore photographer/filmmaker George Harrison Marks in 1993. "I was in [Soho's] Gerrard Street at the time. There were dozens of heavy porn bookshops and a very big porn [production] industry, which doesn't exist now, strangely enough. Proper hardcore stuff. The Old Bill [i.e., police] were paid off regularly. The stuff came from abroad, not home-grown." Crime novelist Robin Cook, alias Derek Raymond, whose novels of the London underworld like *The Devil's Home on Leave* and *I Was Dora Suarez* rest on first-hand observation, managed a Soho porn shop in the Fifties. He was taken aback when a group of policemen walked in and demanded "the films." After denying there were any on the premises, he called his boss, who explained that, far from wanting to bust the shop, the police were collecting entertainment for their Christmas party.

The real reasons for a shortage of porn, however, probably lie deeper, in the collective shame Powell isolated in *Peeping Tom*, and the furtiveness that Britons had come to demand in their sexual dealings. Terence Rattigan, who relished dissecting British embarrassment, spelled it out in *Separate Tables* (1954). When the pompous "Major" Pollock is arrested for groping in a cinema, he explains to a fellow guest of his stiflingly moral Bournemouth boarding-house, "It has to be the dark – always with strangers." In the original of the play, it also had to be men, but the Lord Chamberlain, then Britain's theatre censor, insisted Rattigan, also gay, change this.

For the British cinema of the Sixties, a hardcore film flickering peripherally in a party scene became the accepted signifier of irredeemable decadence. James Fox in *The Servant* (1963) watched stag films at a languid Bayswater orgy as did Michael Caine in the 1971 *Get Carter*. For a scene in *Performance* (1970) where Fox, a gangster this time, puts the frighteners on a porn producer, directors Donald Cammell and Nicolas Roeg resurrected, presumably because nothing local was available, a popular but untitled French S&M film from twenty years before. In it, a personable young woman was bent over a table and languidly flagellated by a lady in a peignoir and a gentleman wearing beret, socks, sweater and – better safe than sorry – both false nose *and* fake moustache. Clearly scornful of the whole enterprise, the victim participates expressionlessly, except for one withering stare into the camera, which Roeg and Cammell use to good effect. (This film in its complete form begins and ends with a nude girl stepping out from behind a curtain with cards reading *Entr'acte* and *Fin*. From what sort of Parisian *divertissement*, one wonders, would such a film have been regarded as light relief?)

Lindsay Anderson, loyally Buying British, commissioned English cineaste Tony Sloman, who had directed a couple of sex romps, to create a porn film for a party scene in his 1973 *O Lucky Man!* John Landis, however, rolled his own for the 1981 *An American Werewolf in London*, creating convincing scenes from a British softcore film, *See You Next Wednesday*, as background for a sequence in the now-defunct Jacey basement sex cinema in

Piccadilly Circus. The film came complete with joke credits: Brenda Bristols (actually Linzi Drew) and Lance Boyle (Lucienne Morgan). The same Linzi Drew later became editor of *Penthouse*, then was jailed in 1992 for her part in a porn video distribution business.

Today, those furtive scenes of *The Servant* and *Performance* have an almost archaeological value. In the Seventies, the floodgates, as moral campaigners liked to phrase it, opened, and London's Soho swelled into what would become, for a few years anyway, one of the vice spots of Europe. Nobody in England would ever really be shocked by hardcore again.

The reality of the sexual pursuits of the well-heeled and well-hung, as well as the accommodations described by Simon Raven as being available only to the rich, came dramatically to light in 1961/2 when John Profumo, Minister for War in the government of Harold Macmillan, confessed to an affair with party girl Christine Keeler. Keeler might easily have been one of the women photographed by Mark Lewis, posing for the 8mm films of softcore producer George Harrison Marks or shivering at the Windmill in body make-up and a bunch of grapes. In fact, she was prancing in careful near-nudity round the miniscule stage of Percy Murray's Cabaret Club in Soho when she and her friend Mandy Rice-Davies were noticed by society osteopath Stephen Ward, who took Keeler in hand and passed her around among his wealthy patients and friends. In Michael Thomas' script for *Scandal*, Michael Caton-Jones' 1989 film about the Profumo affair, the club owner leads his patrons, pointedly identified as "My lords, ladies and gentlemen," in three cheers for the re-election of Harold Macmillan's flabby Conservative administration. Responding was a group that ranged from Lord Astor to slumlord Peter Rachman, united in their wealth and taste for sensation.

One irony of the stand against moral decadence taken by British films in the Sixties was that many filmmakers were themselves involved. Mandy Rice-Davies named Douglas Fairbanks Jr. as a client of herself, Christine and fellow party girl Mariella Novotny. (The actor, though an admitted patient of Stephen Ward, denied knowing them.) The name of producer, scriptwriter and TV executive Harry Alan Towers turned up often in testimony. Another intimate of the Ward circle, Diana Dors, a semi-amateur prostitute before entering movies, took lovers from the shady side of London clubland, including ex-Etonian "Dandy Jim" Caborn-Waterfield, jailed for burglarising the French Riviera home of actor Jack Warner. Dennis Hamilton, one of Dors' husbands, was a friend of Rachman and Ward and a regular guest at Rachman's country house, which was fitted out with one-way mirrors, hidden cameras and tape recorders. Barbara Windsor, busty star of *Carry On* films, married Ronnie Knight, a henchman for the notorious criminal Kray brothers.

Among the events unearthed in the Profumo investigation was a 1961 London party thrown by Mariella Novotny at which a man, naked and masked, was tied between two wooden pillars. Each guest struck him with a whip as they arrived, and he spent dinner cowering under the table. He was Anthony "Puffin" Asquith, director of *The Winslow Boy* and *The Yellow Rolls Royce*. Asquith, who shared with T.E. Lawrence a taste for flagellation and working-class rough trade, ideally with a military flavour, could be found on many weekends serving behind the counter of a tea stall near the military base at Catterick.

It was an accommodation strikingly similar to that arrived at by Lawrence, who, after seeking anonymity in the Royal Air Force as "T.E. Shaw," hired a young colleague to flog him periodically, under the pretext that a relative had insisted Lawrence prove his stamina should it be needed when another war broke out. The man was required to write detailed descriptions of these ritual beatings and Lawrence's reaction to them. These were mailed to a postal address which belonged not to the notional uncle but to Lawrence. Most biographers now agree that the incident at Deraa, described in *The Seven Pillars of Wisdom*, during which, spying in Arab clothing, he was supposedly flogged and sodomised by a Turkish officer and his men, was another such invention. In the way of fantasies, however, it achieved extraordinary longevity, being featured in David Lean's 1962 film and in the play *Ross,* where Terence Rattigan, a connoisseur of British sexuality's more shadowy corners, suggests the beating and sodomy were inflicted on Lawrence by a Turkish general thoroughly aware of his identity and intent on breaking him as leader of the Arab revolt. In the real world, such a general would simply have shot him, but sexual fantasy has its own rules. The man whom Lawrence accused of his torture was still alive in the Sixties, but nobody thought to ask for his version. When truth and legend conflict, print the legend.

Diana Dors

Michael Powell himself had a taste for sexual sadism. In *Peeping Tom*, he cast himself as Professor Lewis' father and his own son Columba as young Mark in home movies on the experiments which turned the young Mark psychopathic. To shoot the scenes, he used the house directly opposite one where he lived as a child. On visits to Australia in the Sixties to direct *They're a Weird Mob* and *Age of Consent*, Powell felt freer to release his impulses. There's more than normal relish in the scene in *Age of Consent* where a nude Helen Mirren is thrashed by Neva Carr-Glyn for admiring herself in front of the mirror, and rumours circulated widely of discomforts inflicted by Powell on his mistress, a local actress.

George Harrison Marks.

If hardcore was rare in Britain throughout the Fifties, there was more than enough softcore to go round. Its king was George Harrison Marks. A publicity photographer of variety shows during World War II, he compiled a few coffee table books of discreet nudes. After a publisher from Denmark approached him to buy these pictures, and whatever else he could supply, Marks metamorphosed into a producer/publisher in the Irving Klaw mould, turning out scores of still photos of pale, breasty young women bathing, posing and frolicking, always with pubic hair discreetly airbrushed out by his wife, model and assistant Pamela Green. The same girls appeared in ten-minute movies. People without projectors to run them bought plastic hand viewers and wound the films through them while holding the appliance up to a light. Since this impeded masturbation, many preferred stills of the same models featured in Marks' magazines such as *Kamera* and black and white booklets, printed in the same sharply incised letterpress as knitting books. Their sisters, less shapely, could also be seen, neutered by airbrush, playing nude volleyball, table tennis and hockey in *Health and Efficiency* – celebrations of nudism and good diet whose editorial was the least-read journalism in Britain.

Nudist magazines and Harrison Marks' one-reelers enshrined the prevailing British ideal of sexuality. Milkmaids and farm girls, wide-hipped, bovine, with soft white breasts, the models seemed kidnapped from eighteenth-century Flanders. Their Junoesque proportions were replicated in a platoon of husky colleagues in modelling and the cinema; Sabrina, Liz Fraser, Pamela Green and Diana Dors, whose charms were emphasised even further by a booklet of "views" employing 3D, the prevailing fad of 1955.

In 1955, the British Board of Film Censors, though busy with cutting or banning such threats to law and order as *The Wild One*, *The Blackboard Jungle* and *The Man With the Golden Arm*, took the time to axe *Garden of Eden*, an American celebration of naturism by journeyman director Max Nosseck. The story of a crusty old man redeemed by his experience of the naked outdoors, featuring Jamie O'Hara as a young widow converted to nudism when she strays into a colony with her six-year-old daughter, *Garden of Eden* was a framework on which to hang scenes of naked men and women, always discreetly photographed from behind or, if from the front, only from the waist up. In erotic charge it barely equalled Nosseck's best-known previous film, an adaptation of Anna Sewell's equine melodrama *Black Beauty*.

Normally a BBFC ban was absolute, but, sensing revolt in the air, the distributors of *Garden of Eden* petitioned London's County Council to permit screening in the capital alone. Not only did the LCC agree, they gave it a "U" certificate, permitting even children to attend. Three hundred more local authorities followed the LCC over the next three years in licensing *Garden of Eden*, but the BBFC wouldn't budge. "Where are we to draw the line?" Board secretary Arthur T. Watkins wrote querulously to a protester: "Long experience has convinced us that it is best to keep nudity off the screen. If we were led to depart from our general rule, we feel sure that we might soon be faced with a dangerous amount of exploitation which we should find it difficult to prevent."

Garden of Eden also became a *cause célèbre* in New York, where the Motion Picture Division of the New York State Education Department, then in charge of censorship, banned it. The distributors, Excelsior Pictures, took the decision to court, and on 3 July 1957 the New York Court of Appeals found that the ban was illegal. A year later, the British Board reversed its stand, conferring a grudging "A" certificate. After that, the nudist wave foretold by Watkins wasn't long in coming.

Predictably, the first such film to go on general release in Britain was produced, directed and co-written by Harrison Marks and starred Pamela Green. *As Nature Intended* follows a secretary, a dancer and a sales girl as they visit a Cornwall naturist camp on their holidays and, after initial nervousness, revel in the experience. The Cameo-Moulin cinema, in the same street as the Windmill, had been reduced to running cartoon programmes, but a double bill of *As Nature Intended* and *The Call Girl Business* galvanised its fortunes. People queued on both sides of the street, in the rain, on opening night. Some were back again at 11am the next day. *World Without Shame*, *Nudist Paradise*, *The Isle of Levant* (set on that French clothing-optional resort), *The Reluctant Nudist* and *It's a Bare, Bare World* repeated the formula, while in America a handful of producers – Bill Mishkin and Joe Brenner in

New York, David F. Friedman in Chicago and Dan Sonney in Los Angeles – each cranked out a nudie every ten or twelve weeks for the fifty or sixty theatres nationwide that dared to show them.

Nudes Around the World, The Bare Hunt, The Nude and the Prude, Hollywood Nudes Report, My Bare Lady and *Career Girls on a Naked Holiday* were as ritualised as their British equivalents. Attractive girls, initially sceptical, encounter nudism while taking a holiday, pursuing boyfriends, looking for a job or, in one extreme case (*Take Off Your Clothes and Live*), searching for buried treasure. After the newcomer is coaxed by her more worldly friends to get naked, the stories unravel into a succession of excuses for distant rear views of the principals. The tone of these films was paralysing genteel. All proselytised as vigorously for naturism as the magazines of which they were little more than movie versions. Since the average nudist was dismally unattractive, most of the performers were professional models. Even then, nudity was confined to rear views and the occasional breast shot, low in what prime time US TV in the Seventies christened "jiggle quotient." Anything more was ruthlessly excised by censor John Trevelyan and his eagle-eyed staff.

"Normally the more genuine the film, the more problems it gave us," Trevelyan recalled. "When real nudist gatherings were filmed, we carefully removed all sight of genitals, if necessary going through the film several times to make sure we had not missed any! I remember one film, however, that caused us trouble because the girls, obviously not genuine nudists, walked about wearing high-heeled white shoes; the makers told me that this was because they had refused to walk on the paths with bare feet. To preserve the sanctity of our rules, we even made a filmmaker insert in his film, which was rather charming and quite harmless, a shot of a notice-board to establish that the film was shot in a nudist camp. It all seems absurd today [1973], but at this time we were concerned about the possibility that we would not find it easy to keep a reasonable control."

As the cycle of what the trade called "nudies" gained strength and direction, producers less interested in health and efficiency than in accountancy cashed in with *Nudes of the World, Some Like it Cool* and *Around the World With Nothing On*. They would continue as an unexceptional part of the erotic movie market until 1966, when *The Raw Ones*, by American producer/director John Lamb, broke the rules by showing frontal nudity. The film had no sex, but the mere fact that one could see what countless other films had hidden was enough to draw audiences. *The Raw Ones* took $3400 in one screening alone at the Paris Theatre

in Los Angeles and cleaned up everywhere else, especially in provincial cities. In a technique that would shortly be adopted by X-rated producer Russ Meyer, Lamb also shrewdly turned the film into a talking point by filling the commentary with libertarian quotes from authorities as eminent as Bertrand Russell, Thomas Jefferson and Hugh Hefner. Critics were disarmed, and though the law took Lamb to court, he won every case. By 1966, however, erotic cinema had outgrown the nude film. A wave of eroticism washed over Britain in the mid-Sixties, changing the rules for good.

9
Danish Blue

Between 1967 and 1969, Denmark removed almost all restrictions on pornography. The adjective "Danish," associated until then with bacon, blue cheese and modern furniture, acquired new connotations as Denmark became Europe's primary exporter of porn, with Britain among its best clients.

"Why should a quiet, prosperous, introspective, Lutheran country like Denmark become the first to liberate pornography?" asked British barrister Fenton Bresler in his book *Sex and the Law*. Lord Longford's 1973 *Report on Pornography* shared his confusion. "At first sight, Denmark, a primarily agricultural country with a population just under five million, would not be expected to provide a relevant comparison with industrial Britain, whose population is twelve times as great."

Among British reformers such as Mary Whitehouse and the staunchly Catholic Longford, the most plausible explanation was a national erotomania, like the waves of *accidie*, a sort of communal despair, that plagued Europe in the Middle Ages. The reason was simpler, and less moral than legal. In fact, the Danes were simply dealing rationally with the growing market in porn, ensuring that local entrepreneurs could continue to make money but at the same time protecting public sensibility. In July 1969, Knud Thestrup, the conservative Minister of Justice, confirmed the official line, that "public authorities should not censor what the adult individual wants to see and to read." It was an attitude that even one member of Lord Longford's committee found persuasive. "The principle of the new law here [Copenhagen]," he wrote, "is that anything goes – providing that you don't impose it on the general public by littering the streets with it or expose it to children at any time. Seems fair enough to me."

The production of erotic books, magazines, films and photographs in Denmark soared during the Sixties, but local consumption barely increased. Almost everything was made for export. The photographs were mostly German or French, though hard-pressed publishers sometimes went as far as England to buy material. At the same time, the rule against public display was rigidly enforced. So much material was confiscated that the police lacked space to store it. In 1967, they asked one wholesaler, Betex Trading, to take back the books, magazines and films they had seized until a court could decide whether or not they should be destroyed.

Danish film producers rushed into production with robust comedies featuring generous quantities of nudity. Not particularly successful at home, the label "Danish" ensured they rated high with other European audiences. The true quality of Danish eroticism, a flaccid jollity reminiscent of English seaside postcards, was well displayed in the popular film comedies written and/or directed by John Hilbard and starring Ole Soltoft. *Bedroom Mazurka*, *Danish Dentist on the Job* (aka *Bedside Dentist*), *Danish Bed and Board* and *Danish Pillow Talk* (all 1973/4) were hugely successful. *Mazurka*, *Dentist* and *Pillow Talk* share the same plot. A naive girl is pursued by overweight captains of industry, horny schoolteachers and randy politicians with dragon wives. *Danish Bed and Board* varies the formula only to the extent of casting Soltoft, usually the young man with whom the liberated heroine ends up, as a schoolteacher troubled with nervous impotence. His students stumble across a recipe for an aphrodisiac which they introduce into the school salt supply, with predictable results.

The Danish decision itself became the subject of films. Cinemas were bombarded with quasi-documentary surveys of sex in Scandinavia, pioneered by Vilgot Sjoman's study of one girl's exploration of the new moral climate, *I Am Curious – Yellow*, and unleashed on America under a 1966 Supreme Court ruling that "redeeming social importance" excused nudity in a film.

I am Curious Yellow.

Alex De Renzy, the San Francisco filmmaker and cinema owner who had hitherto made a good living with ten-minute films of masturbating teenagers, visited Copenhagen to make *Censorship in Denmark: A New Approach* (1970). He was filmed interviewing a (nude) porn actress, visiting sex shops, a pornographers' trade show, a hardcore film in production, and a night club to observe Olga and her Sex Circus, whose performers prowled among the punters, encouraging them to join in the action or masturbate while they watched.

Some films advertised as erotic were anything but. Audiences who hoped for sexual excitement in *The Language of Love*, *More About the Language of Love* and *Sexual Customs in Scandinavia* were often disappointed, as were those spectators for films fronted by American sexologists Phyllis and Eberhard Kronhausen, a humourless couple, determined, it seemed, to place sex on the same excitement level as cost accounting. Their films demonstrated sexual positions with numbing attention to detail and offered more information about venereal disease and impotence than the audience really wanted. Sex for the handicapped was discussed. Men were cautioned to wash under their foreskins following intercourse. When, in the course of a Kronhausen documentary, an audience in London's Charing Cross Road was offered, for the worthiest of purposes, a split-screen display of fifty penises, even the stony British punter was appalled. From the darkness came the weary comment, "Not a pretty sight."

In 1969, Georges Pompidou, President of the French Republic, described his ideal for France as "Sweden, but with a bit more sun." Most of Europe shared his view of its northern neighbour as a beacon of rational humanism and enlightened social legislation, so were not surprised when the Swedes, no less severe believers in total openness than the Danes, followed Denmark by lifting most restrictions on pornography. Tourists visiting Stockholm in the hope of unbridled vice, however, found a sexual climate even more chill than that in Copenhagen. Intensely private people, sombre and introspective, the Swedes hungered not for the pleasures of the flesh but for forests, lakes and a cleansing emptiness. They could be free and open about sex because it didn't interest them very much.

Welsh writer/actor Emlyn Williams visited Stockholm in 1970 to present his one-man show on Charles Dickens, and took time off to check out the porn scene, of which he was a strenuous enemy. *Beyond Belief*, his book on Moors Murderers Ian Brady and Myra Hindley, who tortured a seventeen-year-old and two younger children to death, stressed that the killers read pornography and that Brady owned books by de Sade. Having packed his prejudices when he left London, the actor had them conveniently to hand when his guide conducted him to a neat, well-run sex shop with racks of magazines. He dipped into a few of them, with predictable distaste.

> The Book of Genitalia. Species Gargantua. A public welter, of what used to be called private parts. Fellatio, cunnilingus, anal-oral stimulation, all leading up to the grand finale, the bonne bouche. Visible

> ejaculation. And with every flick, hair, wrinkle, bump, vein and pore continued to glisten as crystal-clear as the apples and oranges in those color ads. A smorgasbord of sex.

Even more disturbing to him were pictures of a woman fellating a horse. Williams' very British love of animals was offended. He rhapsodised about the "beautiful thoroughbred, brown shining coat, fine head in profile, held high in repose..." He also loitered around a live sex show. Though he missed the actual performance, he did glimpse the male of the couple, sipping Coca-Cola and reading while his children played on a swing. The man was "markedly pale. Prison pallor. And all the men who set foot in his place of business, he must hold in the utmost contempt." He was, Williams decided, "being used," as were the women who posed for the books and magazines. In their case, he claimed to see the evidence in their expressions. "The looks on their faces – simulated or real; how can you tell? – are continuously the most driven imploring sort of subjection, involving the drooling of lips, the grinding of teeth and the ecstasy of upturned eyes disappearing under the lids."

Williams spoke to nobody on his tour except his guide and interpreter, a Swedish professor on whom he confers a comic accent ("yolly Christmas presents, yaw?"). He could, with very little trouble, have met the girl in the animal pictures. A celebrity in the Scandinavian porn world, Bodil Joensen was in fact Danish. With her horse Dreamlight and her German Shepherd bitch Smut, she featured in most of Copenhagen's and Stockholm's live sex shows, as well as the magazines through which Williams leafed. She raised all the animals personally on her farm in the north of Zeeland. Her stock included some cattle, twelve pigs, four cats, two horses, two dogs, some geese and a hamster, though not all, she reassured visitors, were sex partners.

Williams' perceptions of the Swedish sex business were as blinkered as his view of the Swedes. The sex performer was pale? So are most Swedes – and, for that matter, most

Britons. As for the girls and their imagined air of oppression, Bodil Joensen at least found her work satisfying and rewarding. In fact, she preferred animals to people. "When we made the last porno magazine," she said, "they gave me a new partner, a man I didn't know, and it was *awful*!"

Shortly after Williams' Stockholm trip, the Longford committee made its own pilgrimage to Copenhagen. The Danish Embassy arranged conferences with bishops and diplomats, professors of jurisprudence and political science, and officials from the Ministry of Foreign Affairs, but, in what was now a well-established tradition, nobody from the porn business itself.

Lacking expert guidance, Longford and his team struck trouble as soon as they took their enquiries into the streets. Their report describes the most memorable moments of the visit, which were (as Longford may have hoped and expected) well covered by accompanying pressmen.

"Two visits were paid to so-called live shows," said one report, "from both of which the Chairman felt compelled to walk out after brief encounters, in the second case with a 'lady' who appeared afterwards to have been a man. In his own words he had "seen enough for science and more than enough for enjoyment." When asked whether he had not expected to meet these phenomena, he replied that he had not foreseen the audience participation required of him. The rest of the team proved to be of sterner stuff, and saw the show through to the end.

Not all the committee shared Longford's closed mind. One member noted later, "Lord L's sole reaction is disgust, no more, no less. The rest of us aren't sure that disgust is a very useful reaction. This is where two very different outlooks begin to emerge. He sees the problem in black and white, while I think the rest of us can detect a certain amount of shading." The committee concluded that the Danish experiment had no relevance to Britain. It was correct, though for all the wrong reasons. The Danes, however briefly, had introduced light and logic into the sexual experience – characteristics antithetical to the British taste for the dark, and strangers.

10
Mary, Mary, Not Quite...

At the end of the Seventies, the Scandinavians, pained at having become the world's sex factory, throttled back on production. By then, however, the British government, notwithstanding the Longford report, had adopted a modified version of the Danish model. The Criminal Justice Act protected pornography against frivolous prosecutions. It freed publishers to circulate hard core magazines, and exhibitors to screen in private clubs the sort of films already seen freely elsewhere. There was even some local production of sex films to match the much greater boom in sex shops and in print pornography.

Campaigners were quick to attack this new liberalism. The Longford committee turned its attention to British entrepreneurs in the mail order market, targeting in particular Bernard Hardingham and David Sullivan, young economics graduates who, in a year, built up a mail-order pornography business serving, they told the committee, up to 25,000 clients. "They did not admit that they were fostering an addiction," Longford said. "Claiming that their customers were just the 95% of ordinary people – mostly men between 19 and 35 – they believe that the chief impulse to buy is curiosity, which is soon sated."

Longford baited David Sullivan with some seductively wriggling generalisations about Unhealthy Cravings and Unnatural Acts, but, as racist MP Enoch Powell enjoyed saying when tempted by journalists to mount the soapbox on his particular obsession, immigration, "In vain is the net spread in sight of the bird." Secure in a buoyant market and an administration that encouraged free enterprise, Sullivan told the reformers that "anyone with any initiative would want to get on, make money, be a success, in any field." With Britain relishing its North Sea oil revenues and negotiating for a seat at the groaning board of the European Economic Community, Longford found it hard to argue.

Sullivan was to become a major beneficiary of the porn boom, with mail order the cornerstone of his enterprises. Like many before him, he realised that a magazine or film arriving under plain wrapper appealed to the British taste for the furtive. To serve this market, he launched Conegate, which published magazines such as *Climax* and *Whitehouse,* the latter cheekily named after the most vocal of Britain's moralizers, Mary Whitehouse, head of the Viewers' and Listeners' Committee pressure group. He also produced softcore feature films starring an actress named Mary Millington.

Robert Hamer's 1949 comedy *Kind Hearts and Coronets* foreshadows the venal and acquisitive Britain of two decades later. A black fable of upward mobility, it follows Dennis Price's Louis D'Ascoyne as he coolly murders the relatives who block him from a dukedom. In a delectable irony, the moralistic Edith, the woman of Louis' dreams (and widow of one of his victims), is played by Valerie Hobson, wife of John Profumo.

D'Ascoyne's nemesis, Sibella (Joan Greenwood) is a diminutive and mock-genteel tart in the mould of Christine Keeler's friend Mandy Rice-Davies whom no Englishman can help desiring. Her very faults and lack of true beauty make her irresistible to any gentleman lusting after "a bit of rough." When she asks Louis how he would describe her, he is moved to eloquence: "I'd say you were the perfect combination of imperfections. I'd say that your nose was just a little too short; your mouth just a little too wide. But that yours was a face a man could see in his dreams for the whole of his life. I'd say you were vain, selfish, cruel, deceitful. I'd say you were adorable."

As role model for the Sixties "naughty girl," Sibella had her incarnation in Mary Millington. She fitted Louis' profile almost exactly, and shared Sibella's trashy charm. Sibella, however, is cunning enough to blackmail Louis into rescuing her from suburban tedium, a shrewd move for which Millington lacked the necessary smarts. "I haven't got much upstairs," she confessed ruefully.

Born illegitimate as Mary Quilter, Mary, in common with most successful sex performers, was bisexual, which contributed to her appeal. Too short, at 4 feet eleven inches, to become a model, she appeared in a number of porn shorts before drifting into the orbit of David Sullivan, who changed her name to Millington. She featured in *Come Play With Me*, written, produced and directed by the tireless Harrison Marks, followed quickly by *The Playbirds*, *Queen of the Blues* and *Confessions from the David Galaxy Affair*. Standard softcore, the films recycled comedy/crime plots from the last days of Ealing's golden period. In *Come Play With Me*, forgers use a health farm as a cover. Bumbling Scotland Yard cops in *The Playbirds* investigate the murder of a number of centrefold girls for *Playbirds* magazine by planting a spy (Millington, inevitably) inside the company. In *Queen of the Blues*, neophyte owners of strip club The Blues, where Millington is the star, are harassed by gangsters.

Sullivan was shrewd enough to enlist some of Britain's army of unemployed character comedians. They gave shape to what are often rambling plots, and helped Millington through her less-than-convincing dialogue scenes. "She speaks her lines as methodically as she strips," one critic remarked. But, leaden lines and all, it was Millington the punters came to see. In all the films, she's that staple of British erotica, the uniformed figure of authority – nurse, woman police officer – who embodies power and sexuality in equal measure. *Come Play With Me* in particular, advertised by a poster of Millington in nurse's uniform, stockings and suspenders, ran for years in the Soho cinemas controlled by Sullivan.

Mary became his mistress, and an emblem of the Sullivan operation. She posed for photo layouts in his magazines, played in his films, toured the country to promote them, then put her name to fanciful reminiscences in *Whitehouse* of prodigiously hung studs in the Gorbals and lesbian encounters in Clacton-on-Sea. A sex shop was opened in her name in the London suburb of Norbury. Supposedly the sister of the owner, she invited punters to write to her there. Game for anything, she tweaked officialdom with

Mary Millington.

well-publicised stunts such as appearing nude in front of 10 Downing Street, arm in arm with the Prime Minister's private police guard.

She developed a line of hot chat, a feature of the sex performer's repertoire that went back to vaudeville appearances in the Thirties by Mae West and Jean Harlow. In modern times it had been perfected by Marilyn Monroe, always ready with a quotable reply when a reporter asked what she had on in bed. Sometimes she responded "Chanel No. 5," sometimes "Just the radio." Fellini sent up the practice at Anita Ekberg's press conference in *La Dolce Vita*:

> Journalist: What was the happiest day of your life?
> Ekberg (*to secretary*): What was the answer to that question, Edna?
> Secretary: It was a night, dear.

On her visit to England to make *Doctor at Sea*, Brigitte Bardot was coached, when asked what person she most admired, to answer – improbably – "Sir Isaac Newton" – because "he discovered that bodies attract one another." Mary Millington's best-remembered contribution to this tradition was a languorous "It's not the sleep of the just I enjoy. It's the sleep of the just – after."

On screen, Mary had the same gamine charm as Ginger Lynn two decades later, but without Lynn's skill at managing her career. Always unsure of herself, she became a drug user and occasional kleptomaniac. She bought a large house in the stockbroker belt of Surrey which she shared with her husband Robert Maxted, but most of her affection was lavished on two pet Alsatians, Tippi and Reject.

1977 was Mary's biggest year. It also, however, marked the high tide of official tolerance of pornography in Britain. In June, Prime Minister James Callaghan appointed a committee under Professor Bernard Williams to overhaul the system. The Williams committee wasn't anti-porn, but it did signal new official interest in the business. In particular Internal Revenue investigated a number of people, including Mary, and began court cases for the retrieval of unpaid taxes.

On 18 August 1979, Mary was arrested for shoplifting. She was already facing another similar charge, and had begun seeing a psychiatrist – "because she was doing silly things," her husband explained. The next day, she was found dead at her home. Police reported that "pills were all over the bed and a half-empty bottle of vodka was nearby." She was 33. She had written a long letter before her death – presumably intended for David Sullivan, who used extracts in his magazines and later in *The Naked Truth*, a grisly documentary summarising her life. The letter's poignant combination of rationalisation, sentimentality and self-pity was typical of porn:

> I can't face the thought of prison. They said I'll definitely go to Holloway and told me how bad it is there... I do hope so much porn is legal one day. They called me obscene names for being in possession of it. I can't go through any more...The tax

> man has finished me as well. Please put in your magazine how much I wanted porn legalised but the police have beaten me. I do hope you are luckier... Re my arrest in which it was suggested I stole a bracelet. I am innocent but have stolen things in the past. I am a kleptomaniac but try so hard to control my illness. I can't go on any longer... Can I have photos of Tippi and Reject with me?

Squeezing the last drop of usable scandal from the incident, *The Naked Truth* shows Mary in her coffin, photographs of her dogs curling on the shroud.

David Sullivan went on to publish *The Sport*, Britain's gamiest tabloid. Derisory in news content, it relied on spurious stories skimmed from the same pot as the *National Enquirer*. Space not filled with semi-nude "stunnas" and details of celebrity "bonking" was devoted to the sort of small ads Mark Lewis might have seen in tobacconists' windows. *Phone Girls W**k You on Any of the Following..., M**turb*With Me... Ring These Dirty Tarts Now – They are Waiting to Talk Filthy to You... Peeping Tom* seemed increasingly prescient.

11
Naked Lady Movies

"I was the spark who lit up flaming youth," boasted Scott Fitzgerald. "Colleen Moore was the torch." If anyone ignited the sex revolution in movies, it was Russ Meyer. The torch was a picture called *The Immoral Mr. Teas*.

A World War II combat cameraman, Meyer was a virgin until 1944, when his commanding officer, Major Ernest Hemingway, persuaded a brothel just outside Paris to open up for his men. From among the fifteen girls, Meyer, exhibiting a lifetime preference, chose the one with the biggest breasts.

After the war, he took up stills photography, specialising in pin-ups. One of the six centrefolds he shot for *Playboy*, which Hugh Hefner launched in 1953, was the steatopygous ex-Miss Sweden, Anita Ekberg. Based on such commissions, Meyer concluded that American men enjoyed looking at women with large breasts more than at women with small breasts. He knew *he* did. Enshrining this insight, he produced and directed over four days in 1959 his own script of a 64-minute film called *The Immoral Mr. Teas*.

The plot was perfunctory, a stand-by of adolescent porn. After a visit to the dentist – Meyer borrowed the real surgery of a friend – a Los Angeles deliveryman, Bill Teas (played by Teas himself, another old pal), finds himself miraculously endowed with the ability to see through women's clothing. As he moves around the city, various young, beautiful and busty girls appear to him – and to the audience – naked. Or as naked, at least, as the conventions of the nudie film allowed. Meyer, an artist in his fashion, wasn't content simply to present a succession of animated pin-ups. Turning the cost-cutting lack of dialogue to advantage, he gave Teas a rueful/philosophical internal monologue, written and spoken by Edward Lasko, that turned this unattractive man into a sympathetic figure. The audience empathised. They too were troubled by overactive sexual imaginations. But, also like him, they would end up at home alone, and wake up next day, as the old blues has it, with their troubles in their hands.

By accident, Meyer claims, *Mr. Teas* was sent to a San Diego cinema as support for the dour Gary Cooper Western *The Hanging Tree*. Within twenty minutes, police were milling round the box office and the film's success was assured. Six months later, Seattle, Washington, the first city to accept the film, gave it a censorship certificate. It ran there for two years. In January 1960, it opened at the Monica in Los Angeles, and even the *Los Angeles Times* took notice. "Last Friday evening," it wrote, "the peep show finally moved across the tracks from Main Street, and to judge by the concourse of solid-looking citizens, presumably all aged eighteen or over, the film is going to be a *great* success."

Russ Meyer and his wife Eve.

Leslie Fiedler, author of *Love and Death in the American Novel* and one of the country's most respected cultural commentators, wrote a long and approving essay on the film. "As old restrictions crumble in our society," he said, "the naked flesh assumes its proper place among the possible subjects for movies, the place it has always held in the other, less public arts; but meanwhile, in the United States, we have been long corrupted by the pseudo arts of tease and titillation, conditioned to a version of the flesh more appropriate for peeking than love or lust or admiration or even real disgust."

In many states, *Mr. Teas* was cut or banned. Mayer fought such decisions and, in most cases, won, though in New York it lost eleven minutes of footage. For even more nervous locations, including the state of Maryland and countries such as Australia, both of which banned it entirely, Meyer produced a doctored version. Fake steam, snow and rain, crudely inked onto the negative, obscured all but the broadest detail of the well-endowed cast. This device did, however, allow cinemas to advertise the film as "Complete and Uncut," and the profits continued to flow.

Between 1959 and his retirement in 1979, Meyer produced, directed, wrote and shot twenty films. In most of them, heavy-breasted heroines played by actresses such as Candy Samples, Edy Williams, Uschi Digard and Francesca "Kitten" Natividad are grossly imposed upon by a succession of villains, only to surge back triumphantly and knee their traducers in the groin.

Vixen (1968), his first major production, cost $76,000 and grossed over $10 million, a pattern that Meyer, having precisely targeted his market, repeated in *Supervixens* (1975) and *Beneath the Valley of the Ultravixens* (1979). Directing always at the top of his visual voice, Meyer punches home his scenes with zooms, pans, and fast cuts from long shot to close up. He relishes physical violence. Characters employ cars, pickaxes, chainsaws and dynamite as weapons. There's no shortage of blood, nor of raw language. Character names are as broad as the fake casts of stag films: "Mr. Peterbilt" and "Semper Fidelis" in *Beneath the Valley of the Ultravixens*, "Babette Bardot" in *Common Law Cabin*, "Martin Bormann" in *Supervixens*. Meyer shares the stag film's fondness for outdoor locations as well but – at bottom a child of Hollywood – he photographs his lake, forest and mountain settings with as much glamour as a Sixties backwoods melodrama.

"Women are superior beings in all my pictures," Meyer says. "The men are dumb and klutzy, the willing tools of Meyer's women and their insatiable desires." The poster for *Faster, Pussycat! Kill! Kill!* (1977) promises "Superwomen Belted, Buckled and *Booted*!", a guarantee on which the ferocious Tura Satana delivers, beating most of the film's male stars to death. As Angel unlimbers her breasts from her tank top in *Supervixens* to coax local cop Harry Sledge out of giving her a ticket, his feet curl visibly inside his boots. When she unzips his flies, Meyer uses a V-shaped wooden shutter sliding diagonally across the frame to give us a crotch-eye shot of her staring down at what's been hidden. There's no balloon saying "Wow!" but we get the point.

Meyer avoided the label of "porn" by introducing a political or social subtext into his films. *Vixen*, a romp in the Canadian woods, with the buxom Erica Gavin pleasuring almost all the male cast, ends with a 20-minute discussion about draft-dodging, plane hijacking and civil rights. *Vixen*'s impeccable political credentials ensured respectful treatment from censors almost everywhere. Yale University devoted a retrospective to Meyer's work in 1970 and *Time* magazine film critic Richard Schickel praised *Lorna* as "a preachment against hypocrisy, exhibiting no more skin than the plot absolutely requires." The French enjoyed the insouciant crossover connections to pin-ups and comic strips, and, in line with the *politique des auteurs*, respected Meyer, as they did Chaplin and Jerry Lewis, for controlling every aspect of his films in the face of Hollywood's hegemony. Many, of course, just didn't get the joke of the political arguments and took Meyer for a radical.

Meyer played up to his ambivalent image as both money-maker and intellectual. Richard Zanuck, production head of 20th Century Fox, invited him to make a sequel to Jacqueline Susann's *Valley of the Dolls*. Cheekily hiring up-and-coming film critic Roger Ebert to script it, Meyer made *Beyond the Valley of the Dolls* (1970) for $2 million. Zanuck was all set to commission another three features when his father, Darryl, called back from Europe by an irate board, fired his son and cancelled the deal.

Russ Meyer's *The Immoral Mr. Teas*.

Shrewd enough to retain ownership of almost all his films, Meyer made millions when video transmogrified the sex film business. Rated X in the days when even a whiff of sex was enough to win condemnation, his films remained on the adult shelves next to far harder material. Asked after his retirement how he felt about them, Meyer said genially "They do a lot for me. They titillate me, they turn me on, they excite me, they rejuvenate me." He shared his life with a succession of busty actresses, including Francesca "Kitten" Natividad, star of his last production, *Beneath the Valley of the Ultravixens*, and stripper Melissa Mounds, forty years his junior. Asked how he spent his days, Meyer, always in character, said, "I get up, I sit around, I write, I fuck." Rejuvenated indeed.

The Immoral Mr. Teas transformed the sex film market. Over the next three years, an estimated 150 variations were unleashed on a disbelieving but growing audience. The world of stag film, Tijuana bibles, blue comedy and male mythology was looted for subjects. Filmmakers who, a decade before, would have disdained porn, were seeing it as, if not their life's work, then a means to an end. At the UCLA Film School in 1961, Francis Ford Coppola, bored by the academic curriculum and hungry to shoot films, was approached by friends of his brother to make a short nudie film in the style of *Mr. Teas*. Coppola acquiesced.

> We shot *The Peeper*, about a little man who has reason to believe that pin-up sessions are being photographed near his house. The whole movie was the equivalent of a Tom and Jerry cartoon, with the guy trying to see what's happening. He peeks through a telescope and sees only a belly-button, or he hoists himself up with a block-and-tackle, and then falls down... Some people saw it, and offered to buy it, but they themselves already had shot a vast amount of footage of a Western nudie, about a drunken cowboy who hits his head and sees naked girls instead of cows. They wanted me to intercut my film with theirs to leaven it and thus make the package saleable. So they gave me money, and we devised a plot gimmick whereby both characters meet and tell their stories, and that's how we'd unveil the two films, under the title *Tonight for Sure*. Sixty to seventy percent of it was not my work, but I was so eager for recognition that I shot

the credit sequence and printed "Directed by Francis Ford Coppola" up on the screen!

Coppola also later shot twelve minutes of buxom model June Wilkinson for cutting into a German movie, work that prepared him well for similar tasks he was to perform for Roger Corman a few years later.

Independent producers with little or nothing to lose moved into the porn business from parts of the fringe. At a time when his wife was pregnant with the future star of *Iron Man*, Robert Downey, soon to be acclaimed for *Chafed Elbows*, *Putney Swope* and other eccentric comedies, directed *The Sweet Smell of Sex* on a three-day schedule for a fee of $750. Playwright Tom O'Horgan contributed a bizarrely inappropriate jazz score, but Downey's gags about chickens, dogs and fat men who keep pigeons in their apartments were cheerlessly un-erotic. The producer, Bernard L. Sackett, who rated his sex films as one-, two- or three-hatters, to signify the quantity of headgear brought into the cinema by patrons to masturbate into, rated this a no-hatter, ending Downey's career in the porn business.

Harry Smith, a sound man who had worked on A features, broke into directing with *Kipling's Women*, an ingenious porn film based on Kipling's poem *The Ladies*, in which an old soldier reminisces about his sexual career, ending with the considered (and much misquoted) opinion that, "the Colonel's Lady an' Judy O'Grady / Are sisters under their skins." Men such as Smith, on the bottom rung of the movie ladder and with little prospect of moving higher, were the prime movers of nudie production. Pat Henry, an overweight comic and master of ceremonies who was part of Frank Sinatra's Rat Pack and has small roles in films such as *The Joker is Wild*, *Ocean's 11* and *Lady in Cement*, featured in Ted Paramore's *Not Tonight, Henry*, in which henpecked Henry dreamed of sex with Cleopatra, Delilah and Pocahontas, all to become staples of porn film fantasies. Another comic, Tom Noonan, who had played second banana all his life in films such as *A Star is Born*, where he is Judy Garland's pianist confidante, made *Promises, Promises* in 1963, a comedy about infertility featuring Jayne Mansfield, often in the bath.

Barry Mahon, an ex-air freight pilot and small-time film producer, befriended Errol Flynn in his debauched later years by introducing him to King Farouk of Egypt, who wanted a film made about his nation's military hero Mohammad Ali. Flynn refused the role but asked Farouk for a look at his famous collection of porn. The king obliged and Flynn, convinced Mahon could arrange anything, made him his agent and business manager. Mahon made twenty low-budget nudies a year in New York during the early Sixties. By personally producing, directing, writing, shooting and editing, he could produce a 65-minute colour film for $15,000. Little more than animated pin-ups, *Nude Scrapbook* and more than fifty others grossed about $60,000 each. Most were semi-documentaries, featuring a painter at work (*1000 Shapes of a Female*), college art classes (*Naughty, Naughty Nudes*) or glamour photographer Bunny Yaeger (*Nude Las Vegas*).

In the wake of the 1957 Supreme Court decision in Roth vs. USA and others which followed, progress in porn became a question of inching forward, testing the limits of "community standards" and, where possible, stretching them. With the legal way clear, the social revolution added freedom from censorship to such planks of the libertarian platform as decriminalisation of marijuana and abortion on demand. The media adopted the new belief that sex was not so much a function of human relationships (and as such inextricably entwined with cumbersome verities such as Family and Love) as a marketable product of which women were the raw material and middle-class white males the consumers. Sex as the sensual equivalent of marijuana, pleasurable in effect but leaving no dangerous residues nor emotional addiction, was a seductive concept, and magazines which celebrated the idea, especially *Playboy*, flourished. Its bunny emblem became, after the Coca-Cola wave, the most readily recognised trade mark in the world, and Hugh Hefner an avuncular ideologue of the sexual revolution; Walt Disney with an erection.

In 1953, the same year that Hefner launched *Playboy*, Maurice Girodias started the Olympia Press in Paris to publish a better class of pornography. Most people first encountered professionally printed erotica in his Traveler's Companion paperbacks. Although he published his share of frank porn, most of the Olympia Press output was timidly outrageous, aimed at the notional individual of the "What Kind of Man Reads Playboy?" ads created by Hefner's marketing division to attract advertising. Girodias, pornographer to the literati, maintained an urbane image. The pseudonymous works of "Marcus Van Heller" and "Akbar del Piombo" appeared alongside Nabokov's *Lolita*, Donleavy's *The Ginger Man* and Burroughs' *The Naked Lunch*, all bound in the same Establishment Green card Sotheby's used for catalogues of *objets d'art*.

Olympia's output was often composed tongue-in-cheek by moonlighting novelists and expatriate intellectuals such as Alexander Trocchi ("Frances Lengel"), Christopher Logue ("Count Palmiro Vicarion") and Terry Southern, who, with Mason Hoffenberg, wrote *Candy*, a parody of the pornographic novel distantly derived from Voltaire's *Candide*. *Candy*, retitled *Lollipop*, was reissued in 1958 under the pseudonym "Maxwell Kenton" for fear the association with Girodias would impair Hoffenberg's chances of selling a children's book he had just finished. He needn't have worried. In 1957, the Traveler's Companion series found an American publisher. Over the next decade, most of Girodias' successful writers and books would be published to acclaim and good sales in the US. In 1964, *Candy* was reprinted under Southern and Hoffenberg's real names by ultra-respectable Putnam's.

Intellectuals, often with more enthusiasm than forethought, embraced the softcore culture. There was a hasty, even unseemly scramble to board the bandwagon. Parodies such as *Candy*, as well as unhurried views of erotica, evasively suggestive novels translated from the French, manuals of joyous (but always conventional) sex illustrated with discreet pen-and-ink sketches, European movies with soft-focus nudity, and naughty nineteenth-century ribaldry illustrated by Aubrey Beardsley were all hailed equally. To protest against censorship became essential to one's liberal credentials. To be acquainted with erotica was stylish. To participate... *that* was chic. For the underground newspaper *Suck*, feminist ideologue Germaine Greer, later the author of *The Female Eunuch*, posed naked with her ankles behind her neck.

In New York, at least, porn won intellectual acceptance in 1968 when Andy Warhol made *Blue Movie*. Warhol had always been interested in and amused by the phenomenon. Most of the films he made in his East 47th Street Factory shared porn's seedy settings and minimal technique. "Art will be remembered with distaste," he proclaimed. "Westerns, pornography, science fiction, rock 'n' roll, Pop Art paintings are the supernatural truth, the unreal place where you really are, the place where your vision is." His 1963 *Blow Job* tweaked the staid straight establishment by showing a 40-minute act of fellatio, but recording only the handsome face of the young man being fellated. *Blue Movie*, also known as *Louis and Viva* or, simply, *Fuck*, was shot in 1967 while Warhol was lying in a New York hospital, "stitched up like a Schiaparelli gown," in his words, after being shot three times with a .32 pistol by Valerie Solanas, founder of SCUM, the Society For Cutting Up Men, her manifesto for which Maurice Girodias had published. The irony of Warhol's wounding was that Solanas' intended victim had been Girodias, with whom she had been carrying on a sulphurous correspondence about her manuscript. Finding he wasn't in his Gramercy Park offices, she went on to those of the unlucky Warhol.

Blue Movie was an extended (133 minutes) coverage, unedited, of a sexual encounter between Factory regulars Louis Waldron and Viva. The couple fuck for about half an hour, but most of the film is taken up with domestic activity – washing, frying eggs – some lengthy, often laboured preliminary chat ("You think I'd do this in a movie? You're crazy, my Mama would never let me do that") and post-coital discussion of Vietnam, civil rights and sexual politics. When the film was prosecuted in New York, Warhol claimed

that *Blue Movie* was political rather than pornographic, a defence not accepted by the judge, who banned it.

After the Solanas attack, Warhol distanced himself from films, concentrating on his prolific printmaking and portrait work and on *Inter/view* magazine. Convinced that the greatest art was making money, he now wanted his films, according to Billy Name, the Factory's superintendent, "to be financially successful, like the rest of his art; when he realised that they wouldn't be profitable, he lost interest." Paul Morrissey, who had filmed most of *Blue Movie*, took over entirely on *Flesh* (1968), *Trash* (1970), *Heat* (1972) and the so-called Warhol versions of *Dracula* and *Frankenstein* (1974). With *Blue Movie*, Warhol had, however, endorsed, however backhandedly, the idea of sex cinema, which for one section of the intellectual elite was enough. If Andy liked playing with porn, so did they.

Porn had even more prestigious enthusiasts, though they disguised their interest. Early in 1964, when Federico Fellini visited the United States to receive his Oscar for *8½*, he met with Groucho Marx in New York to try and persuade him to appear in his next film, *Satyricon*. Marx declined, but he and Fellini got on well. Strolling through

Times Square, the comedian asked Fellini if he liked porn films and, when the director said he had never seen any, took him into a shop where hundreds were on sale. "He himself had seen an enormous quantity," said Fellini. "He said to me, 'You're Italian, yes or no? Then you can't have not gone to see porno films.' He was convinced that Italians spent their life going to porno films and masturbating." Fellini, who, despite his taste for buxom women in his films, was undersexed, even impotent, became fascinated with porn films and accumulated a large collection.

12
Behind Behind the Green Door

Publicity changed life for America's porn merchants. Until then, with the mails barred to them and the police always at their shoulder, they had needed to rely on each other. Theirs was a tight, private world. Cinema owners worked directly with producers. Information was exchanged, money borrowed, dope or performers acquired. Friendships formed and loyalties were established which, in the years that followed, would prove crucial to some people but a grave disappointment to others.

Bill Rotsler was among the old-style entrepreneurs who collided with the hit-and-run economics of the business in the form of two fly-by-night financiers drawn to the porn business by the prospect of quick returns. As the writer John Warren Wells said of such people, the only thing they had ever produced was a credit card. "I came up with a bunch of capsule story lines for them," said Rotsler,

> and they picked two. And I worked and worked and worked on them, meanwhile trying to get a budget without a script – ball-park figures. And they kept saying, "It's too much money." Finally, I got mad – it's a lot of work – and I said, "Let's look at it the other way. How much do you want to spend?" So I came up with some new storylines that would fit that very very small budget, and they picked two, and said "Let us see the script." I don't know what got into me that day, but I said "No." They'd just put me to so much damned work, you know.
>
> They said, "What do you mean 'No'?"
>
> I said, "Do you want the movies or do you want the script?"

> "We want the movies."
>
> "Well, then give me the money and I'll come back later with the films."
>
> They got very upset about it, but they gave me the money and I went out and did a film called *Four Kinds of Love*. I only scripted one scene. The rest, we ad-libbed. But I knew what the other scenes were to be. And I explained it to the actors. And I cast personalities. And I also helped that I was in it and a buddy of mine was in it, a real actor who could ad-lib.
>
> We said, "OK, the scene is about this and he's going to come in, do this…" And everyone reacted naturally. And only once, in two movies, did nobody talk, or did someone talk on top of somebody else. You get naturalness and speed of production. You usually don't get great lines. But with this sort of thing, great lines are not what they're looking for.

Archetypes of the Californian porn gang were the Mitchell brothers, Jim and Artie. Most porn films exist in a stylistic limbo that makes them difficult to date, but those of the Mitchells are redolent of the late Sixties. In 1991, when disaster had overtaken them, critic Jared Rutter offered a measured epitaph. "The Mitchells were unique. Their product seemed to come out of the sex revolution of the 1960s and early 1970s. There was an emphasis on actual lovemaking. It was very Bay Area. Generally, they were seen as eccentrics by the rest of the business."

War babies, the Mitchells had been brought up in the San Francisco industrial satellite town of Antioch. Their mother was a schoolteacher, their father a drifter and small-time professional gambler who occasionally worked security for illegal card games. Later, Artie, the younger by two years and the more mercurial – he was known as "Party Artie" – liked to emphasise their louche background.

"We were raised to be torpedoes against the state," he said. "Being an outlaw, it helps to come from an outlaw family. The pressure is less." In truth, their outlaw standing was mostly a front, a prop of their street credibility, like the letter of thanks from Yippie leader Abbie Hoffman framed on their office wall.

As the legend runs, the boys were watching stag films at a smoker when one turned to the other and suggested that someone who improved on these joyless efforts might make money. Jim took some courses in film at San Francisco State University. When he had mastered the basics, the Mitchells bought that Model T of 16mm cameras, the Bolex. Neither had any illusions about their cinematic skills. "We were only clumsy film students making pornography," Jim said. But they learned.

Among the myths that surround the Mitchell Brothers was one which credits them, suffused with the spirit of the Summer of Love, with elevating porn cinema from a tawdry trade to art. In fact, their first one-reelers were anything but artistic. They initially showed nothing but women masturbating and pulling open their vaginas for lingering close-ups. San Francisco in the Sixties was full of girls who had drifted west in search of fulfilment. They hung around the Haight-Ashbury area, short of money but not especially attracted to jobs as waitresses or clerks at the A&P. A model who worked, if not for the Mitchells, then for Californian producers like them, told Laura Lederer, "The average pay was very good. You could make $45 for half an hour of filming for a peep show." Nor, for most of the women, was there any particular stigma attached to pornography. "Runaways were a very big part of the business," said Lederer's informant. "This fed right into the 1960s hippie movement. I remember feeling nudity was okay and natural, so photos of it must be okay too."

The standard unit of porn was the ten-minute 16 mm "One Day Wonder." Known in the trade as loops, they could be run singly in 25c peep shows, or linked in series. Also in San Francisco, Alex de Renzy turned out five or six loops a week which he showed in his cinema, The Screening

Room, and sold on to other exhibitors. Having paid a model between $15 and $30 and spent $30 more on film stock and processing, a filmmaker had a product that would sell at $75 or $100 a copy to scores, even hundreds of sex shops and peep-show arcades across the country. "It's a very hard business to lose money in," confirmed Bob Sumner, one of the Seventies' most successful porn producers.

There was, to give Jim Mitchell credit, a rationale of sorts behind his emphasis on masturbation. "The purest form of titillation," he told George Csicsery, "is the single girl 'auto-masturbation' film [...] and the beaver film was a lot truer form for getting off on some kind of autoerotic fantasy. When it opened up and you added fucking, you had to show the man and you covered up the girl. It disrupted the autoerotic trend of sex films. It was boring because all anyone really wanted to see was the close-up penetration shots."

After Roth vs. USA in 1957, avoiding prosecution for making sex films became, given the elastic morality of a city such as San Francisco, merely a matter of staying exactly abreast of changing community standards. The Mitchells were past masters at this game. "We started with single girls," Jim said. "Then there were scenes with two girls (who were not yet allowed to touch each other), and when the competition imitated us, we went to three."

When the Mitchells couldn't satisfy the demand for loops, they bought them from Bill Osco in Los Angeles. Self-styled "Boy King of LA Porn," Osco was a gaudy operator who, while still in his mid-twenties, became the biggest producer of porn loops in the country. Affecting a full-length fur coat over jeans and boots, and cruising LA in a $35,000 Rolls, he lived in a walled mansion in Encino and emulated on a slightly smaller scale the lavish lifestyle of Hugh Hefner on the other side of the Hollywood Hills.

An ambition to be a professional baseball player brought Osco to Los Angeles from his native Ohio, but after his failure to make the grade with the LA Dodgers and a few months off, he claimed, running with a chapter of Hell's Angels bikers, he drifted to movies, and to porn. In 1967, he went into partnership with Howard Ziehm to form Graffiti Productions and make loops. Within a year, they were turning out fifteen or twenty a week.

From the start, Osco gave his films a hint of Hollywood polish. He varied the unblinking stare of the Mitchells' films, changing camera angles to show off the models, many of whom were attractive wannabe starlets. Rarely among loop-makers, Osco put his name on his films, and the cognoscenti of porn learned to look out for Graffiti's logo of the earth, in imitation of Universal's opening credits in the Thirties, being circled by a tiny plane which in this case jerked and sputtered.

In January 1969, the Mitchells bought an old garage on the corner of Polk and O'Farrell Streets and turned it into the O'Farrell Cinema, painting the outside sky blue, with, this being the period of Flower Power, giant floating multi-coloured blooms. The O'Farrell showed their own loops and those of Osco. Audiences queued round the block. Mitchell loops were so popular that Jim later admitted, "If the cops hadn't bothered us – business was good – we probably wouldn't have ever gotten into stories."

The Supreme Court reflected a new national tolerance for porn in its 1969 decision in Stanley vs. Georgia. "If the First Amendment [to the US Constitution, enshrining freedom of speech] means anything,' decreed Justice Thurgood Marshall, "it means that a state has no business telling a man, sitting alone in his house, what books he may read or what films he may watch." Later cases defended porn on public display. To be declared obscene, decided the court, a work must be "patently offensive" and have no "serious artistic, literary, political or scientific value when taken as a whole."

Like Russ Meyer, the Mitchells realised that these decisions would protect them from prosecution if their films at least aspired to artistic merit. A space behind their cinema became a studio. A more sophisticated Arriflex BL replaced the Bolex and they bought a Nagra tape recorder to add synchronised dialogue. Tentatively they began making hardcore shorts with casts of both men and women. They also started looking for a story, and performers who could act.

Underground culture was at its most vigorous in San Francisco. Newspapers such as the *Berkeley Barb* were the community notice board. People met at the rock concerts promoted by Bill Graham at the Fillmore, attracted by his psychedelic posters with their all-but-unreadable wobbling letters in Day-Glo orange, lime and cerise. Everyone read comic artists such as Ron Crumb, and Gilbert Shelton, whose hairy, anarchic dope-dealing Fabulous Furry Freak Brothers, with their motto: "Dope will get you through times of no money better than money will get you through times of no dope," were first cousins to the Mitchells, themselves bearded and often, in Artie's case at least, stoned.

The Mitchells had already in the late Sixties made it socially permissible to view porn – if not with your wife or girlfriend, at least with a male companion. George S. McDonald saw his first porn film there in 1969.

> I was impressed: it was in colour, it had sound. It was a clean theatre, and on this Saturday night it was full. Unfortunately the guy on screen couldn't get it up. Nervously, I kept laughing, and the guy I went with – because you went in pairs at that time – said "What are you laughing at?" And I said, "With a girl like that, you'd have to be dead not to get it up." And he said, "You think you can do that?"
> "Yeah, I can do that,' I said.
> I answered an ad in the *Berkeley Barb*. But it took a month of ringing and talking to the guys at the O'Farrell Theatre before I got to make a film.

Coincidentally, the girl with whom McDonald acted in his first hardcore porn picture was the girl he had seen in that film at the O'Farrell. "I was scared to death," he recalled. "I couldn't sleep the night before. I did fifty-four films and I never could sleep the night before." But he persisted, to become famous in the trade as "Big Mac" and, as Jim Holliday put it twenty years later when he inducted McDonald into the X-Rated Film Critics' Hall of Fame, "porn cinema's first hard dick." It was McDonald who played the male lead in the most famous of all early Californian porn features, *Behind the Green Door*.

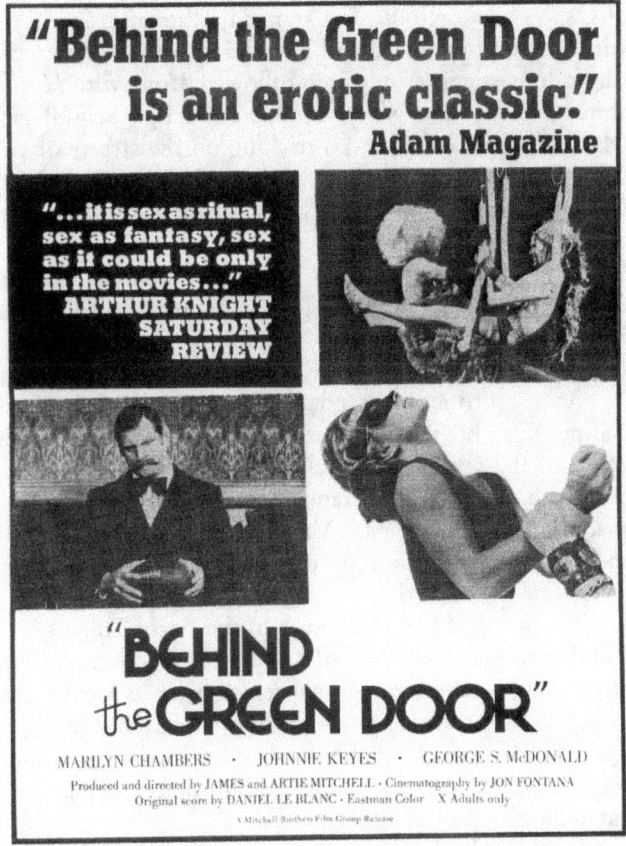

The most famous – but not the first. That honour goes to the now-forgotten *Mona, the Virgin Nymph*, made by Bill Osco in 1970. The ever-ambitious Osco had graduated to longer films in 1967/8, plunging $7000 of Graffiti's profits into the forty-minute *Whatever Happened to Stud Flame*? Trying to keep within the parameters of that year's community standards, the film had ample nudity but no penetrative sex. The result pleased nobody, and the film flopped. Undeterred, he embarked on a feature.

Unlike *Behind the Green Door* and *Deep Throat*, *Mona, the Virgin Nymph* was shot largely outdoors, a characteristic of Osco's productions. The star, Fifi Watson, has oral sex with a man in the middle of a field and with a woman in a sunlit domestic interior. Osco followed *Mona* with *Harlot*, about Melody and Mary, Hollywood High School girls who take the day off to go tricking on the streets of LA. Inventive for porn, *Harlot* was shot, like *Mona*, outdoors. In slow motion, one of the girls, Melody (Patty Alexon) runs naked with her overweight biker boyfriend through a shopping centre, watched in astonishment by passers-by, and a scene between the girls and a man on top of the Federal Bank Building ends unexpectedly in a helicopter shot pulling away from the writhing bodies on the roof.

As a sop to moral standards, the film has a cautionary ending. Caught, the girls are forced into an orgy in the office of the school principal, and Melody, after falling in love with the biker who raped her, is killed with him in a road accident. At the end, Mary stands by Melody's grave and swears eternal celibacy – only to break her vow with the handsome driver of the hearse.

Taking a leaf from the book of the Forty Thieves who had distributed their own films around the country, Osco hired small cinemas in regional centres such as Denver and Phoenix and presented the films himself. In some cities, he took as much as $25,000, unheard-of figures for porn, and a promise of the bonanza to come: a bonanza in which Osco, paradoxically, would not share.

In 1972, Marilyn Briggs was a nineteen-year-old model living "on love, fresh water and marijuana" in San Francisco.

There are numerous versions of how she became Marilyn Chambers and a porn star. She tells it this way.

> I was eighteen or nineteen and living in San Francisco in the hippie days. I had never done a porn film – it wasn't such a hip thing to do. Jim and Art [Mitchell] saw me and yelled out "Wait! We want to talk to you!" I remember thinking they were really nice guys. Art had on this sweater vest and a button-down shirt – I mean, really preppie. They told me about their families and about their kids. They were so family-oriented and down-to-earth and honest, and that was the kind of person I was, so we clicked.

The Mitchells, she claimed, looked through her portfolio, noticed a packet shot she had done for Ivory Soap the year before, cuddling a delighted baby, with the slogan "99 and $^{44}/_{100}$% Pure" and said, "You're just what we're looking for – the girl next door."

This was almost total fiction. Chambers, daughter of a New York advertising man, was living with her boyfriend Doug Chapin and working in a topless bar. She had already done a few TV commercials before moving to California, and played a small role opposite George Segal and Barbra Streisand in Herbert Ross' story of a hooker and her client, *The Owl and the Pussycat* (1970). It was an experience Marilyn didn't relish. She was pestered by propositions from members of the production and offers from producers of more work if she would sleep with them.

Nor was Chambers a stranger to sex films. In 1971 she appeared, as Marilyn Briggs, in a quasi-documentary by Sean S. Cunningham, later to direct *The Case of the Smiling Stiffs/Case of the Full Moon Murders* (1975), the widest-circulated of all softcore comedies. Called *Together*, Cunningham's film might, in view of its content, have been better titled *Altogether*. Employing the documentary format, it used extracts from the *Kama Sutra* and interviews with jaded teenagers, a worried psychologist and a liberal priest to grapple with the concept of "togetherness." This ideal state was demonstrated at the film's conclusion by a visit to the seaside clinic of a Dr Roy Curry, where couples (including Chambers) romp in liberated empathy and nothing else.

Marilyn Chambers.

It stretches credulity that an actress who had already made a film like *Together* and had an intimate acquaintance with San Francisco would not have heard of Jim and Artie. As for the Mitchells, can it have escaped them that a girl who looked like Jane Fonda and was shortly to feature on soap packets across America was God's gift to hardcore? The realisation had not eluded Jim at least. Later he confessed to having seen *Together*, after which he described Chambers as having "a face every boy would love to put on his cock."

The Mitchells offered Chambers a generous deal. In New York, 8mm One Day Wonders were being delivered at $100 each. Linda Lovelace was paid $1200 for *Deep Throat*, while her co-star Harry Reems would, on a good week, according to Lovelace, take home $700 in tax-free income. For *Green Door*, Chambers received $2500, plus a percentage of the film's profits. In the Eighties this still amounted to $2000 a month.

She also had the right to choose her own partners. George McDonald was one. Another was African-American Johnnie Keyes, who happened to be in jail at the time on a minor charge. The Mitchells, accustomed to such problems, waited until he was free.

With Adrienne Mitchell, Artie and Jim had come up with a script, named for a hit song of 1955, in which a sleepless singer frets about the wild party going on behind the green door of a nearby house. Both the song and the film owe their title to what the Mitchells credited as an "anonymous European novel" but was, in fact, a pornographic pamphlet which circulated among American soldiers during World War II.

The author, whoever he was, dipped liberally into the same collective erotic unconscious from which Dominique Aury had drawn *Histoire d'O*. As refined for the film, the story starts in a roadside diner, where a truck driver (McDonald) is asked by the cook to tell him and a fellow driver about "the green door." As he describes the existence of an exclusive sex coven who prey on young girls, we see Gloria (Chambers) checking into a hotel. That night, she is abducted by two men (Jim and Artie Mitchell) and taken to the club where, after being "calmed" by some intensive lesbian caresses, she is paraded before an audience of masked men and women in evening dress. For their entertainment, she submits to a variety of sex acts – with a black man (Keyes), a trio of men on trapezes, and members of the audience, among them the truck driver. At the climax of the orgy he runs on stage, snatches up Gloria and flees from the club.

Back in the diner, the cook asks, "What happened next?" Leaving, the driver says, "Tell you next time." As he drives away, the film dissolves to him having sex with Gloria, an extended sequence that uses lavish optical colour effects, including giant gouts of semen leaping in multi-coloured slow motion.

True believers ever, the Mitchells used the film to sneak in a short sermon appealing for public acceptance, not so much of kidnapping and rape as of the pornographer's right to fantasise about them and audiences to enjoy the fantasy without guilt. Before Gloria is brought out, the master of ceremonies addresses the crowd: "Ladies and gentlemen, you are about to witness the ravishment of a woman who has been abducted; a woman whose initial fear has mellowed into expectation. No harm will come to those being ravished. Tomorrow she will know that she has been loved as she has never been loved before. So with the knowledge that you can do nothing to stop the performance, just relax and enjoy it."

Directing *Green Door* was so arousing, Artie Mitchell claimed later, that "we just wanted to throw down the cameras at the end of each day of filming and fuck and suck our way to oblivion." Others have a different story. "I'll tell you what it was like," George McDonald recalled of shooting the final scene of gaudily ejaculating semen.

> We got up at 6 a.m. and went down to the bad part of town, to a sound studio called Stage 8. It was the size of a 747 hangar. It was my forty-seventh film. We had full body make-up; that had never been done

> before. We got to stand round on a cold concrete floor, naked, till ten, when the lights were set up and we were ready to go. Then they moved us over to a three-quarter-inch plywood platform covered with black photo paper so the shot could be run through an optical printer. An optical printer! That was new too. We've got full body make-up on black photo paper, so we can't move. Under full direction, the first scene took two hours. When they said "Stop," not only did you have to think about keeping it up, but, with fourteen technicians, they could afford to have a make-up girl come over and touch up your testicles.

The Mitchells were too involved in the technical problems of their first big film to contemplate joining in. "There were a lot of sharp words on the set," McDonald says: "Sometimes it was funny. I'd be sitting on a bed naked, waiting for a scene to begin. Jim would be on one side of me and Art would be on the other and I'd be getting conflicting directions of what they wanted. I'm sitting there trying to get it up and keep it up and I'd say, 'Couldn't you guys have worked this out ahead of time?'"

The solarised colour effects of *Green Door* signify its hippie heritage. So does the unconventional filling of lesser roles, which cast a net far wider than did Osco, with his preference for beautiful young performers. The final orgy, which was to become a Mitchell Brothers trademark, brings together an awesomely heterogeneous mix of characters. They range from midgets and cross-dressers through middle-aged baldies and a few tattooed people to one woman so enormous that fat hangs round her in valances of white blubber. The prototype of other grossly overweight performers in so-called "chubby-chaser" films of the Eighties such as *Tons of Love* and *Too Fat to Fuck,* this lady (or her twin) figured in a number of Mitchell productions under the *nom du film* "V. Venus." Bill Rotsler encountered her on *The Resurrection of Eve* (1973). "She was sitting there by herself and she had this big smile on her face. She had just done this big orgy scene. As I walked by, I said something like, 'My, you look happy.' And she said, 'Y'know, if it wasn't for these films, I wouldn't get laid at all.'"

The Mitchells opened *Green Door* in New York City, alerted wire services to the Chambers/Ivory Snow connection and, with typical *chutzpah*, took ads in the trade press recommending the film to Academy members when choosing the Oscars. A scandalised Procter & Gamble announced in March 1973 that it was withdrawing packets of Ivory Soap that featured her. Unconcerned, Chambers said of her new image, "That's me. That's how I plan to continue."

The film cost $60,000. Mythology sets its profits as $60 million, though, even if true, little of it stuck to the Mitchells' fingers. Neither lived luxuriously, and in 1988 they estimated their worth as only $1 million. But one senses that with the Mitchells, money was never entirely the point.

13
The Sound of One Hand...

In the early Seventies, a porn cinema anywhere in the world generally showed a non-stop programme of "loops," occasionally with a perfunctory accompaniment of canned music. A decade later, critic Nick Roddick found such "grind houses" still operating in London's Soho as "Film Clubs," and accurately evoked their atmosphere.

> Cinemas using film – almost always 16mm film, whatever the sign outside may say – rely on two projectors with thirty minutes of film in each. A typical reel will consist of three or four short narratives, often starting in the middle of a scene, with leader and countdowns between them. In many of the cinemas, when a reel ends the film will come out of the gate and flap around on the take-up reel until someone comes and turns on the other projector. At the Queen's Cinema Club, one of the projectors was silent (or at any rate its sound system did not work) and a record was put on. The film itself was obviously a talkie, since there were numerous dialogue scenes. There were signs of a sense of humour in the choice of record – the theme from *Midnight Cowboy*. "Everybody's talkin' at me/Can't hear a word they're sayin'" – which suggested that this was more than a temporary measure.

Most porn features were not made with any more attention to detail than loops. Tina Russell has given an unglamorous picture of the cheaper two-day shoots. *The Magic Ring* (1970) was an early film by Gerard Damiano, later to direct *Deep Throat*. Typically down-beat, it opens in Central Park with a bum panhandling for a meal (his first rejection is from Damiano himself, playing his usual cameo). Russell finally shares half of her sandwich with the bum. Less than an hour later, after a succession of sex scenes and a climactic four-way orgy, she's strangled with a whip.

The Magic Ring was re-issued in 1974, oddly retitled *Bottoms Up*. Russell watched it at New York's Hudson cinema with her husband Jason and a slightly aghast journalist, who took down her comments.

"This film has been on and off since I made it, they were afraid to distribute it. It was never finished. I was supposed to get another day or two… The sound is a voice-over, that's not me talking… I've never seen this film before, it's the first time."

The journalist asked who did the wardrobe and make-up. "Me. In these lousy two-day things you do everything yourself. I put on my own face, you don't have make-up artists or costume people."

She continued to watch dispassionately as the screen filled with more naked bodies. "That girl had a big long tongue. We did those scenes a week in between. I worked one day, then a week later I was called in again for the second day's work. That's Jason, without a beard, working on me."

After the 52-minute film, the Russells and the journalist went outside, where they were joined by the cinema manager and someone from the distributor. They were proud Russell had come to the theatre and wanted her to sign autographs, but to their surprise she declined.

Producers of porn in New York still worked on the lean filming ratio of 1.5:1 – one usable metre of film for every 1.5 metres shot (Hollywood routinely shoots 1:10). Retakes were almost unknown. Nick Roddick saw a film called *Dirty Weekend* in London in the Seventies: "Two New York secretaries on holiday in California run out of money and decide to earn $300 by selling themselves. They make a good deal more with a variety of men (some of whom have difficulty maintaining their erections, causing one of the girls to look despairingly at the camera; a hand appears and waves her back to work)." *Vice Academy/Vice Busters* (1988), one of the series of softcore parodies of the successful *Police Academy* films with which Ginger Lynn managed to extricate herself from hardcore, involves undercover policewomen exposing porn. In the great tradition of One Day Wonders, its filmmaker directs with a series of placards, which he holds up for the performers: *Fall On Bed*, they read, *Moan Louder* and *Degrade Her More* – not too far from the truth.

Exhibition and distribution remained a risky business. Some cinema owners still pocketed at least half the admissions and many dragged their feet about paying the rest. If a film was confiscated in a police raid, the producer had to provide a $750 replacement print at his own expense, with little hope of seeing either copy again. At the height of its success, three-quarters of the eight or nine hundred legal prints of *The Devil in Miss Jones* were estimated to be in police hands. Bootleg copies circulating on the projectionists' grapevine further eroded profits. Fortunes could, however, be made. The producer of a one-hour film would shoot it in three days, pay the talent whatever he could get away with, then strike fifteen prints. The prints cost $8000. He could sell them outright to a distributor for $1500 each – a profit of between $15,000 and $20,000 for perhaps a fortnight's work. Even short features such as *The Magic Ring*, running under an hour and shot for $10,000, could play in the two thousand X-rated cinemas spread across the United States and later be sold to Europe.

The common currency of the business remained loops, which were produced on a production line. Unlike Bill Osco's, those made in New York bore no credits. Most were funded by the Mafia, for whom porn was just another product, like narcotics. They would no more put a name on them than boutique dope dealer Zachary Swann would personalise the bags of cocaine he distributed all over Manhattan via a colleague who used the cover of a dog-walking service. Nobody made them, nobody sold them...

Wherever possible, faces were disguised, in part to preserve anonymity but also to allow shots of better bodies and more erect penises to be intercut with less impressive material. Chuck Traynor, later the husband of Linda Lovelace, and, later again, of Marilyn Chambers, was proud to have produced two reels in which the action consisted only of feet walking, until they met – after which the camera moved up as far as the navel. A wholesaler paid $100 each for them, unaware – or, if he was aware, unconcerned – that Traynor had re-invented a narrative idea which dated back to the cinema of 1914.

Marc Stevens, a male model who had begun his show business career in live sex shows on 42nd Street but later starred in porn features, evoked the atmosphere of those days.

> You work in dirty cellars mostly, [for] sleazy dirty porno makers, all of them. One guy named Harold Kovner is sick. I walked off the set on him, the only director I ever walked off the set. He was directing me eating (i.e., performing cunnilingus). I don't mind being directed when I'm eating, but when he told me not to smile... This man is not going to tell me how to eat a cunt! Then there's Bob Wolfe with his cellar on 14th Street. Sleazy. The girls he hired were the pigs of life. I've balled some dirty, filthy people, lesbians, gay chicks, junkies, whores, in these hundreds of loops. I'd do two or four loops a day and I was paid by the loop. $20 to $75, or a package deal for so much a day, doing a lot of loops. I bet I'm in every film that's around. Part of me, anyway.

"Imagine a huge loft," recalled one actress, "where ten different sets are built in a circle with three walls and one open side – all cubicles with different kinds of bedroom set-ups, baby cribs, walls with harnesses, high school locker rooms, dungeons. Chip [the producer] put a crew on a

24-hour day. While one scene is being shot in a bedroom, people are warming up with whips for the dungeon scene. At the end of five days Chip has eight films in the can. Scripts are written on the way over in a cab, but most of them are improvised."

Loft studios with standing sets were, if anything, the luxury end of the business. Another actress evoked an atmosphere even more distasteful. "A filthy loft in Manhattan, sheets draped over the furniture, floors that had never been mopped, a bathroom sink that had never been scrubbed. Two other actors were waiting there, a young man named Rob and his wife, Cathy. The director giving us the story line. 'All right, Rob, you lie down on that rubber sheet and Cathy, you and Linda come over and piss on him.' Not believing my ears, watching Cathy try to do it in vain, her saying finally 'I just can't.' The director announcing 'Well, fine, if you can't be the pisser, you can be the pissee. Cathy, you lie down and Rob, you and Linda piss on her.'"

"Linda" was Linda Boreman, a pale-skinned, dark haired woman of average prettiness, soon to be metamorphosed into a household name as Linda Lovelace.

With no acting training and a face that, on film, looks tight and expressionless, she was an unlikely candidate for stardom. The daughter of a policeman, she ran away from an overbearing mother in Yonkers, New York, with an engaging Florida bar owner named Chuck Traynor. Speedily revealed as a drug dealer, gun freak and pimp, Traynor, Lovelace claims, forced her to undergo silicon breast transplants, to marry him, and, finally, to appear in porn films.

Lovelace's most famous film – more notorious even than *Deep Throat* – was a one-day wonder in which she has sex with a dog. In the ghosted *Inside Linda Lovelace*, she denied categorically that she ever appeared in such films, and accused editor Al Goldstein of faking the photos published in his magazine *Screw*. In her two later volumes of memoirs, however, she admits to the appearance, but claims she was forced by Traynor, literally at gunpoint, to perform.

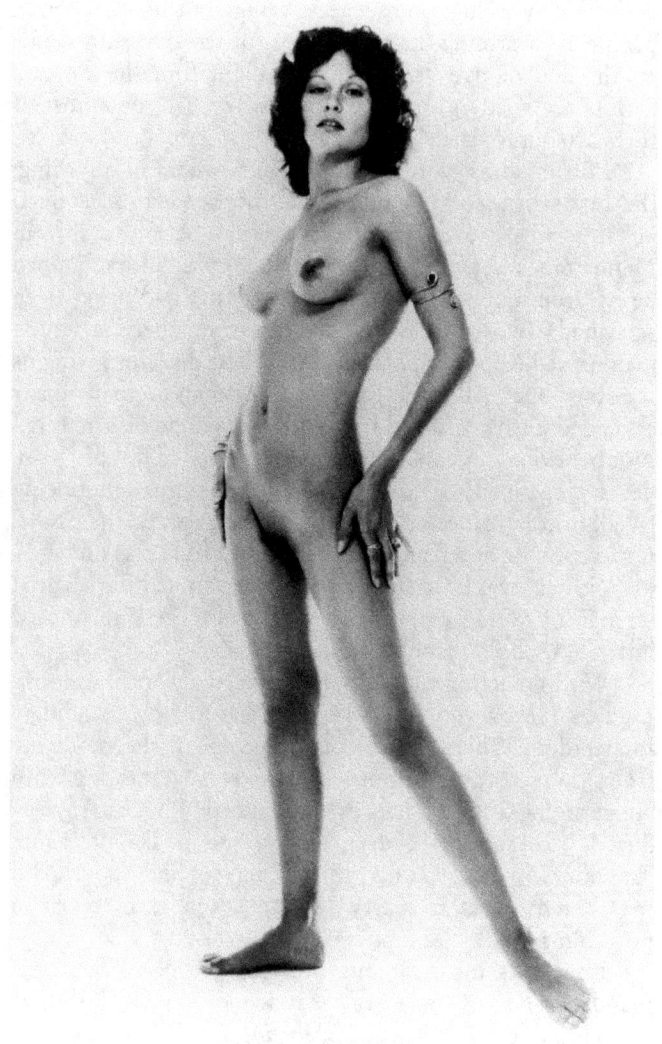

Linda Lovelace.

If she was coerced, there is little evidence of it in her surviving films. Nor do most of her early films have the look of productions from the seedier end of the porn spectrum. The short generally known as *Dog Fuck* was, in its technique and setting, modestly up-market. The set was dressed to imitate (or may well be) a hippy-style apartment, with calfskin rug, Chinese trunk, wall hangings and a low bed with a colourful cover. Lovelace, naked but for a long string of beads and much jewellery, has seldom looked more beautiful. Her long black hair is elaborately curled, her false nails lacquered an unchipped black.

As she fornicates with well-known porn stud Eric Edwards at the start of the film, she appears cheerful and energetic. Edwards leaves, however, despite her protestations, and Lovelace, after shooting him the finger, begins romping with a large and affectionate dog. Over the next ten minutes she masturbates and fellates the dog, then encourages it to mount her twice from behind. It's obviously difficult to keep the animal positioned and aroused, but the filmmaker devotes considerable effort to showing the acts in detail, shooting from a number of angles and moving in frequently for close-ups. Production must have taken at least a day, and the editing much longer. At no point does Lovelace appear to be under pressure. Smiling, moving sensuously, visibly conveying pleasure in the act, she shows no sign of fear or distress.

Like most hookers, Lovelace looked on a sex movie as just one part of her working week which might include turning tricks in a hotel, stripping for a "smoker" and satisfying any or all the guests who could pay. The only skill which set her apart from her sisters was the ability to take, sword-swallower style, the whole length of a penis into her mouth. Traynor, she claimed, taught her this using arcane hypnotic skills he had supposedly learned in Nicaragua, but since it was soon a part of every porn actress' repertoire, one can safely discard this claim, like many others made by Lovelace. What she mostly had was good luck. While she was serving a number of men at a party, demonstrating her novel fellating skill, a director of porn shorts named Gerard Damiano saw her and decided that here was a gimmick on which he might build his first feature.

On paper, Damiano's career looks not much different to that of a hundred filmmakers who entered movies in the

Sixties. In 1967, the 38-year-old New Yorker owned two Queens hairdressing establishments. At the same time, he was learning low-budget movie-making as assistant cameraman, grip and occasionally actor in a variety of starvation productions. When it became evident that his first film as director, *Night of the Rain,* was failing to gel, he added some improvised erotic scenes. Retitled *We All Go Down*, the film was a modest success, and Damiano moved permanently into porn with a succession of documentaries, hardcore loops and shorter features. One of these short films, *Teenie Tulip* (also known as *The Doctor Makes a House Call* and *Doctor Love*), featured a girl so sexually voracious that she approaches a sexologist for help. Driving back to Queens over the 59th Street Bridge after observing Linda Lovelace's novel fellation technique, Damiano saw how this story could be expanded into the script that became *Deep Throat*.

Lovelace, who denies Damiano's version of her discovery, claims she signed on the crew of *Deep Throat* as script girl to be near Traynor, who was to be its cameraman, and was cajoled into starring. She also paints Damiano as a talentless hack in thrall to his mobster producer. Yet his later films reveal a personal filmmaker who, within the restrictions of hardcore, has created a consistent and disturbing body of work. His films, often violent, cynical and suffused with what some critics identify as Catholic guilt but was more likely simple misanthropy, stand in contrast to the yea-saying Pleasure Above All message of the porn world at large. Damiano's work was often called "Bergman-esque." The proposition of *The Devil in Miss Jones*, that endless sex without satisfaction could be a form of hell, certainly originated with Bergman's *The Devil's Eye* (1960), and while he is hardly in the same league artistically, his films, the most joyless in sex cinema, share some of Bergman's despair. "In the beginning we are born. In the end we die," runs a line in Damiano's *Odyssey*. "The middle is called life."

Throat was shot over six days of January 1972, in suburban bungalows around Miami, Fort Lauderdale and

Coral Gables, with three months of post-production in New York. The "Lou Perry" listed as producer was Louis "Butchie" Peraino, son of Anthony "Big Tony" Peraino, a member of the "family" of Mafia don Joseph Colombo. Described by Lovelace as "a 250-pound hulk," Lou Paraino had a long career in porn distribution. In 1971, with $25,000 borrowed from his father, he moved into production with Gerard Damiano Productions Inc. *Deep Throat*, of which the Parainos owned two-thirds, was their first major film.

Paraino's use of a pseudonym typified *Deep Throat*. Damiano, who signed the film "Jerry Gerard," sought out Harry Streicher, who, as "Harry Reems," a name coined by Damiano (as was "Linda Lovelace"), had already played the doctor/nurse scene for his earlier *Doctor Love*. Dinner theatre, summer stock, Off- and Off-off-Broadway were the nurseries of porn. Actresses with fair looks and not much talent could always find work in sex films, and actors, well-built, well-hung, with an ability to maintain an erection, were equally employable. Streicher, a stocky man with a bushy moustache, wasn't classic leading man material, but he had worked at La MaMa in New York and the National Shakespeare Company, as well as appearing in commercials for such squeaky-clean products as Wheaties breakfast cereal. In his account of his casting, he was out of work at Christmas 1969 when a friend told him they were paying $75 for a morning's performance in 8mm porn films. Over the next three years, he appeared in more than four hundred of them. He never planned to act in Damiano's film, he says, but signed on as part of the crew ("Ned Reems" gets screen credit as Assistant Cameraman). When Marc Stevens, a well-known stud, failed to take the role, Reems stepped in as the doctor.

Like most porn plots, *Deep Throat* follows one girl's search for sexual fulfilment. Liberated Miami bachelor girl Linda confesses to housemate Dolly Sharp that, despite plenty of experience, she gets little pleasure from sex: "a lot of little tingles" but no "bells ringing, dams bursting, or bombs going off." Doctor Young (Reems) discovers that Linda lacks a clitoris in the normal place. He finally locates it deep in her throat, where it can be stimulated only by the form of fellatio in which the woman relaxes her throat to engorge the penis totally. When he illustrates by allowing Linda to fellate him, she experiences orgasm for the first time. Damiano illustrates her reaction with footage of fireworks, rockets taking off and the Golden Striker figures on Venice's Piazza San Marco battering a bell with sledgehammers. Linda begs the doctor to marry her. Instead, he persuades her to become a therapist, treating his sexually dysfunctional patients, but returning to him frequently for total satisfaction. Combined with his regular screwing of his nurse, this is too much for Young, who collapses, a bandaged victim of overindulgence. Linda has meanwhile met Wilbur, a well-hung young man addicted to burglar/voyeur/rapist fantasies. She straightens him out, but his penis proves too long for her ideal satisfaction. The doctor, however, reassures the couple that it can be trimmed to any size Linda desires.

Deep Throat was simply the standard stag film writ large. Anyone familiar with porn knew these characters; the naive heroine, eager for enlightenment; the burglar/rapist, and the louche doctor. Its incidents are an anthology of popular fetishes, e.g. the money shot, the orgy, voyeurism, rape, even the insertion of a bottle into the vagina, here updated with a glass tube. It also includes a few not seen since the Thirties. Linda shaves her pubic hair, for instance, an act elaborately parodied by portentous music and the commercial theme for Old Spice toiletries.

Reems, who tended to walk through all his performances with a look of private amusement, makes no pretence at establishing Young as any more complex than a comic character in a vaudeville sketch. Though a porn film with original music and even a title song was remarkable in 1972, the latter, written by Damiano, was abysmal even by the standards of porn themes. Even Lovelace, no *literateuse,* scoffed at lyrics such as "Deep Throat / Don't row a boat / Don't get your goat / That's all she wrote/Deep Throat" though she missed the point that the song, like all the film's music, was a parody, in this case of the Mickey Mouse Club Theme.

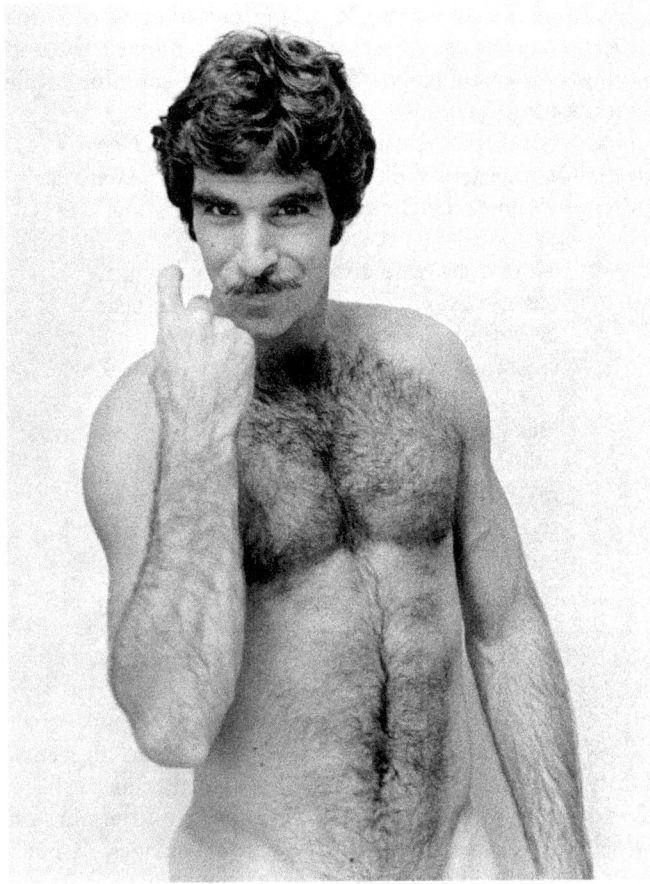

Harry Reems.

Damiano's dialogue, mostly broad one-liners, would work equally well – or perhaps better? – as intertitles in a silent stag film. Linda to Reems, when he's amused by her plight: "What if your balls were in your ears?" "Then I could hear myself coming."

Gay man (played by Damiano himself, as "Al Gork") arriving at the height of an orgy and glimpsing a familiar member: "What's a nice joint like you doing in a girl like that?"

Helen (Dolly Sharp), enjoying cunnilingus with the grocery delivery boy (Ted Street), lighting a cigarette and saying conversationally: "Excuse me for smoking while you're eating."

Lovelace later described the production of *Deep Throat* in nightmarish terms. She was, she claimed, systematically beaten by Chuck Traynor throughout the filming.

> Next door, where the crew is partying, it has got as quiet as a tomb. They can hear everything. The first punch sends me crashing onto the bed. Chuck is berserk now, picking me off the bed and throwing me against the wall. I fall to the floor, rolling myself into a tight ball, protecting my stomach and breasts from his boots, screaming "Stop! Please stop! You're hurting me!" Screaming. "Help! Oh, God, please help me! Someone help me!" But help does not come and the beating goes on. Why is there no help? Why do the men stay in the next room?

Nobody has ever corroborated her version of events. Harry Reems dismisses both her stories, as well as Traynor's claim to have worked creatively on the film, on which he receives credit as Production Manager. "Chuck was an asshole, but he was hardly around for the filming. Damiano sent him away because he would get jealous of how much she was enjoying the sex. She was really into it." Independent reports of the Lovelace/Traynor relationship confirm Traynor as overbearing and Lovelace as vague and inarticulate, but there is no reliable evidence of personal violence, nor any sign of it in the film. Given that Lovelace was nude for most of *Deep Throat*, one would expect some sign of injury, especially on such white skin, but aside from a small bruise on her thigh, there is none. Pressed on why no other star has complained of the coercion she describes as rife in porn film, Lovelace responded vaguely, "In a sense the whole world is a victim. The people who make porno, the audience…" Valid as a truism, it's dubious as testimony. Boreman was as bad a liar as she was an actress.

14
Cutting Throat

Deep Throat opened in June 1972 at the New Mature World Theater on New York's West 49th Street, just off Times Square. It took $33,000 in its first week. That cinema had a history of headline presentations. In February 1946, then simply known as the New World Cinema, it established a tradition for gaudy, if misleading advertising by promoting Roberto Rossellini's neorealist drama *Rome, Open City* as "Sexier Than Hollywood Ever Dared To Be," backing the promise with a giant close-up of Anna Magnani's eyes. *Deep Throat*, however, would be its last film. As part of a "Clean Up Times Square" campaign in that year's mayoral election, owner Sam Lake was arrested twice for obscenity, and the cinema was finally ordered closed in March 1973.

During the court hearings, the judge called *Throat* "indisputably and irredeemably obscene," "a feast of carrion and squalor" and "the nadir of decadence." "This," he concluded, "is one throat that deserves to be cut." Lake sarcastically announced the closure on the cinema's marquee: "Judge Cuts Throat: World Mourns." By then, *Deep Throat* had been seen by a quarter of a million people and grossed $1 million – on one occasion $96,000 in a single week. Damiano saw none of the profits. He had sold his one-third interest in the film to the Parainos for $25,000, almost exactly what it cost to make. Asked why he had accepted such a derisory amount, he said, "You want me to get both my legs broken?" Nevertheless, its success launched him into the higher echelons of the business and he had no trouble finding money for a second feature.

With Lovelace appearing in *Playboy* and on the cover of *Esquire*, *Deep Throat* was among the year's most widely publicised films, porn or straight. Al Goldstein of *Screw* magazine called it "the very best porno ever made" featuring "the greatest on-screen fellatio since the birth of Christ." But the film had far more prestigious supporters.

Ralph Blumenthal of *The New York Times* revealed that a large group from the paper's staff saw *Throat* during their lunch-hour in the first week of the run. In a long article, he classified it as the latest manifestation of "porno chic." During the courtroom proceedings, Arthur Knight, author of the then-standard work of film history, *The Liveliest Art*, the text he used in his classes at USC which included George Lucas and other future luminaries, praised the film "for expanding the audience's sexual horizons and producing healthier attitudes towards sex." Other enthusiasts included Warren Beatty, Frank Sinatra, who screened it for Vice President Spiro Agnew, and Mike Nichols, who saw it three times and recommended it to Truman Capote.

It became commonplace for couples to catch *Deep Throat* together, the first film to crack that barrier, and the last, until the softcore features of the Eighties. It was this fact more than any other that surprised Ned Tanen, head of production for Universal, and the executive responsible for cultivating new talent. "The thing that shocked me most about *Deep Throat*," he said, "was that nobody in the audience was a dirty old man with a raincoat."

"Not to have seen it," wrote Manhattan journalist and novelist Nora Ephron in *Esquire*, "seemed somehow derelict." Unlike her male colleagues, however, Ephron was alarmed by scenes such as one in which a client places a glass tube in Linda Lovelace's vagina from which they share Coca-Cola through a plastic tube to a few notes from Coke's "It's the Real Thing" jingle. "All I could think about was what would happen if the glass broke," said Ephron. She was reassured when she interviewed Lovelace. The actress, who said she had been paid $1200 for *Deep Throat* and was then making $250 a week, told Ephron, as she told everyone at the time, that she was an exhibitionist who loved doing the film and hoped it would encourage everyone to discard their sexual inhibitions.

In those cities where it was permitted to play, *Deep Throat* continued its phenomenal release. At the Pussycat Cinema in Santa Monica, the beachside suburb of Los Angeles, the uncut version played thirteen times a day for

THE ONE AND ONLY...
DEEP THROAT
ADULTS ONLY IN COLOR

Shows Daily at: 12:15 - 2:00
3:30 - 5:00 - 6:30 - 8:15 - 9:55
11:30 - 1:05 - 2:40 and 4:10
For additional information,
call 654-5744

OPEN DAILY 12 NOON
OPEN ALL NIGHT

PUSSYCAT • 654-5742
7734 SANTA MONICA BL., HLYWD
And Now Playing At The
PUSSYCAT BUENA PARK

THE STIMULATORS

EASTMANCOLOR • ADULTS ONLY
OPEN DAILY 12 NOON
PUSSYCAT BUENA PARK
6177 Beach Blvd. 521-5337
Formerly The Grand

ten years, grossing $6.4 million. Delegates at CBS's 1972 Convention abandoned a party at the home of singer Neil Diamond to stand in line, in some cases for hours. The entire Russian basketball team tried to see it in Albuquerque, NM, but couldn't scrape together the cost of admission. In New York, even the censored version, double-billed with Damiano's second film, *The Devil in Miss Jones*, and with the penetration scenes in both rendered legally acceptable by dividing the image diagonally (which deleted the lips and penis), then optically repeating the remainder eight or sixteen times, a fly's eye view of fellatio, ran for years.

The Paraino family prospered on the profits of *Deep Throat*. Lou formed Bryanston Distributors Inc. (not to be confused with the British Bryanston Films) which grossed $20 million in its first year, and financed a number of non-porn productions, including the kung-fu movie *Return of the Dragon* and Tobe Hooper's debut *The Texas Chainsaw Massacre*. The good times, however, didn't last. The California Department of Justice charged that Bryanston coordinated the nationwide distribution of full-length films for organised crime. In 1976, as part of an FBI campaign, "Big Tony" Paraino, Lou and his brother Joe, as well as Harry Reems, were convicted in Memphis, Tennessee of "transporting obscene materials" (*Deep Throat*) across state lines. Reems' conviction was overturned in 1977. The Parainos appealed their case to the Supreme Court which, in November 1981, refused to reverse the decision. A month later, jail terms of up to three years and fines ranging from $2000 to $10,000 were handed down on Lou Peraino, Bryanston and Gerard Damiano Productions.

Meanwhile, on Valentine's Day 1980, four hundred FBI men and local police raided the offices of porn distributors in thirteen US cities, arresting fifty-eight people, including Lou and Joe Paraino. Among the offices invaded was that on 150 Lafayette Street in New York's Little Italy occupied by Star Distributors, the East Coast's largest distributor of porn – and also, incidentally, of *Screw* magazine. Mickey Zaffarano, a major figure in porn and the producer of films such as *Debbie Does Dallas*, died of a heart attack during the raid. Though the FBI called their strike "Miporn" (for "Miami Porn") they were actually more interested in crushing the theft and bootlegging of Hollywood features, a sideline of the porn business so widespread that Hollywood demanded a crackdown.

Deep Throat remained the Paraino's sole major success, and a source of deep satisfaction, not to mention profit, to the mob family. Asked how much money he had made from the film, the elder Joe Paraino replied, "Well, Lou's got eight kids and Joe has kids, and their kids and their grandkids have nothing to worry about the rest of their lives. Does that tell you how much the movie brought in?" By then, *Deep Throat* had played in seventy cities across the United States. In 1980, the FBI estimated that, if one included the income from sequels, spin-offs and merchandising, it could have taken as much as $600 million, making it the most profitable movie up to that time.

A heightened awareness of porn cinema's recreational possibilities vastly expanded its scope and options. Stars and even directors found they had admirers who would seek out their work. Filmmakers such as Bruce Seven, John Stagliano and Rinse Dream could depend on new videos selling largely on their reputation, and while critical acceptance in the United States was confined to the porn trade press, the French in particular accepted and discussed their work. Critic Pierre Gras coined the label "*Auteur noir*" for Gerard Damiano. One French magazine called him respectfully "The Godfather of Porn" and, under the title "Between the Bed and Death," *La Revue du cinéma* ran a long interview that probed his dour philosophy.

Damiano continued to be the most consistently interesting of porn directors. *The Devil in Miss Jones* (1972) could hardly be less like *Deep Throat*. There is none of *Throat*'s sophomoric humour. The story begins with a bloody suicide and subsides seventy minutes later in a cackle of laughter at the aimlessness of a life devoted to sensuality. Justine Jones, a frustrated middle-aged spinster, slashes her wrists in a bath. Waking up in a cheerless modern Hell, she is assessed by its custodian, who concludes that, since she has enjoyed none of the experiences for which one was normally condemned, she should return to earth for the kind of spree that might justify damnation. With the encouragement of a corporeal adviser (Harry Reems), Miss Jones explores lesbian sex, simultaneous vaginal and anal penetration, sex with another couple, and a sensual encounter with a python, as well as more routine encounters. Returning to Hell fulfilled, eager for more experience, she discovers that damnation is an eternity of sex without orgasm.

Justine Jones was played by one of the legendary figures of porn cinema, Shelly (sometimes Chelle) Graham. Thirty-seven years old in 1972, she possessed hard blonde good looks that disguised a crackling sexuality. As a child, she had run away from home to join the circus. Later she danced in USO shows, in the chorus of Broadway productions of *The Pajama Game* and *Cabaret*, acted off-Broadway, worked as a dance director, appeared in TV commercials, where she met Damiano, and held a desk job in advertising. In 1962, she played a brief lesbian scene for American director and distributor Radley Metzger, who wanted to liven up the US version of a French film called *Les Collegiennes*, which he had renamed *The Twilight Girls*. Thereafter, she regularly appeared in porn loops, which she spoke of bleakly as "fuck films."

Divorced three times, Graham was living in a homosexual relationship when she answered an advertisement in 1972 for a cook on *The Devil in Miss Jones*, then being shot at a ranch owned by Harry Reems. Damiano had already cast a younger actress for Justine but he saw Graham and changed his mind. His offer added another one-liner to the porn lexicon. "They told me, 'We'll give you $100 a day and all the cock you can eat,'" says Graham. Out of some residual prudery, she adopted as her *nom de porn* "Georgina Spelvin," a version of "George Spelvin," the pseudonym used in American theatre programmes when an actor doesn't wish to be identified.

Despite the obvious affinity between *The Devil in Miss Jones* and Sartre's existential *Huis Clos*, the bleakness of the tale was belied by Spelvin's evident pleasure in the sex. Her lesbian *pas de deux*, played with her own real-life lover, Claire Lumière, was believably sensual. Whether shot, as legend has it, during what the performers believed was a rehearsal, or, as Marc Stevens asserts, over a period of four days, the scene of her penetration by two men simultaneously was remarkably convincing. Spelvin's obbligato of muttered encouragement, murmurs of pleasure and "Left hand down a bit" orders to her partners lifts the performance above choreography into erotic reportage, with a corresponding voyeuristic charge.

Damiano's next production, *Memories Within Miss Aggie* (1974) intended, he has said, to be the story of Justine Jones' life had she not committed suicide, was even darker. In a secluded farmhouse in the snow-bound hills of Pennsylvania sometime in the Thirties, an ageing Miss Aggie (Deborah Ashira) describes to a companion Richard (Patrick L. Farrelly) a series of youthful sensual experiences, with the Aggie character played in each case by a different actress. A young blond Kim Pope chooses to lose her virginity with Eric Edwards in a sequence notable for its extended, carefully observed foreplay. Edwards then visits a whore (Darby Lloyd Raines) who inflames him with a long episode of masturbation. And finally a girl (Mary Stuart), having excited herself by masturbating with a small doll, seduces a delivery man (Harry Reems). After every recollection, Richard casts doubt on Aggie's veracity. It's finally revealed that she is insane and the Richard to whom she speaks is the ghost of her first and only lover. She murdered him when he threatened to leave her. Now, *Psycho*-like, his corpse shares the lonely house with her, a truly captive audience for her erotic ramblings.

Memories Within Miss Aggie decisively dispels Linda Lovelace's picture of Damiano as a hack. The shooting is atmospheric, the direction of actors both in the erotic scenes and the framing story skilful, the music unassertive and atmospheric. It ends, in what must surely be its only use in a porn film, on a few bars of the hymn *Amazing Grace*. *Miss Aggie* was shown in the market at that year's Cannes Film Festival and became the most widely circulated of all Damiano's early films.

In Damiano's 1975 *The Story of Joanna,* his version of *Histoire d'O*. Jamie Gillis, largely type-cast at the time in S&M roles, plays Jason, a rich European sadist who invites Joanna (Terri Hall) into his chateau to "perform a task I am unable to perform for myself." After a series of humiliations and punishments, to all of which Joanna adoringly submits, and an unexpected homosexual interlude between Gillis and his servant Griffin (Zebedy Colt), she takes the upper hand and shoots Jason, who is suffering from an incurable disease. The task he could not perform was to kill himself – a quietus he prefers to be administered by someone who loves him.

As his films indicate, Damiano had more talent and better ideas than most X-rated filmmakers. MGM offered him a contract after *Deep Throat* and was briefly in contention for an Oscar for *Memories Within Miss Aggie*.

Despite this, he remained in the porn world, preferring, it seems, the role of renegade. However, a certain resentment at the complacency of Hollywood is evident in his most bizarre film, the 1975 *Water Power*. A thriller based on actual events, it deals with a Los Angeles rapist (Gillis again) who inflicts enemas on his victims, and his final tracking down by a cop (C.J. Laing, an actress known for her interest in S&M) who becomes a victim.

Nobody who has not lived in Los Angeles can hope to grasp the eerie accuracy of *Water Power*. The twitching Gillis is excited to orgasm while watching an enema being administered to a woman at the Garden of Eden, a club for bondage freaks, sadomasochists and cross-dressers. As his first victim, he chooses that most seductive of uniformed women, an airline stewardess. Having spied on her through a telescope making love, he feels justified. "She's dirty," he reflects. "Just a toilet. If I cleaned her out she would be clean again. She'd thank me. She'd be glad I cleaned her out." The French critic Pierre Gras called the film a "sulphurously Gothic masterpiece," describing it as "joyously murky… a metaphor for the fantasy world of American hardcore which would like to rid, by sexual violence, Hollywood of its prudery. Jamie Gillis, a barbarous and Dionysiac brute, officiates genially over this Satanic Hollywood."

Damiano's subsequent output was prodigious (more than twenty features) but uneven. Catchpenny projects such as *Damiano's People. Whose Fantasy Is This Anyway?* (1984), a collection of his loops, and *Fantasy* (1979), a parody of the TV series *Fantasy Island* with Georgina Spelvin, alternated with more serious films such as *Odyssey* (1977) and the 1980 *For Richer, For Poorer*, both attempts at "thoughtful" porn in which couples look for new meaning in relationships that have begun to decay into boredom. *Throat: 12 Years After* (1984), far from celebrating his first success, is an extended critique by two modern couples of the earlier film.

Damiano worked almost entirely out of New York's Adventureland Studios, and on 35mm film. With the introduction of video his output slowed to a trickle, but his reputation continued to rise. He has been called the Godfather of Porn and (by performer Jerry Butler) its Leonardo. Damiano, however, seldom returned the compliment. Preoccupied with the mechanics of the world hardcore is creating (the theme of *Water Power*), he made a number of jaded quasi-documentaries, cynical reports from the front line of the sexual revolution.

Consenting Adults (1982) is typical. Produced by Damiano but conceived and co-directed by his then-mistress, Ellen Steinberg, better known as porn star "Annie Sprinkle," as well as veterans Marc Stevens, Joey Civera/Silvera, Veronica Vera, Sharon Mitchell and Ron Jeremy, it includes scenes from a nude beauty contest at the Ponderosa Sun Club in Roselawn, Indiana, a piece about the fad for labia piercing pioneered by Marilyn Chambers, another on female wrestling, and a long interview with Damiano himself on his sexual tastes. Hell, Sartre said, is other people. Damiano seems to agree. Does *Consenting Adults* endorse the hedonistic life-style? Or are these people (and Damiano himself), solemn in their obsession as stamp collectors, meant to excite our derision? To many, the film resembled a final hoot of laughter, signalling Damiano's contempt for the entire business.

In a venerable tradition dating back to the earliest days of American cinema, production of porn migrated in the Seventies from the chilly east coast to a sunnier and more liberated California. *Behind the Green Door* established the Mitchell brothers as the nation's preeminent screen pornographers, a reputation they seemed determined to live up to, if not positively to exceed. Not frightened to spend money, they expanded the horizons of porn, adding expensive costumes and better production values.

Jim Mitchell directed *The Resurrection of Eve* with Jon Fontana, the cameraman given much credit for papering over the technical cracks in *Green Door*. It used Chambers and Keyes again, this time in a more complex story of a girl who discovers sexual pleasure after her face is reconstructed following a road accident.

The Autobiography of a Flea (1976), directed by Sharon (Mitchell) McKnight, the ex-porn star/singer who was later to appear in, and co-direct, *Behind the Green Door: The Sequel*, was adapted from a piece of Victorian erotica as a vehicle for Annette Haven and the best of the new stud stars, John Holmes. The period costumes of *Flea* – the film was set in the France of 1810 – cost a fortune, but the Mitchells regarded this as a reasonable expense, since their films by then were being shown in conventional cinemas all over America, a dozen of them belonging to the brothers themselves.

Never long out of the limelight or the courts, the Mitchells throughout the Seventies and Eighties lived up to their renegade image, fighting a running battle with the "straight" world. The O'Farrell Theatre ranked as a Bay Area landmark alongside Alcatraz and the City Lights Bookshop, cradle of the Beat Generation of writers. Refurbished, expanded to a combined cinema/strip club, with its frontage incongruously decorated with a mural of dolphins, salmon and mating whales – the Mitchells loved to fish – it became a local monument. Later they renamed it The Eros Centre and gave it a new decorative motif of rain forest and aquaria, embedding it even deeper into the Californian ethos.

Those who attacked the Mitchells, such as San Francisco Assistant District Attorney Bernard Waller, a long-time adversary, often unwittingly augmented their lustre. "The First Amendment was the Mitchells' licence to make millions selling oral copulation and digital intercourse to thousands of tourists," Waller complained – a statement not likely to offend anyone, least of all the Mitchells' happy customers. "I ask those who say flattering things about the Mitchells," he continued. "Would you say the same about two brothers from Sicily or two handsome black pimps?" Given the racial diversity of San Francisco, this argument was hardly designed to win friends, especially since the Mitchells were, in the best tradition of the Seventies, scrupulous in distributing work in their films among ethnic and cultural sub-groups. Nor was Waller's final accusation likely to sway their supporters. "The Mitchells had the money to hire the same legal talent that defended Huey

Newton, the Weather Underground, IRA gun runners, and other First Amendment Communist front organisations." To which the citizens of California, most litigious state in the union and home to 11% of its lawyers, would generally have responded "Right on!" Waller dubbed the O'Farrell "a Cadillac of whorehouses." This didn't deter tour buses from depositing passengers for an hour's browsing in its Kopenhagen strip theatre, cinemas and X-rated video store. It may even have encouraged them.

The Mitchells used their street smarts and reputation as gonzo porn merchants to harry and influence the law. Some of their coups were ingenious. When San Francisco mayor Dianne Feinstein turned on the heat, the Mitchells displayed her unlisted home phone number on the O'Farrell marquee. A New York judge compared the activities in *Green Door* with those of Sodom and Gomorrah. Jim and Artie promptly announced that this was a great idea, and that they would shortly produce a film on the twin cities of vice. *Sodom and Gomorrah: The Final Days* (1977), a lavish and erotic retelling of Old Testament incidents as viewed from the future, cost $350,000, making it the most expensive porn film ever made to that date. It was also one of the most disastrously unprofitable.

The O'Farrell became an informal hang-out for members of the press, law enforcement and the political establishment, and for writers such as gonzo journalist Hunter S. Thompson, who worked there as "Night Manager" for a year, researching a book. The San Francisco establishment routinely turned a blind eye to the Mitchells' activities. Critics charged that public officials often did so in return for free sex, though most were simply content to bask in the O'Farrell back-room ambiance, which included closed-circuit TV observation of the strip stage and dressing room. In 1985, during Marilyn Chambers' triumphant return to the O'Farrell as a stripper, the SFPD sent thirteen cops to arrest her when it was reported she had allowed men in audience to fondle and finger her. Later, in a series of indignant articles, journalist Warren Hinckle, an O'Farrell habitue, claimed the bust took so much time and so many men because each cop wanted his picture taken with Chambers. The tendency of police to overstaff such raids was international. When the London police invaded a club screening Andy Warhol's *Flesh* in February 1970, 32 officers converged on the tiny theatre. As Ben Hecht had remarked on American law enforcement in the Thirties, "the forces of law and order did not advance on the villains with drawn guns but with their palms out like bellboys."

15
99 ⁴⁴⁄₁₀₀% Sexy

"Dirty movies have gotten better, I'm told," Joseph Heller wrote in his 1972 novel *Something Happened*. "Smut and weaponry are the two areas in which we've improved. Everything else has gotten worse." Coming from the writer whose *Catch-22* had merchandised anarchy to Middle America, this was a powerful statement of, if not acceptance, then at least recognition of an art form which until then had been considered too trivial even to insult.

The success of *Deep Throat* propelled its principals into the spotlight, and the fast lane of the porn business. Carol Connors, who played Doctor Young's long-suffering nurse, turned her blonde good looks to advantage. She starred in two rip-offs of *Candy*, *The Erotic Adventures of Candy* and *Candy Goes to Hollywood*, then metamorphosed into a more knowing performer to direct herself in the Mitchell Brothers' *Desire For Me*. Harry Reems became, briefly, the most sought-after stud in porn. His stocky body and bushy moustache appeared in scores of porn features, including two, *Young Butterflies* and *Bel Ami*, made in Germany and Sweden respectively.

Lovelace, the first trophy porn star, was pursued by every bedroom athlete in the world. Chuck Traynor handed her around like candy among those who could further her career. When Czech director Miloš Forman and his writer, Buck Henry, approached her to appear in Forman's first US production, *Taking Off*, about the parents of teenage runaways trying to re-educate themselves in Seventies mores, Traynor, she writes, responded enthusiastically: "If you guys really want to make a movie with Linda, you can have her for a week." They declined. Spotting Lovelace on a London street, an aged Rex Harrison had his chauffeur halt his car and piled out onto the footpath so hurriedly to meet her that he sprained his ankle. Sammy Davis Jr., famously priapic, was also her frequent sex partner, as he was of other porn stars. (He presented Marilyn Chambers with one of the diamond-studded rings she wore through her pierced labia.) Lovelace also became a valued guest at Hugh Hefner's *Playboy* mansion in Beverly Hills. She joked about Hef, a somewhat undersexed participant, prowling the overcrowded jacuzzi, bottle of baby oil in hand, searching for Targets of Opportunity, and finally sodomising her.

Among the people who emerged from Lovelace's account of her career in no good light was Al Goldstein. In a *Playboy* interview, the editor recalled their first meeting. "We met in a small, cold $17-a-night hotel room, and it was the most difficult interview I ever conducted, because she's really inarticulate. Chuck Traynor, then her husband and 'manager,' did most of the talking. After the interview, I said, 'Listen, I'd like you to suck my cock.' I figured she was just a hooker anyway, so I wasn't embarrassed. She said fine. Chuck said OK, and she blew me. I ran the photos of her sucking my cock and my description of it. It was a paradigm of personal journalism."

After *Deep Throat*, Lovelace stumbled through a few farces such as *Linda Lovelace for President,* propped up by elaborate plots and a supporting cast who, unlike her, knew what they were doing. For an advance of $100,000 from Pinnacle books she put her name to a ghosted memoir, *Inside Linda Lovelace*, and appeared in quasi-documentaries where, as in the book, she rhapsodised about the life of a sex goddess and urged everyone to follow her path to sexual fulfilment. She remained, however, a dismal performer in anything that required acting ability. Sammy Davis Jr. offered to include her in his Las Vegas stage act but, after a few rehearsals, thought better of the idea.

Lovelace avoided prosecution in the federal case against the Parainos and *Deep Throat* by insisting she was forced into making the film, a claim she pressed in her book *Ordeal*. Critics, with some justification, attacked *Ordeal* and its sequel *Out of Bondage* as improbable and slanted. Both rely almost exclusively on reconstructed conversations and Lovelace's patchy recall. There are many detectable exaggerations, and numerous shadowy areas.

If Lovelace or her collaborator Mike McGrady checked any part of the story in more than superficial detail, there is no sign of it. Traynor, married to Marilyn Chambers, rejected Lovelace's version of their life together, but, as Mandy Rice-Davies famously responded when a judge pointed out that a client denied her description of their liaison, "Well, he would, wouldn't he?" Nevertheless, her accounts of the porn milieu, the need to suck up (in many cases literally) to backers, the problems of low-budget shooting on remote locations, always one step ahead of the law, the attraction of drugs and alcohol, all confirm other reports.

While Lovelace faded away after her great screen triumph, Marilyn Chambers flourished in the porn milieu. There are interesting parallels between the careers of Lovelace and Chambers. Both entered movies at the same time, both were famous in the Seventies, both married the same man. Neither was classically beautiful. Lovelace's legs were thin, and she walked without grace. There was also a glassy vacancy behind her eyes that recalled the pouting stare of the inflated sex doll. Chambers has an odd mouth, wide and duck-like, that gave her face a rubbery, amused quality, as if she was always about to break into a grin. Nor was her body, small-breasted, thin and muscular as Jane Fonda's in middle age, the standard instrument of the porn performer.

In her better moments, there was something almost nun-like about Lovelace. Her pale skin bruised easily, a fact she traded on in her books. She seemed remote, unreal, a natural ascetic. "The most amazing thing about Linda," said Gerard Damiano, "is that she looks so sweet and innocent."

Chambers' innocence, on the other hand, was never more than skin deep. She pointedly planted packets of "99 and 44/100% Pure" Ivory Snow soap powder in films such as *Insatiable* to underline the improbability of that early association. At her best, she exhibited star quality, and, specifically, the star quality demanded by porn, which combined charisma with a repertoire of sexual tricks and the instinctive knowledge of how and when to employ them. Whoever directed Chambers, she was always the *auteur*.

What made Chambers so expert? In the late Seventies, Robert Stoller of Yale University began analysing erotic performers, models and dancers. He called their personalities "hysterical" or "histrionic," with a "chronic erotic tenseness."

> Women of this subcategory think and feel erotically day and night and have consciously done so since early childhood – three, four, five, six. They are profoundly exhibitionistic: always feeling that they are being watched, always preparing themselves for being watched, and therefore always alert to their physical appearance... They may spend hours on – are highly focused on – cosmetics, fashions, sexy underwear, erotically provocative movements, performing before mirrors, fantasising being in or engaged in the professions of exhibitionism, such as acting, dancing, singing and modelling. They are not only always "on stage" but, in being so, transmit their... excitement about being watched. This then stimulates the necessary reciprocal fantasies in the audience, which is composed of men who will want the woman and of women who will admire or envy her. This unending performance creates an aura – a miasma, when the overtones are darker – of erotism. Such a woman grabs her culture's definitions of femininity and drives them to extremes.

Chambers fits this definition in almost every respect. Even in *Behind the Green Door* her relish for sex was obvious, and clearly went beyond simple performance. Bill Rotsler watched her on the set of the 1973 *The Resurrection of Eve* and was deeply impressed.

> The way they shoot orgy scenes, they just get a big room full of people, and everybody just starts sucking and fucking, and the camera goes round from person to person. I was walking across to the other side of this thing, trying to keep out of the way of the camera. And I saw Marilyn Chambers go down on Johnnie Keyes. Keyes was laying sprawled on a couch and she was kneeling between his legs. What was remarkable about this is that, as she came up on him, her whole body was sinuous. It was like she was sucking him to her toes! It stopped me dead in my tracks. It was the most physically beautiful act of that nature I'd ever seen, and I just stared at this. It was just gorgeous. And it never got on film.'

Like most porn stars, Chambers aspired to a career in legitimate films. However, her appearance in the 1977 *Rabid* by Canadian director David Cronenberg as a girl who is infected during reconstructive surgery by a bug that turns her into, in Kim Newman's words, "a rabies-spreading vampire with a penile barb in her armpit," didn't result in any more serious offers. She also starred in an unsuccessful play, *The Sex Surrogate*, and assembled a cabaret show for Las Vegas. Both won meagre reviews.

Finally, and perhaps gratefully, she returned in her midthirties to her metier. Almost as if she had caught it from *Rabid*, she brought with her a new edge of violence. Her films of this period, mostly made for the Mitchells, have no story. *Beyond De Sade* (1979) shows her performing at the O'Farrell's Kopenhagen Lounge to an audience of masked men, all of whom wield large phallic flashlights. The performance is overtly masochistic. *Never a Tender Moment* (1979) is a compilation of shorts, including *Southern Belles*, in which a mixed-race cast of ladies in *Gone With the Wind* costumes pleasure one another with dildos, and *Hot Nazis*, an S&M fantasy to German martial music. Chambers' contribution to the anthology is a nude dance which focuses on her famous labial ring.

The vehicles of Chambers' success in the Eighties were *Insatiable* (1980) and *Insatiable II* (1981), both directed by Godfrey Daniels II. Shrewdly, she exploited the fact that she was no longer the innocent of *Behind the Green Door*. By choosing to play Sandra Chase, a retired model who, born rich, has never lacked luxury nor had to deny herself anything, she could set her films in the glossy milieu of *Dallas* and *Dynasty*. In each film, Chambers co-stars with another mature actress. In *Insatiable*, it's Jessie St James, star of *Easy* and *Hot Legs*. She plays Sandra's friend and agent Flo, whom she flies to London to visit; an excuse for a Rolls Royce tour of London, conversations with the Houses of Parliament in the background and chilly-looking sex scenes in the pool of a country mansion. In *Insatiable II*, set in a series of mansions back in the States, Sandra submits to an interview with reporter Juliet Anderson, another veteran. Anderson's series of films about porn movie producer Peggy Norton, aka Aunt Peg (*Aunt Peg*, 1980. *Aunt Peg's Fulfilment* (1982) gave her an image as a tough professional woman whom Chambers as the hedonistic Sandra plays against.

There is a marked difference in tone between the two films. *Insatiable* is an *Emmanuelle* clone, aimed at a crossover audience, partly female. The male performers include John Leslie and John Holmes, though following his arrest the latter's name was crudely scratched out of the negative. *Insatiable II* is tougher, reflecting the growing violence of Chambers' work. Two extended sexual "numbers" in *Insatiable* II are powerfully masochistic.

In the more striking of them, she submits to Jamie Gillis, star of *The Story of Joanna* and *Water Power*, allowing him to place a dog's choke lead around her neck, flick her with a dog whip and drip hot wax on her nipples, a cliche S&M fantasy of the sort in which Gillis specialised. An earlier sequence, however, is less formalised and ritualistic. Chambers, playing the naive seventeen-year-old

Sandra, finds a hired handyman (Richard Pacheco) shooting snooker in her father's billiard room. She orders him out, but instead the man seduces her.

The set-up is cliche. Marilyn wears a ridiculously demure pink nightie. He's in a T-shirt and jeans, dripping with "attitude." But the performers lift the scene. He doesn't mistreat Chambers so much as bully her, prodding, urging, ignoring her weak protests. Occasionally he even uses his long pendulous penis as the equivalent of Gillis' whip, to flick her face and vagina, urging her into action.

Chambers' sexual choreography is precise. Though her hips undulate constantly on the edge of the billiard table, she keeps the rest of her body immobile until her lover demands it. In a gesture that is now part of the iconography of eroticism (Edward Weston uses it in his Mexican nudes of Tina Modotti) her near-camera arm is kept tucked under her body until he directs her to fondle his penis. Then her hand emerges nervously to grasp it. Her head remains on the table until he also demands that she fellate him. Then she swivels eagerly on the baize to take him in her mouth. At the end of the scene, her face turns suddenly towards the camera and the image freezes on her wide-eyed my-god-what-have-I-done? gape.

The supposedly virginal Sandra is clearly in her thirties and has unaccountably shaved her pubic hair. Chambers, however, is confident her audience won't mind. She knows her way round in the dark far better than we do. But because that expertise is so personal and so resistant to analysis, it will always stand between the porn film and those who seek to apply standard critical criteria. There can be no taxonomy for something so subjective as arousal.

At the start of the Seventies, the grind houses and storefront porn palaces with their semen-smelling booths at the back had turned porn cinema into something between a joke and a crime. By the middle of the decade, however, the kudos won by *Deep Throat* and *Behind the Green Door* was such that it had acquired production, distribution and exhibition systems and turned into an industry. The audience was large enough now to be profitable. Most American cities had at least one X-rated cinema that showed features and not simply the ubiquitous loops. "The day of going into a sleazy theatre and having a rat crawl up your leg is over," the president of the Adult Film Association of America, Ann Myers Perry, said reassuringly in 1977. The occasional X-rated film found its way into distribution even when its cultural credentials were uncertain. *Exhibition*, a semi-documentary about the life and work of French porn star Claudine Beccarie, played the New York and Los Angeles Film Festivals and went on a national art house release.

Filmmakers no longer relied on the Old Pals' Network for distribution. Professional distributors bought porn, promoted it, sent stars on personal appearance tours and subsidised national advertising campaigns. People who once bolted for the fire escape when the doorbell rang now leased Fifth Avenue offices and handed out engraved business cards. Porn had sales conferences, conventions, even film festivals. New York launched its Erotic Film Festival in 1972. Among its judges were former prostitute and now madame Xaviera "The Happy Hooker" Hollander, Andy Warhol and his star Holly Woodlawn, Miloš Forman, Terry Southern and America's pre-eminent novelist of the homosexual experience, Gore Vidal. A Dirty Dozen of the arts perhaps – but who, ten years before, would there have been to ask?

Though porn and its performers were not exactly socially acceptable in the United States under Nixon, it was hip to be familiar with them. Bob Woodward initially named his source inside the Nixon administration simply "my friend" but *Washington Post* managing editor Howard Simons suggested "Deep Throat." The coining was at once an acceptance that this piece of porn had entered the popular culture and an implied criticism of an administration under which such a film could become common property – an echo, in fact, of Groucho Marx's remark about not wanting to join any club that would have him as a member.

A coy consciousness of sex as Entertainment rather than Cause had transformed the attitude to western intellectuals towards pornography. In his indignant 1967 anti-bomb film

The War Game, British director Peter Watkins quoted a cleric who decreed that there was nothing intrinsically evil about nuclear weapons providing they were "clean, and of good family." It was much the same with porn. Everyone had read the well-bred *Candy*. Hardly anyone, though, admitted to knowing the raunchier works of its co-author Mason Hoffenberg, such as *Until She Screams*.

Someone who might well have read *Until She Screams*, since he later knowledgably dismissed the Girodias product as "sometimes good art [...] but always bad pornography," was Kenneth Tynan, Britain's most flamboyant arts journalist. An enthusiastic eroticist, Tynan had a taste for lingerie and for bondage photographs. When his first wife discovered his cache, Tynan, drawing for topical references on the scandal surrounding a distinguished musician who had been arrested trying to smuggle porn into his native Australia, disarmed her with doggerel: "Dear Mrs. T/You tied to me/The knot that never loosens/How sad that I/Turn out to be/Yours truly Eugene Goossens."

In 1966, Tynan conceived a theatrical revue about sex to which major artists would be asked to contribute films, sketches or music. Among those invited to participate were Roman Polanski, Federico Fellini, Jean Genet, Terry Southern, John Lennon, Harold Pinter, Sam Shepard, Kurt Vonnegut, Joe Orton, Jules Feiffer, Edna O'Brien, David Mercer and Samuel Beckett. (Pieces by Beckett, Feiffer, Lennon, Shepherd and O'Brien remain in the finished version.) French Surrealist Clovis Trouille had painted a nude displaying her ample backside and called it *Oh! Calcutta!*, a pun on *O quel cul t'as!*/"O what an ass you have." Tynan, at the suggestion of his wife Kathleen, lifted the title for his revue.

His initial suggestions for the show (few of which made their way into the Broadway production) summarise the sexual preoccupations in the late Sixties as concisely as any time capsule. They included a double strip, with one performer a woman and the other a female impersonator, a serial silent film, a sort of sexy *Batman*, American burlesque and Parisian music-hall routines, dance numbers including ballets based on Aubrey Beardsley's *art nouveau* erotic drawings and one on Trouille's paintings, with nuns in sexy underwear doing the splits and circus performers who are half girl and half horse. Other proposals included items on the history of underwear, and tableaux representing national erotic obsessions. As summarised by Tynan, these were "a nun being raped by her confessor (Italy), a middle-aged bank manager bound hand and foot by a Superwoman (USA) and a St. Trinian's sixth-former being birched (Great Britain)."

In particular the show would have celebrated one of Tynan's favourite Paris hangouts, Alain Bernardin's strip club the Crazy Horse Saloon. Tynan eulogised the club's "classic bath number in which a stripper is first seen in silhouette, projected on a downstage screen, and later perched on a black marble bath, meditatively soaping herself; and of course Bernardin's famous *La Veuve*, in which a widow, sitting in a pew at her husband's funeral, devoutly strips as the organ plays."

To European eroticists such as Tynan, the Crazy Horse had an almost devotional importance. Bernardin had managed to make erotica both socially and culturally acceptable. One couldn't mention Plato's Retreat in a Hollywood film, but in *What's New Pussycat?*, Woody Allen, who also wrote the film and appears as a Paris expatriate, tells Peter O'Toole that he's employed at the Crazy Horse to help the strippers out of their costumes. ("How's the money?" asks O'Toole. Allen names a pittance. "That's not much." Allen agrees. "But it's all I can afford.")

In real life, Allen was one of many stars who admired the Crazy Horse and its owner/founder Alain Bernardin. A good proportion of the two hundred thousand clients who strolled past his burly bouncers in Mountie uniforms every year were celebrities. John F. Kennedy caught the show while still a Senator, though he diplomatically slipped away as soon as it was over. Uri Brezhnev, son of the Soviet leader, was a regular. Salvador Dalí, Max Ernst, Orson Welles, Graham Greene and Federico Fellini all made the pilgrimage.

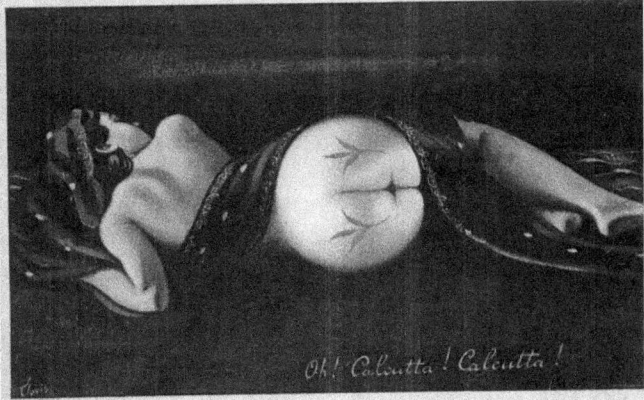

Bernardin, nicknamed "Boy," a slight, genial, dapper man with the look of Noel Coward, had laid carpets and dealt in junk before opening a restaurant in 1930. After the World War II Nazi occupation, he tried to introduce square-dancing to Paris, with disastrous results. In the bitter winter of 1950, crusading priest Abbe Pierre asked his help in housing Paris' homeless. Deciding ends justified means, Bernardin staged a highly successful strip show.

An off-shoot of American burlesque, striptease was little-known on the Continent. "I brought striptease to Paris – to all Europe," Bernardin later claimed (though he did acknowledge that Mata Hari might have experimented with it first). Realising he had found his metier, he leased two basement rooms at 12 avenue Georges V in the fashionable 8th arrondissement, a walk away from the Champs-Élysées and Paris' best hotels. Still convinced that Americans found the cowboy mythos seductive, he decorated them as a sumptuous Wild West bar. Recruiting five dancers and his friend Charles Aznavour to sing, he opened the Crazy Horse Saloon in May 1951.

"I do 'soft' shows; chaste," Bernardin said, "that make you dream. The more frustrated you are, the more you imagine." Instead of simply stripping, his dancers performed in playlets that owed much to the traditional *tableaux vivants* of Paris' *belle epoque* brothels. Sensitive to his location and potential market, he even tried to give the club an historic cachet, insisting, on dubious evidence, that Joséphine de Beauharnais once danced naked behind a veil on exactly the same spot to seduce the young Napoleon Bonaparte.

By the Seventies, the elegance of its staging and the beauty of its performers had won the Crazy Horse an international following, and its famous phone number BAL6969 ran hot. A painter *manqué*, Bernardin increasingly aimed at painterly and sculptural effects in his staging, even inviting veteran sculptor César to plan some routines. Veils, steam, smoke, and in particular patterned scrims that dappled the dancers with patches of colour became widely recognised Crazy Horse trademarks. In an anthology film of the Fifties on sex and the French, a besotted fan tells a stripper's husband that watching her is like contemplating Chartres cathedral by moonlight. When she comes home, the husband demands a demonstration. She obliges with a stately and heavily veiled display to devotional music. A British visitor who yelled an encouraging *Get 'em off!* at the Crazy Horse was almost thrown out. "It was like listening to one of Beethoven's late quartets," he muttered later.

Alain Bernardin.

An enlightened and paternalistic employer in a business where sleaze is the norm, Bernardin paid his dancers $5000 a month, but deducted taxes and automatically banked a fifth of their salary. He personally assigned fanciful stage names to all of them. Labels such as "Rita Cadillac," "Vodka Samovar," "Akky Masterpiece," "Vanity Obelisk" and "Polly Underground" were helpful later when many went on to other careers or to marriage. Since they habitually performed in half-light at the Crazy Horse and often wore wigs, few were recognised.

The typical Crazy Horse girl, like the most successful performers in porn films, was seventeen or eighteen, with an understated, athletic body, calm face and equable temperament. Bernardin estimated he auditioned 16,000 over the years to find the twenty-four used in each show. He insisted that all his girls be between five feet four inches and five foot six, identically proportioned. Most were from eastern Europe; French girls sulked, he complained, or arrived late. Yet it was a French girl with whom he fell in love. In 1985, to general astonishment, he married Marie-Claude Jourdain, aka "Lova Moor", the tiny Nordic-looking blonde star of his show. Retiring from the Crazy Horse, she embarked on a pop career under his management. Sadly, her voice didn't match her looks and the hoped-for stardom never eventuated. It was amidst gossip of a breakdown in their marriage that Bernardin shot himself in the head at his office at the theatre in September 1994, a victim of the sexual revolution he had helped to foment.

Oh! Calcutta! made it to Broadway in 1966 and, in 1971, to film, in a version directed by its stage producer Jacques Levy. The critics, however, were hostile. Tynan's belief, that middle-class intellectuals who had enthusiastically reviewed sexy French movies and novels such as *Lolita* were ready to accept erotica in the glare of the footlights under the full gaze of their families and colleagues, was mistaken. The revue was notorious enough, however, to run until 1972, and enjoy a later successful revival. Tynan also did a sort of *Oh! Calcutta! II*, *Carte Blanche*, but the critical reaction was, if anything, even more hostile.

Because of his outspoken ideas on sexuality (he had been the first man to say "fuck" on BBC TV), Tynan was appointed a Contributing Editor to *Playboy*. He articulated his support for porn in its pages and took a swipe at the critics of *Oh! Calcutta!* in a forthright 1971 essay called "In Praise of Hard Core." Many artists, Tynan commented, had come out during the Sixties in favour of liberalism. But between the lines, he wrote, they are most likely saying:

(a) I hate censorship in all its forms, but that doesn't mean that I actually like pornography.
(b) In fact, I don't even approve of it, except when I can call it "erotic writing" and pass it off as literature.
(c) I wouldn't go into a witness box to defend it unless it had educational, artistic or psychiatric value to make it respectable.
(d) I read it only in the line of duty, and feel nothing but pity for those who read it for pleasure.
(e) Needless to say, I never masturbate.

Tynan, though, was a lone voice. *Playboy* refused to publish "In Praise of Hard Core." It appeared finally in *Esquire*. Hefner didn't care either for a light-hearted history of ladies' underwear Tynan submitted, nor a long 1970 conversation with Alan Coren, intended for its celebrity interview series, in which he scorned well-bred erotica such as Louis Malle's *Les Amants*, praised *Histoire d'O* for its religious undertones, and wondered why fellatio (which he defined as "the sin that dare not speak its name – because its mouth is full") was so popular among New York professional women. These rejections just confirmed Tynan's suspicions about Hefner's liberal pose. "I'd just begun to believe that *Playboy* approved of sex," he said when they rejected the knickers essay, "and wasn't the titillating fraud that everyone says it is."

Hollywood proved just as coy in its attitude to the sexual revolution. Full frontal nudity was a long time coming, and penetrative sex never arrived at all. On the same principle which assigned the first 3-D feature, *House of Wax*, to Andre de Toth, a director with only one eye, MGM handed its 1962 *The Chapman Report*, about Kinsey-type sex researchers uncovering lust among suburban housewives, to sexagenarian homosexual George Cukor. The big Hollywood sex film of 1972, porn's *annus mirabilis* and the year of *Deep Throat*, was Woody Allen's *Everything You*

Ever Wanted to Know About Sex (But Were Afraid to Ask), a series of satires on David Reuben's pop sexology book of the same name. It managed to avoid showing intercourse altogether, except from inside, in a sketch where Woody played a nervous sperm about to go Over The Top.

A few mavericks used the new liberalism outside Hollywood to loosen ancient restrictions. Among the taboos contravened by Robert Altman's *M*A*S*H* in 1970 had been one against jokes about penis size. Dentist "Painless" (John Schuck), best-hung member of the *M*A*S*H* staff, deludes himself he's homosexual and determines to commit suicide. He is given a sedative by his male friends and a new reason for living by homebound nurse Joanne Pflug, who inspects the organ with awe and reverence, selflessly impales herself (in a new definition of "Active Service") and leaves for Stateside wreathed in beatific satisfaction.

Sex on the Big Silver Screen became the domain of exploitation filmmakers, with whom Hollywood went into uneasy partnership. 20th Century Fox commissioned Russ Meyer to make *Beyond the Valley of the Dolls* (1970) and *The Seven Minutes* (1971). Foreign product was titillatingly retitled for the American market. Roger Vadim's *Chateau en Suede* became *Nutty, Naughty Chateau* and *Le Repos de Guerrier* emerged as *Love on a Pillow*. Occasionally an established director essayed a timid try at the sensational. In 1969, British-based American Cy Endfield made *De Sade*, a bowdlerised biography of the celebrated eighteenth-century flagellant with Keir Dullea as the Divine Marquis. The film Sade's most outrageous act, at least in the version, shorn of twenty-one minutes, which surfaced outside continental Europe, was to smear jam on ladies' breasts, then lick it off. (A discomfited Dullea looked, said Pauline Kael, "as if he'd rather be beaten.") Critics attending the London press show were presented with pots of Tiptree Raspberry Seedless Conserve.

British critic Nick Roddick was unsurprised at Hollywood's response to the new popularity of porn.

As with horror films before them, the ensured profitability of porn flicks meant that a number of directors found that as long as they provided the bare minimum of the genre, they could produce an art movie masquerading as an exploitation flick (or vice versa). Only some filmmakers – Gerard Damiano, Radley Metzger and Wakefield Poole, for example – took up the challenge, but they were rewarded by becoming briefly chic: blue movies were "in."

Although Damiano was approached to make a film for MGM and some companies flirted with the idea of featuring Lovelace in mainstream productions, the majors still barred porn makers unless, such as Russ Meyer, they were prepared to toe the studio line. Bill Osco, ever audacious, tried to crash the big time in 1972 with Mike Light's *Flesh Gordon*, a spoof of the Thirties comic strip and its movie serial version. Ming the Merciless of Mongo became Professor Wang of planet Porno (William Hunt), Flash's girlfriend Dale Arden was transformed into Dale Ardor (Suzanne Fields, who seldom gets to wear any clothes at all), and his colleague Doctor Zarkoff into Flexi Jerkoff (Jason Williams). Instead of directing a ray on earth which induces earthquakes, Wang causes the earth to be overcome by an urge to copulate. Racing to the planet, Flesh, Dale and Jerkoff save the world, but only at the expense of various sexual acts, including Flesh submitting to homosexual fellation and Dale being raped by rampant lesbians.

Osco began the film in 16mm but upgraded to 35mm halfway through, hoping to make a killing in the new liberal climate. Porn star Candy Samples made a guest appearance, along with one-time featured player John Hoyt. Technicians who had worked on *Star Trek* and *When Dinosaurs Ruled the Earth* were coaxed into supplying better sets and special effects than were common in porn, and Osco, with typical *chutzpah*, won widespread publicity by claiming that the effects had been nominated for an Oscar, but that the

Academy got cold feet at the last minute and substituted *The Poseidon Adventure*. He even hired pickets to protest at the Oscar ceremonies. In the resultant publicity, Osco cut the raunchier moments of the $2 million film and won a limited general release in 1974.

The dismal quality of the porn made on the fringes of mainstream American cinema disguises the fact that many filmmakers were eager to plunge into adult cinema, had Hollywood found the courage to rise above its innate conservatism. No project illustrates this eagerness more vividly than *Blue Movie*. During the 1963 production in London of *Dr. Strangelove or: How I Learned to Stop Worrying and Love the Bomb*, screenwriter Terry Southern brought a porn film to the home of *Strangelove*'s reclusive director Stanley Kubrick, who watched part of it, then left the room. Later, however, he said to Southern, "It would be great if someone made a movie like that under studio conditions." Southern was inspired to start writing *Blue Movie*, a novel about director Boris Adrian and his ambition to make *The Faces of Love*, Hollywood's first big-budget porn film, with the stars having full penetrative sex, without benefit of doubles. "I thought Kubrick would be the ideal person to direct such a movie," says Southern. "I would send him pieces [from the novel] from time to time. I still have a great telegram from him saying, 'You have written the definitive blow job!' in the scene with the Jeanne Moreau type, Arabella."

Once *Blue Movie* was published in 1970, however, Kubrick, to whom the novel is dedicated, blew cool on the idea. "It turned out he has an ultra-conservative attitude to things sexual," said a disappointed Southern, who was himself a friend of *Hustler* publisher Larry Flynt and, like many radical journalist/writers of his generation, in particular Hunter S. Thompson, an *aficionado* of porn. During the next five years, the project circulated around Hollywood until, around 1974/5, John Calley, then president of Warner Brothers, decided to produce it on a $14 million budget. He was living with Julie Andrews at the time, and persuaded her – "for love, art and a lot of money," says Southern – to play Angela Stirling, the film's squeaky-clean star. On this basis, Mike Nichols, whose eyes had been opened to the possibilities of porn by his three visits to *Deep Throat*, agreed to direct.

All seemed set, until Warners tried to re-acquire the rights to Southern's book and script from Ringo Starr, who then held an option. "He was quite ready to step aside now that there was an actual production ready to roll," recalls Southern. "He didn't want any participation. He just wanted to see the book made into a movie. Enter the villain of the piece: Ringo's lawyer (who shall remain nameless) in absolute hysteria, ranting about how he (the lawyer) was 'going to look like a *schmuck* if the picture gets made and we [i.e. Starr and his company] don't have a piece of it.' John Calley and I were prepared to give him a piece, but it turned out that Mike Nichols wanted to retain all points so he could use them to make deals with actors. That proved to be the deal-breaking stipulation." *Blue Movie* was thrown on the heap of other discarded projects.

In *A Clockwork Orange*, Kubrick toyed with nudity, showed Malcolm McDowell making love with two girls, but speeded up the film to neutralise its eroticism. In 1981, Blake Edwards, then Julie Andrews' husband, fictionalised the incident in his comedy *S.O.B*, in which a director with a flop on his hands decides to rescue it by adding sex scenes. Andrews appears demurely but defiantly bare-breasted, a pale shadow of what *Blue Movie* might have been.

16
Evil

In a well-reasoned 1975 article, the American critic Wayne Losano pointed out how optimistic American porn cinema had become since 1968. The rash of quasi-documentaries on new liberal attitudes to sex had been followed by even more cheerful, often facetious sex films which, like *Deep Throat*, took the heavy humour of stag cinema and blew it up to feature length. Citing 1973 titles such as *All In the Sex Family*, Jerry Deney's *Whatever Happened to Miss September?*, *The Nurses* and the Amero Brothers' *Dynamite*, which ends in a sex scene on a theatre stage where a spotlighted couple make love while three people dressed in red, white and blue costumes tap-dance around them to a Sousa march, Losano argued,

> All these changes towards greater artistry have contributed to the death of the sex film as it was once known. Now that the films are well made, with more respectable and elaborate settings and more attractive and wholesome actresses, the experience is no longer that of descending into a new and evil world. Rather than giving us an opportunity to see how we should not live, the films set out to show us how to live more fully. If the sex film is to continue as a viable genre it must somehow recapture its lost sense of evil.'

Any such hopes were in vain, at least in the optimistic Seventies. The films Losano cites, with their sunny hedonism, attractive performers and occasional comedy, reflected the nature of porn on video. He could not have known that video, in subtracting from porn the element of public viewing, would also remove the collective guilt, shame, and sense of the forbidden that were cornerstones of the stag/smoker/X-rated cinema experience. Video confirmed porn as an element of American domestic life.

The new middle-class taste for porn was reflected in the stars who made their debuts in the mid-Seventies. Annette Haven, who appeared in her first film, *China Girl*, in 1974, won a huge following that included Hollywood directors such as Brian De Palma, who would try to cast her as the porn actress Holly Body in *Body Double*.

Born in Las Vegas, Haven came from the same repressive background that produced most porn stars. Her parents were both veterans of the Korean war, and the family had a long background of Mormonism. Though she clearly entered sex movies because of a natural aptitude, she soon adopted the proselytising attitude that was to become better known in the Eighties through the outspoken advocacy of Nina Hartley and Candida Royalle, who saw adult movies as a route to sexual freedom for women. "Everybody is watching adult videos," Haven told film critic Susan Dworkin in 1982.

> The ladies watch the films while the men are away at work and the men get together and watch the films after the ladies have gone to bed. People are watching them separately because they're nervous about them now, you know. They'll watch them together maybe next year. Then a couple of years after that, they'll be watching them with their neighbours, and a couple of years after that, it'll be, "Come on, Mabel, why don't we go down to the local theatre and watch this adult movie on the big screen." It's going to be very interesting to watch how people adjust.

Mainly because of the rise of the video cassette, Haven's forecast of a mass family audience for X-rated cinema never did fulfil itself, except in the success of European high-budget erotica such as *Emmanuelle* which began to flood the world market in the mid-Seventies. However, middle-class Americans, especially those within reach of New York or Los Angeles, didn't lack opportunities to spend an entirely reputable evening with family and friends watching attractive people performing naked, if that was their taste. Nor did they have to risk their wallets and safety in the peep-show arcades of Times Square. Three live sex shows of impeccable credentials, *Oh! Calcutta!*, *The Dirtiest Show in Town* and *Let My People Come* were running on Broadway or in respectable midtown locations.

Let My People Come, playing in an uptown basement cabaret, attracted a sober collar-and-tie audience, sprinkled with couples. Thirty minutes before curtain, members of the cast, in a practice borrowed from dinner theatre, circulated among them, fully dressed. "Hi," said the fresh-faced blonde as she visited each table. "I'm Cindy, and I'll be in the show tonight." The proper reaction was a smile, a nod and maybe "Good luck." Anyone who tried to prolong the conversation – by asking, for instance, if this was an Equity production, was everyone being paid scale, and how it had been cast – was gently discouraged. "You don't have to *talk*," the girl or boy would tell them, before moving on, smiling, to other tables.

Those who questioned them didn't realise the performers were circulating for other than social reasons. In this part of the show, they weren't actors at all, but Tonight's Specials in the sexual restaurant, to be displayed like a platter of Maine lobsters or a whole salmon so that, by the time they were served up nude on stage, the audience would have developed an appetite. Later, in a sketch called *Fellatio 101*, Cindy would be seen as a college girl being taught cock-sucking on a banana.

Let My People Come, like *Oh! Calcutta!*, the revue which inspired it, was the acceptable, up-market face of sex in New York in the early Seventies. Only *Oh! Calcutta!* attracted a mass audience, and both *Let My People Come* and its competitor *The Dirtiest Show in Town* petered out, but a demand for "boutique" public sex among the carriage trade had been identified. Later in the decade it would be satisfied, in Manhattan at least, by what Gay Talese circumspectly called "clothes-optional recreational centres for couples." The pioneers of such establishments were initially entirely gay. The most famous in the early Seventies was Steve Ostrow's Continental Baths, known colloquially as "The Tubs." Patrons drifted about in nothing but a towel, the method of knotting of which was a code indicating sexual preferences. Between bouts in the private rooms, they relaxed watching shows that featured rising unknowns such as Bette Midler and her pianist/arranger, Barry Manilow. The Baths and other gay spots such as the Tambourlaine became part of the Manhattan celebrity tour.

Porn, no longer the trade that dare not speak its name, was not only a subject for conversation in polite society but *the* subject. In 1974, homosexual activist Dennis Altman visited the Continental Baths and fell into conversation with

> a tall dirty-blonde man, who was wearing a button proclaiming himself a member of the ten-and-a-half-inches club. And did that refer to...? Yes. His name was Marc Stevens, he'd acted with Linda Lovelace in *Deep Throat* – "Linda Lovelace," he said, "is such a pig" – and like all good '74 swingers was bisexual. All of which sounded like an elaborate put-on – I didn't stay around long enough to test the first of his claims – except that a week later flying from Los Angeles to Honolulu I sat next to the wife of the editor of *Screw* magazine who confirmed the whole thing.

The same year, the Continental was celebrated in the *Saturday Night at the Baths*, a crossover comedy aimed at winning wider acceptance for the sexual liberalism the Baths represented. Financed by Jim Buckley, publisher of *Screw* magazine, the *Variety* of the porn trade, the film was directed by his brother David. A pitch not so much for homosexuality as bisexuality, it starred Michael Aberdeen as a straight pianist who gets a job at the Baths, is seduced by the MC (Don Scotti, playing himself) but returns to his girlfriend to reassure her he still wants to swing both ways.

It was only a matter of time before heterosexuals eased out the renegades. As New York began to think of promiscuous sex not as a vice but a right, the Continental moved into the sexual mainstream and closed, to re-open as Plato's Retreat. In carpeted, mirror-walled rooms, with piped music, discreet lighting and a well-stocked bar, you could cruise the (usually nude) talent of both sexes, goggle at low-rent celebrities such as Sammy Davis Jr., Margaux Hemingway, Richard Dreyfuss, Buck Henry, Jill St. John and George Hamilton, slip into one of the alcoves for a semi-private orgy, take steam in the tiled sauna with its suggestive Classical Greek statues or catch the action in the Mat Rooms, where couples fucked in crepuscular proximity on pads laid out on the floor of a gym-like space. The club, a regular stop-over on the porn tour of New York, was featured in a number of films, including the softcore feature *New York Nights*.

The gay and S&M community regarded such middle-class ecumenicalism with scorn, and quickly shifted their patronage to raunchier establishments. At The Sanctuary, a converted church at the corner of 10th Avenue and 48th Street, black drag queens consorted with white truck drivers on the prowl. None of the furnishings had been removed; Bob Colacello, editor of Andy Warhol's *Inter/View*, recalled leaning against a confessional and watching "a zonked-out DJ spinning soul songs on the altar, the after-hours hustlers heavy petting in the side pews, the stiletto-heeled transvestites twirling under the strobe lights that flashed across the nave."

For those in search of authentic sleaze, there were The Toilet, The Anvil, the Eagle's Nest and The Mine Shaft. Situated in a series of basements and sub-basements in the meat-packing district, these clubs catered to most variations of gay sex. At the Mine Shaft, the bar and a lounge showed non-stop gay porn on the ground floor, there was simple semi-public fucking on the next levels down, while in basements members could enjoy a group grope, bondage or beating. Others crouched in metal bathtubs to be urinated on: genuine Golden Showers – "the Real Thing," noted one report righteously, "as distinct from the warm ammonia squeezed from a rag onto dupes as they lie back, eyes obediently closed, at some of the city's more expensive brothels."

The Mine Shaft's dress rules, posted at the door, were like a summary of pre-AIDS gay style, and a decisive rejection of the chic of places like Plato's Retreat.

> *No Cologne or Perfume*
> *No Suits or Ties*
> *No Lacoste or Rugby Shirts*
> *No (Designer) sweaters*
> *No "Disco" or other drag*
> *No Sandles (sic) or Guccis*
> *No Ruffled shirts*
> *All attire subject to inspection*
> *Please open your coat*
> *We welcome jock straps, T-shirts,*
>   *and SWEAT*

These clubs enjoyed a vogue among the international glitterati. When he was in New York, German director Rainer Werner Fassbinder convened meetings with his backers at the Mine Shaft. Towards the end of 1977 Andy Warhol visited the Eagle's Nest and watched fascinated as a man filled a beer bottle with his urine and left it on the bar for someone else to drink. "They were all fighting over it," he told his colleagues at The Factory the next day. "It was so abstract." Inspired, Warhol in December 1977 began his "Oxidation" or "Piss" Painting and the "Torso" series. After treating canvases with copper paint, he paid men to urinate on them, sometimes feeding them vitamin pills to change the chemistry of the urine. For the "Torso" pictures, Victor Hugo, a protege of the designer Halston, arranged photo sessions for Warhol in his 19th Street loft, paying young gay hustlers to perform in orgies. Warhol hovered around the edges, snapping Polaroids, then hurrying into the toilet for a private "organza."

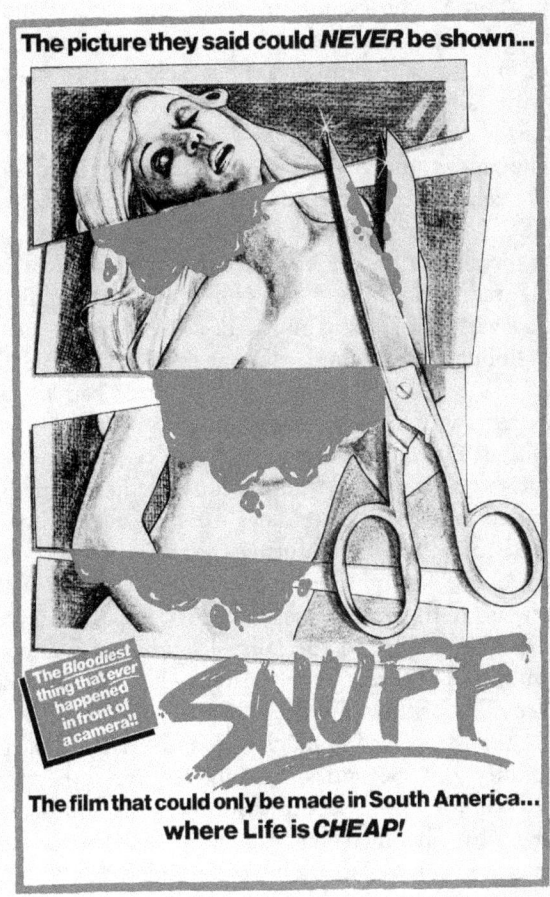

The Tambourlaine was closed in the early Seventies when a Cuban drug dealer castrated a Puerto Rican drag queen in its washroom, but the Mine Shaft survived until

1985, when it was put out of business by the city – not, ironically, for its sexual activities, but for the poor hygiene of its kitchens. By then, the ambiance and wardrobe, thanks in some part to Warhol, had been enshrined in the work of gay filmmakers and photographers such as Robert Mapplethorpe, whose shots of well-hung models shoving whips and, occasionally, their arms up the anuses of their friends in the practice known as "fist fucking," were usually taken after all-night sex sessions which often began in clubs such as the Anvil.

The sado-homoerotic chic of those pre-AIDS days has become celebrated in gay porn as a vision of prelapsarian delight. *Nighthawks* (1987), a gay *Behind the Green Door*, shows members of a gay elite circulating *entrees* to a club called Paradise, a visit to which is like a tour through a lost world. Every door opens on hard, oiled, hairless, healthy bodies, lounging, fondling, or in one case dangling in straps while a brute in a leather harness and biker's cap languidly greases a brawny forearm to the elbow.

One area in which the reputed "evil" of porn continued to flourish was in talk of "snuff" films in which participants committed murder. "There has been... a rumour that persisted for a long time during the years 1975-78 about 'snuff movies,'" wrote French critic Michael Caen in 1991, "that is to say films in which the actors, the actresses were really put to death. No specialist – I think of [editor and later publisher of *Screw*] Al Goldstein – has seen them. Nor could the FBI or the police find them."

No topic occupied so much time and energy in the porn debate during the Seventies. To some feminists, the murder of a woman for male sexual pleasure was the apotheosis of pornography. That men were capable of such things, radical campaigners such as Andrea Dworkin didn't doubt:

> Men love death. In everything they make, they hollow out a central place for death, let its rancid smell contaminate every dimension of whatever still survives. Men especially love murder. In art they

celebrate it, and in life they commit it. They embrace murder as if life without it would be devoid of passion, meaning, and action, as if murder were solace, stifling their sobs as they mourn the emptiness and alienation of their lives.

Did snuff films exist? The evidence was entirely anecdotal. In 1979, an ex-porn actress told Laura Lederer:

> I heard about "snuff" films right after I stopped modelling. Stories came down the grapevine. One agency in Los Angeles sent a woman out on an assignment with a man who killed her and took pictures of how he tortured her. The business just froze. Models went to work with their boyfriends, and some stopped coming in altogether. Everyone was terrified. That didn't last long though. People need money in order to live. My agency told me that that man had come to them, and that they had checked out his credentials and found that they were false. Obviously the murdered woman's agency didn't check. We valued ourselves so little.

The actress wasn't identified. Nor was the filmmaker or the agency. Gloria Steinem was equally vague in 1983. "Though 'snuff' movies in which real women were eviscerated and finally killed have been driven underground (in part because the graves of many murdered women were discovered around the shack of just one filmmaker in California), movies that simulate the torture murder of women are still going strong... The last screening of a snuff movie showing a real murder was traced to the monthly pornographic film showings of a senior partner in a respected law firm; an event regularly held by him for a group of friends including other lawyers and judges."

Which filmmaker? Which lawyer? In the decade since Steinem wrote this, no harder evidence of snuff films has emerged.

In 1977, a film called *Snuff* opened at the National Theatre off Times Square in New York City. The poster showed a woman's body cut into pieces by giant scissors, under the slogan "The Bloodiest Thing That Ever Happened In Front of a Camera." Hyping the film as "an overwhelming assault on the senses too real to be simulated, too shocking to be ignored," distributor Allan Shackleton called *Snuff* "the film that could only be made in South America, where life is *Cheap!*"

Snuff deals with a Manson-type cult in some unnamed Latin American country whose members vow revenge on the rich. A man is castrated, another shot, and a pregnant woman butchered. At the conclusion of this scene, the director and film crew are seen walking into shot. A pretty blonde production assistant tells the director she found the scene sexually arousing, and he invites her to join him on the bed. Feminist writer Beverly LaBelle, describing the film, writes:

> They start fumbling around in bed until she realises that the crew is still filming. She protests and tries to get up. The director picks up a dagger that is lying on the bed and says, "Bitch, now you're going to get what you want." What happens next goes beyond the realm of language. He butchers her slowly, deeply, and thoroughly. The observer's gut revulsion is overwhelming at the amount of blood, chopped-up fingers, flying arms, sawed-off legs, and yet more blood oozing like a river out of her mouth before she dies. But the climax is still at hand. In a moment of undiluted evil, he cuts open her abdomen and brandishes her very insides high above his head in a scream of orgasmic conquest. The End...

> Fade into blackness. There are no credits
> listed in the final moments of the film.

Indeed, no credits are listed – perhaps from embarrassment. *Snuff* was a fake. Originally called *Slaughter*, it had been made in Argentina by Americans Michael and Roberta Findlay in the mid-Sixties, a fact readily apparent from the dated costumes. Ten years later, Shackleton resurrected it in the wake of rumours about snuff films being made in Argentina and transmogrified it into *Snuff*. The final "murder" was shot in New York with some cheap special effects and an actress bearing only a passing resemblance to the woman she replaces. As the final touch, Shackleton himself arranged for protestors to picket the theatre – "Pickets sell tickets," he told the press, and admitted he was "out to make money and to be noticed by the motion picture industry." New York DA Robert Morgenthau quickly uncovered the hoax but refused to prosecute. Feminist groups all over the USA, however, harried *Snuff*, turning it into a *cause célèbre*.

Given the extent of human perversity, the cheapness of life, and the easy access to video recording, one has to assume that amateur snuff films exist. In his 1990 *Henry: Portrait of a Serial Killer*, John McNaughton shows the confederate of murderer Michael Rooker taping a rape/murder and later replaying it repeatedly. In the real case on which the film is based, no such video was made. However, if the killers among us hadn't thought of doing so already, they are doing it now.

But fears that such films would find their way into porn cinema were unfounded. The strongest evidence against the existence of snuff films is neither repugnance on the part of filmmakers nor fear of retribution, but the fact that there's no audience.

There is an analogy in the treatment of blood in porn films. The shedding of synthetic blood will always find an audience in horror films. Sex filmmakers, however, have never found real blood, virgin or otherwise, attractive as a subject. In *Pretty Baby* (1978), Louis Malle dealt, controversially, with the market value of a virgin in the New Orleans' brothel district of Storyville around 1917. The virginity of Violet, daughter of a whore, brought up in the brothel and happy in its society, is auctioned to the highest bidder. We see no blood, however, during her deflowering, and Malle's interest is almost entirely in the sex appeal of his star, the pre-adolescent Brooke Shields.

Anthony Burgess, protesting about the 1977 English ban on Hubert Selby Jr.'s *Last Exit to Brooklyn* did point to one link between pornography and blood. "Blood-drinking murderers have admitted to the stimulation of the sacrifice of the Mass. One multiple child-murderer in the United States was, on his own confession, haunted by the Abraham-Isaac episode in the Old Testament. Ban the Marquis de Sade and you will also have to ban the Bible." Since, however, neither blood nor death itself are sexually fetishised for most of us, the number of people interested in seeing a virgin deflowered or a woman killed is infinitely smaller than that which will pay to see a "golden shower," in which a girl urinates on her partner – itself a sight almost unknown in serious porn.

The lack of interest extends to Hollywood. George C. Scott views a snuff film in Paul Schrader's *Hardcore*, but the only director to explore the idea more extensively was maverick David Cronenberg. In his *Videodrome* (1982), low-rent cable TV operator James Woods scorns the art porn offered to him by a Japanese dealer and goes looking for something "stronger." He finds it in a private cable channel on which, it seems – the signal is hard to decode and appears only intermittently – a naked girl is being tortured against an electrified wall of wet clay. The show turns out to be called Videodrome – "just torture and murder. No plot. No characters. Very realistic." Searching for its producers, Woods finds himself in a phantasmagoric world where TV sets come alive and his own body appears to become a VCR into which the villains shove cassettes.

In a world eager for snuff films, *Videodrome* would have drawn large audiences. But Kim Newman confirms in his book *Nightmare Movies* that "it was not a commercial success [...] Its cerebral, enquiring tone and Woods' uncomfortably good performance won it too few friends." Nor did *Snuff/Slaughter*, despite its free publicity, make money. Insiders were unsurprised. Pornography is more conservative than sex, porn film more conservative still, and utterly driven by market forces. If there was profit in sex with blood on it, the X-rated shelves of video stores around the world would be dripping.

Had someone unearthed a real snuff film, it is unlikely anyone would have been prosecuted, at least not in New York. In a city which, by 1988, suffered 3400 rapes and 1900 murders a year, winning a conviction on a simple vice charge was next to impossible, especially if it related to the wide-open and well-protected porn business.

By then, however, snuff films were no longer a fashionable topic for protest. The focus had switched to so-called "Kiddy porn" – sex films with underage performers. Much of what purported to be kiddy porn was, however, like the spurious killing of *Snuff*, a scam. "*Teenage Hussy*," Philip Tambasco of the NYPD paedophile unit was quoted as saying, "invariably turns out to be an anorexic 22-year-old in pigtails and clip-on braces." On one occasion when the heat was on in Times Square, a hand-printed sign over a peep-show booth for something called *Jail Bait*, described as featuring a "14-year-old teenage girl, blonde hair and blue eyes," had been crudely amended with felt pen to read "18-year-old..."

There was little official enthusiasm for prosecuting such films. Attempting a "sting" operation on the child-porn industry, Tambasco and three of his detectives set up a fake production unit and shot three loops which, though they used adult performers, were aimed at the "kiddy" market. However, as they were about to feed the loops into the system and track them up the distribution chain, the Police Commissioner axed the project. He was "morally outraged," he sputtered, that a female detective on the team had watched X-rated scenes being filmed. The kiddy porn market remains, of course, as lively as ever.

17
Sophistiqué soft

In *Reversal of Fortune*, Barbet Schroeder's 1991 film about the drug poisoning of American socialite Sunny von Bulow and the attempts to convict her Danish husband Klaus of attempted murder, Jeremy Irons, in an Oscar-winning performance as von Bulow, is farewelled by his attorney, Alan Dershowitz (Ron Silver) after a conference.

"You're a strange man, Klaus," the lawyer muses as his frosty client slips into his chauffeured limo. Von Bulow (who always denied haunting the nameless bar on New York's West 48th Street, the decor of which included an authentic corpse; the rumour started, he claimed, when Prince don Eugenio "Dodo" Ruspoli said he *looked* like a necrophile) stares at Dershowitz. "You have no idea," he says tonelessly, and the smoked glass window slides up, cutting us off from the world of European decadence.

Von Bulow had a cinematic counterpart in Barbet Schroeder. Critic for *Cahiers du Cinema*, jazz impresario, producer for Eric Rohmer and Jacques Rivette, director of such eccentric films as *Maitresse*, the best to deal with the underworld of sadomasochism, Schroeder seems the image of the sophisticated filmmaker visualised by Americans when they thought about the European industry.

His first feature as director, *More* (1969) was the opening salvo of what was to become the European art cinema's sexual assault on the Anglo-Saxon world. Despite its Pink Floyd score, trendy drug theme, sensual evocation of European decadence and above all its central performance by renegade Hollywood starlet Mimsy Farmer as Estelle, *More* is mostly ignored by books of film reference. Yet it foreshadowed *Emmanuelle* and a hundred other European softcore films. Shot in English, it became the precursor of *Body Heat*, *Body Double*, *9½ Weeks* and *Basic Instinct*, sufficiently up-market not to panic a prospective sexual partner but suggestive enough to induce a receptive frame of mind; the genre the late Sixties labelled "Date Movies."

Roger Vadim had already tried to retail European eroticism to America in *La Ronde* (1964), *La Curée/The Game is Over* (1966) and *Barbarella* (1968), all with his then-companion Jane Fonda, but, except for the *succès de scandale* of *Et... Dieu Crea la Femme* (1956), which, as *And God Created Woman* (or, in the carefully doctored American print, *And Woman Was Created*), introduced Fonda's predecessor Brigitte Bardot to world audiences under the slogan "And God Created Woman... But The Devil Created Brigitte Bardot," he failed. Vadim's stylistic decadence, his penchant for flowing robes, plunging horses and hot-eyed stares, and his bizarre heroines – space girls, incestuous lovers, women who believe themselves the reincarnation of Don Juan or who want to die of an orgasm – didn't attract American audiences. The promotion in America for his films was insidiously lubricious. It seemed to hiss at the audience like the pimps on New York's Times Square spruiking for the Big Live Nude theatres and 25c peep-show arcades – "Pussy, pussy, pussy...Che-e-ck... it... *out*!" Pauline Kael decided he was "redolent of shallow morals [and] the screen's foremost celebrant of erotic trash... who has the scandalous habit of turning each wife into a facsimile of the first and spreading her out for the camera."

In *More,* Schroeder avoided this problem by scaling down European sex to the level of the tourist brochure and the backpack Grand Tour. Its Ibiza location was significant. "The sun was important in *More*," cameraman Nestor Almendros said, "almost like another character." Mimsy Farmer has her experience of triolism when she consoles a friend who's just lost her lover, a scene shot in soft focus through veils, giving it a dreamy eroticism to which women respond. There's a hint of S&M as well when a girl flicks her desultorily with the thin gold chain she wears round her waist. Any American girl making her first trip to Europe in the post-1968 euphoria might well have experienced any or all of the above. Given the model of *More*, many of them would.

The race to put sexual penetration into a commercially released film was won in 1967, inevitably by the Swedes, with Stefan Jarl's *Don Kallar oss Mods/They Call Us Misfits*. The breakthrough took longer to reach the US, though traditionally the sex between Donald Sutherland and Julie Christie in *Don't Look Now* is authentic, and Bruce Dern claims that, in his love scenes with Maud Adams at the climax of the 1980 *Tattoo*, they Went The Whole Way, though given that film's mass of writhing limbs, heavily tattooed, it's hard to see who's involved, let along what's going on. (For the record, Adams denies the story.)

A score of European or Europe-based directors had meanwhile decided it was time to create the erotic epic they had talked about for years. By 1974, Pier Paolo Pasolini had completed his adaptations of *The Decameron*, *The Canterbury Tales* and *The 1001 Nights*, Ingmar Bergman *The Touch*, Stanley Kubrick *A Clockwork Orange*, Bernardo Bertolucci *Last Tango in Paris*, Liliana Cavani *The Night Porter*, Luchino Visconti *The Damned*, *Death in Venice* and *Conversation Piece*, Federico Fellini *Satyricon*, Dušan Makavajev *W.R: Mysteries of the Organism* and *Sweet Movie*, while, among the lesser (but more commercial) talents, Just Jaeckin had made *Emmanuelle*. Significantly, this was, for most of these directors, except Jaeckin, the limit of their sexual activity on film. Pasolini later made *Salo or the 120 Days of Sadom*, Visconti *The Innocent* and Makavejev *Montenegro*, but none was as celebratory of sex as their work of the early Seventies.

By mixing Anglo-Saxon stars and European high style, the producers of these films were aiming at the non-European audience which, they hoped, was ready for a more discreet eroticism than Vadim had tried to peddle. "The Film You Can See Without Being Guilty" ran one US promotional line for *Emmanuelle*. But long before any of these films got in front of the camera, the rival claims of intellect and sensuality had been settled in favour of the former. Bertolucci, Cavani, Bergman and the rest discussed and described eroticism but evoked it only perfunctorily. More stimulated by the subject's peripheral ironies, they refused to involve themselves in the tawdry and, in their eyes at least, lesser task of arousing their audience.

Bertolucci and *Last Tango in Paris* are a case in point. Jean-Louis Trintignant had been cast as the bereaved hero Paul, who submerges the grief at the recent suicide of his wife in a savagely carnal affair with a casual pick-up, Maria. However, Trintignant withdrew from the role at the last minute, panicked by its physical demands, which included nudity and much simulated sex, including – notoriously – sodomy with the assistance of a handful of butter. When Marlon Brando stepped in, *Last Tango in Paris* inevitably became more interesting, by virtue not only of Brando's magnetism but also of the contribution of his personal experience to the script. Since, however, Brando was six years older and fifty kilos heavier than Trintignant, the emphasis was bound to shift. What had begun as another step by the self-absorbed Bertolucci in his screen self-psychoanalysis became more Hemingway than Freud, with Brando the wounded, tormented Alpha male licking his wounds and burying his pain in an obliging younger member of the pack. As Danny Peary has commented, "the film is not about sex *per se* but about a broken, tortured man." And, however electric Brando's presence and however erotic Maria Schneider's, the change in direction robs the film of sensuality. The sex is undercut by a tragic melancholy, making it only intermittently stimulating but undoubtedly more interesting than if Bertolucci had followed his first impulse of exploring a personal sexual fantasy.

As ever, it was trash directors who struck the popular nerve. Jaeckin's *Emmanuelle* became the most popular erotic film of all time, mother to a hundred imitations and rip-offs, some of which carefully misspelt the name as "Emanuelle" to stave off charges of plagiarism. Simply to list some of the titles is to show how tenuous is the connection with Emmanuelle Arsan's bestseller that triggered the film. In addition to the official and semi-official *Emmanuelles II* through *VI*, there have been *Emmanuelle and Joanna, Emmanuelle The Queen of Sados, Emmanuelle on Taboo Island, The Joys of Emmanuelle, Emmanuelle*

Around the World, a *Yellow...* and *Black Emmanuelle* (I and II), *Emmanuelle in America*, *...in Bangkok*, *...in Soho*, a *Goodbye, Emmanuelle* and, inevitably, *Carry On, Emmanuelle*, which sent up the whole cycle. Joy Laurey's frankly imitative novel *Joy* also triggered a series of films (e.g. *Joy and Joan*, *Joy in Africa*) in which the eponymous fashion model heroine, fleeing from an unhappy love affair, rebounds around the beds of a dozen exotic locales. Some of these featured Brigitte Lahaie, the most sophisticated of

Marlon Brando and Maria Schneider in *Last Tango in Paris*.

France's newer X-rated stars, whose serious, absorbed face and husky voice gave class to the trashy stories, but they couldn't hope to compete with *Emmanuelle*'s extraordinary success.

Critics were baffled by the *Emmanuelle* phenomenon. In London, critic Alexander Walker dismissed Jaeckin's films as "a fashion model's daydream of sex." *Emmanuelle*, he charged, "simply transports the daydream of a travelogue setting." But to most Anglo-Saxons, the travelogue and the tourist brochure *were* the most familiar experiences of "abroad." *More* had put sex into the context of *Europe on $5 a Day*. *Emmanuelle* upgraded it to Club Mediteranée.

Before *Emmanuelle*, Just Jaeckin has said, sex in movies was like "a hair in the soup," a disagreeable surprise that disturbed your appreciation. With *Emmanuelle*, he aimed for a film in which the characters, the setting, the costumes, the locations, the dialogue and the music immersed you in sensuality. In such an environment, he hoped, sex would arise naturally, shocking no one. Columbia Pictures, who picked up the film for American release, agreed. *Emmanuelle* was merchandised with the slogan "X Was Never Like This," and its success with the nervous US audience assured.

Emmanuelle Arsan, writer, director and actress, was the daughter of Thai politician and diplomat Knun Bibidh Viregggakia. As "Marayet Andriane," she played the Chinese slave/prostitute Mally opposite Richard Attenborough and Steve McQueen in Robert Wise's 1966 *The Sand Pebbles*. Married to French diplomat Louis Jacques Andriane, who was stationed in Bangkok as administrator of the South East Asian Treaty Organisations, Mme Andriane hosted receptions for visiting dignitaries and modelled in the informal fashion parades run by Queen Sirikit. In her free time, however, she was more unbuttoned. Her memoir of her Bangkok days and nights, *Emmanuelle*, was published in 1957, and promptly banned by the de Gaulle government as yet another slur on its foreign service, already battered by books such as Roger Peyrefitte's *Les Ambassades*. Although Grove Press issued the book in the US and made it an international bestseller, it remained on the official French banned list until 1992.

Arsan became an instant celebrity. No exhibition of erotic art was complete without her patronage, no new piece of up-market porn launched without, if not an introduction, then at least a cover quote. She published five volumes of collected essays on sexual subjects, and went into film production. In 1975, she also wrote and starred in *Laure*, the film intended as a comeback for Linda Lovelace until the *Deep Throat* star backed out.

Whether *Emmanuelle* is a fanciful autobiography or total fiction has never been settled, though there is little doubt that, despite following a classic porn novel structure, the book has some basis in fact. When Sylvia Kristel, *Emmanuelle*'s eventual star, was asked if Arsan had invited her to play in *Laure*, she replied sniffily, "No, because that's her drug. For her. Finally, more for the fantasies of her husband, I believe."

Shrewdly, Jaeckin, an ex-fashion photographer, chose a north European rather than an Eurasian for his film. Anglo-Saxon audiences would relate more readily, he gambled, to the milky charm and look of open-mouthed wonder of 20-year-old Dutch model Kristel, if not to her rabbity overbite and celery-stalk legs. It would also prove more erotic to see such a woman thaw in the heat of Thailand.

The film follows Emmanuelle, nineteen and inexperienced, as she flies out to Bangkok to join her diplomat husband Jean (Daniel Sarky). After a vigorous reunion in their luxurious house, Emmanuelle is cast adrift in the society of bored embassy wives. "You may play tennis, golf, explore the canals," Jean tells her as he heads back to the office, "and you can make love." That she is ripe for sexual adventure is demonstrated in a flashback where she recalls fucking with her seatmate during lights-out on a 747 (in First Class, naturally; coitus in Coach would rupture a contortionist). The sight so inflames another passenger that he hauls her into the lavatory for a second, cramped climax. (Producer Jennings Lang – whose sexuality, not to mention his sense of humour, had survived being shot in the testicles by fellow producer Walter Wanger in a fracas over Wanger's wife Joan Bennett – cast Kristel as an air hostess in *Airport '79: The Concorde*. Hopes of an *Emmanuelle* replay at supersonic speed with Hollywood production values were, alas, unfulfilled.)

Initially hesitant about joining the Bangkok swinging set, Emmanuelle is persuaded by precocious 17-year-old Marie-Ange (Christine Boisson), who concludes their morning coffee by masturbating to a magazine portrait of Paul Newman and persuades her to do the same. Emboldened, Emmanuelle explores the canals of Jeanne Coletin in the showers of the Country Club and embarks on an affair with bossy archaeologist Bee (Marika Green). When she goes on an excursion to the interior with Bee, Jean, unexpectedly jealous, consoles himself by visiting a nightclub where the floorshow includes nude girl/girl romps and a performer who smokes through her vagina.

When Emmanuelle returns, Jean, deciding she's now ripe for graduation, assigns her to Mario, the standard Older Man, embodied with suave reticence by veteran Alain Cuny. The star of *Les Visiteurs du Soir* plays a small but crucial role. French porn producer Henri Zaphiratos pointed out at the time that "the success of *Emmanuelle*, to tell the truth, is not Sylvia Kristel, it's Alain Cuny. The other films of Kristel haven't made anything. Alain Cuny, perhaps the greatest of our actors, gives a façade of respectability. He reassures the conservative bourgeoisie and right-thinking people, and it's those people who are going to see the film."

Mario takes Emmanuelle on his own unique Bangkok By Night tour. She's groped by a drunk chosen by him at random as they clop through the streets in an open carriage, tries hashish in a dope den, is raped by two fellow smokers and given as the prize in a Thai boxing match, after which she joins a trio with Mario and another man. The final shot of the film shows her primping before a mirror after her experience, now hard-eyed, heavily made-up but, presumably, totally liberated. She's ready for *Emmanuelle II: L'Anti-Vierge* (Hong Kong: massage, tattoos, acupuncture) and, impersonated by a score of actresses, white, black and yellow (most notably Laura Gemser, the black masseuse of *Emmanuelle II*), the interminable sequels.

Curtis Harrington directed Kristel in the 1985 *Mata Hari* and found her anything but passion's plaything. She arrived on the set for nude scenes with her pubic area covered in adhesive tape, but wouldn't reveal it on camera. "That part of my body is for my husband alone," she told him primly. She demanded the set be cleared and that black velvet curtains be hung round the bed. During sex scenes, she was absolutely silent. Harrington was told, "I presume you will add the noises and voices later."

Sylvia Kristel and Marika Green in *Emmanuelle*.

Just Jaeckin never escaped his heritage in the glossy magazine and commercials; may never have tried to, in fact, seeing that people accept sex more readily if it's packaged as a product. The method worked for everything. Censors commenting on the scene in his 1975 *Histoire d'O* where O (Corinne Cléry) is seared with a red-hot iron, said it looked like a cigarette commercial. All it lacked was a title indicating "The Surgeon General Has Established That Branding is Dangerous To Your Health."

The *Emmanuelle/Histoire d'O* plot, of an innocent led from sexual encounter to ever more bizarre sexual encounter, dutifully following the orders of an elder who is Doing It All For Her/His Own Good, is a commonplace of pornographic fiction. Such victims always submit cheerfully and heal up with remarkable alacrity. By the last page they not only adore their tormentors but assist enthusiastically in inflicting the same discomforts on others.

It is usual when an outrageous novel appears from an unknown writer to identify it as the pseudonymous work of a master. When *Histoire d'O* was published in 1954, critics as authoritative as Graham Greene, who in his early days had been nominated as possible author of a sensational published-in-Paris novel called *To Beg I Am Ashamed*, hailed it. Insiders confidently identified "Pauline Réage" as *nouveau romancier* Alain Robbe-Grillet, scenarist of *L'Année Dernière à Marienbad* but, more to the point, writer/director of *L'Immortelle* (1963) and *Trans-Europ Express* (1967), both of which boasted erotic and bondage elements. If it was not by him, then the author must be his wife Catherine, who had already published sadomasochistic fiction as "Jean de Berg."

Neither of the Robbe-Grillets ever denied the rumour, but it soon became generally known that "Pauline Réage" was actually Dominique Aury, long-time mistress of publisher Jean Paulhan, to fan whose ardour she wrote this hymn to submission. The fact was an embarrassment for feminist critics, especially in the United States, to whom *Histoire d'O*, especially in its film version, is a particular *bete noire*.

At the start of the film, Parisian fashion photographer O is delivered by her lover René to a lonely chateau at Roissy, on the outskirts of Paris (these days the location of Aeroport Charles de Gaulle). There she is subjected to a regime intended to turn her into the perfect sexual partner. The girls of the chateau are forbidden to meet a man's eyes. They loiter, eyes downcast, dutifully on call, nude under their long dresses, which part front and back for the convenience of the male guests. Periodically, sometimes for infractions but more often just for the fun of it, O is beaten, though always with a thin dog whip, and never so violently that she's marked in the next scene. (Scabs are *so* unsexy.) Later in the story, she is also branded and her labia pierced to accept a metal ring identifying her "owner" (and offering a reward for her return?).

René reappears with an old friend, Sir Steven. For reasons not very clearly outlined, René needs to discharge an obligation to Sir Steven, which he does by handing over O. She obeys, of course, and is passed round among her new master's friends. On the Nietzschean principle, however, of "What does not kill you makes you strong" (and illustrating *inter alia* two other saws of Nietzsche, "Woman is mud yearning to be mire" and "When thou goest to woman, take thy whip"), O emerges from the experience confident, determined, and able herself now to recruit other women for the Roissy experience.

Jaeckin shot O with all the blurring and soft focusing of *Emmanuelle* and adhered rigorously to the TV commercial's guidelines on costume and decor (Rule 1: Always Relate To the Product). There was no sexual penetration, so *Histoire d'O* didn't cross the line that had come to mark the difference between soft- and hardcore porn. The script, written by distinguished crime novelist Sebastian Japrisot, dispensed with the alternative narrative structures of the book which offered different beginnings and endings (a Robbe-Grilletian trick that fed the rumours of his involvement in the script). Nor was Japrisot any more interested than Réage in René and Sir Steven, who remained, like all the men in Jaeckin's films, puzzlingly sexless. Udo Kier, the epicene Dracula and Dr. Frankenstein of Andy Warhol's camp versions, is hilariously miscast as René, while Anthony Steel, a British leading man of the Fifties working out his grey-bearded retirement in Eurotrash, plays Sir Steven. No Alain Cuny, Steel is all grey bouffant and tweeds, a *milord* out of a French whisky commercial.

It is ex-model Corinne Cléry as O, however, by whom the film stands or falls, and while she screams with vigour and pouts agreeably, she is no more effective than Sylvia

Kristel in portraying a devoted sensualist. If feminists have any allies in undermining the soft-focus erotica of the *Playboy* era, it's women such as Kristel and Cléry, who give nothing whatsoever of themselves to these tepid fantasies.

Jaeckin went on to a career in softcore, including a 1981 version of *Lady Chatterley's Lover*. Shot in a dank, wintry England with Kristel as an improbable Connie Chatterley, Nicholas Clay as Mellors, and Shane Briant as her crippled husband, hilariously malevolent in motorised wheelchair and prosthetic eyebrows, the film gave D.H. Lawrence's novel an unhealthy tone it never had in real life.

When Barbet Schroeder's 1975 *Maitresse* was finally shown in Britain in 1979, the censor refused it a certificate. Romaine Hart, resourceful owner of the North London Screen cinemas, turned Hampstead's Screen on the Hill into a cinema club for the run of the film. *Maitresse* is so subversive and takes such pleasure in the game of sadomasochism and bondage that one is surprised the authorities allowed even this stratagem. The S&M world, one in which Klaus von Bulow would be – perhaps was? – perfectly at home, is rendered by Schroeder in all its eerie fascination and seedy glamour, with costumes by Karl Lagerfeld and a poster, of Bulle Ogier in full leather and trailing a stock whip, commissioned from pop artist Allen Jones.

Schroeder was attracted to the theme by his acquaintance with "Baroness" Monique M. K. Von Cleef, who advertised herself in the Paris papers as a "Sadotherapist." Dutch-born Von Cleef was already famous in S&M circles, having run a highly successful "pain parlour" from her penthouse on New York's East 75th Street. In 1967, she was put out of business and encouraged to leave the country when photos of men being whipped in her establishment panicked the FBI into fears that some customers might be members of the Pentagon brass and, as such, vulnerable to blackmail. Von Cleef relocated in Amsterdam and Paris, to become the inspiration for *Maitresse*.

Gérard Depardieu, who had dealt in stolen jeans and whisky as a boy and knocked around the wrong side of the law before becoming an actor, plays Olivier, a naive drifter new in Paris who is roped into some light burglary by a friend. Breaking into an apparently empty apartment, they find it filled with whips, chains and bondage costumes. Before they can escape, a metal staircase unrolls from the floor above and Ariane (Bulle Ogier) appears wearing a black wig and full leather, and leading a Dobermann. After keeping the men prisoner for a period, she releases the friend but keeps Depardieu. Initially he's her assistant but quite quickly they're lovers as well.

Histoire d'O, *The Story of Joanne* and most S&M films strive for the high seriousness of *The Song of Bernadette*, but *Maitresse* is, if not a comedy, then at least visibly entertained by the weirdness of this arcane world. Nestor Almendros, who shot the film, lit much of it in fluorescent light. It gave the images a greenish tone which suited the subject:

> As always, Schroeder had done intensive research. He even got some prostitutes who specialised in sadomasochism to help out. They were present during the shooting, and even brought some of their clients along. The flagellation scenes (and the scenes where people have themselves handcuffed, hung up, etc.) are real, and preserve a specifically documentary tone. These were lit beforehand in the most practical rather than the most aesthetic way, for instance, the light was bounced from the ceiling to avoid cables on the ground or tripods that would get in the way. Since we didn't know how each of the 'clients' would behave, we had to be ready to film anything that happened. Some of us did not find filming *Maitresse* a comfortable experience.

The same could be said of the clients, who are, as they no doubt wish, mistreated pitilessly. One man has his scrotum pinned out on a wooden board. The beatings (administered by Ogier's double) are real – strikingly so in a sequence where Olivier and Ariane visit a rural chateau for what he assumes is a quiet weekend. They're greeted by the butler (Serge Berry), whom Ariane, to Oliver's confusion and dismay, immediately slaps for not keeping the house in order. When he can't produce an ashtray, she grinds out her cigarette on his palm. That night there's an S&M orgy. Berry – revealed as the chateau's owner who plays the menial role for sexual satisfaction – is the most obliging of hosts, and Depardieu vigorously involves himself. From the swollen, reddened buttocks of one Cécile Pochet, tied backwards, naked, to a chair and thrashed with a belt during this scene, it's evident that the beatings aren't faked. Not surprisingly, clips from *Maitresse* seldom feature in TV surveys of Depardieu's career.

Despite the fad for runaway productions to Italy, Yugoslavia and Spain in the Sixties and the relocation in Europe of major directors such as Stanley Kubrick, Hollywood, though it relished Western Europe as a market, never took it seriously as a place to make movies. When James Mason as the ex-matinee idol of *A Star is Born*, drying out in a sanitorium, tells Charles Bickford he's thinking of working in England – "They're doing some very interesting things over there" – it sounds, as George Cukor means it too, desperate and pathetic.

Porn filmmakers could afford to be more ecumenical. British photographer David Hamilton, a specialist in soft-focus photographs of schoolgirls lounging semi-nude in haylofts or cycling through summery fields, carved out a profitable niche in European softcore. *Bilitis* (1977), with his muse Patti D'Arbanville as the heroine experiencing

David Hamilton.

various manifestations of first love during school vacation, inaugurated a series of films, notably *Tendres Cousines*, that are little more than moving versions of his photo albums. This is cinema in the style of Hallmark greeting cards, with every scene shot through a softening filter and slowed to a pace that Hamilton clearly regards as languorous but which to an audience not fascinated by slim limbs in Laura Ashley frocks is simply lethargic.

Radley Metzger, at least in the films he made in Europe under his own name, worked the same side of the street. A chronic sufferer from hay fever, Metzger paid his way through college as a cinema usher to take advantage of movie air conditioning. He graduated to editing trailers for Janus Films, one of the major distributors of foreign films, and was responsible for promoting *And Woman Was Created*. Like many porn directors, he started with a straight film, and failed. *Dark Odyssey* (1961), a heavy drama about a Greek immigrant avenging his sister's honour, was so unpopular that even Greek audiences rejected it.

To retrieve his losses, Metzger formed Audubon Films with his partner Ava Leighton and, using skills learned working for Janus, began buying US distribution rights to European sex movies. One of the first was an Agnes Laurent comedy called *Mlle Striptease* which he renamed *The Fast Set*. He followed this with Mac Ahlberg's *I, A Woman*, and another film starring Laurent, *Les Collegiennes*. He renamed this lesbian romance *The Twilight Girls* and, while he was at it, shot some additional nude scenes and cut them into the film. One of the girls he used was Chelle Graham, later Georgina Spelvin. For *I, A Woman*, which he bought for $20,000, Metzger cut out the *longueurs* and, to underline the fact that this was Art, released it subtitled rather than dubbed.

The $4 million he made on Ahlberg's film launched Metzger as a director. For the next two decades, he was a fixture of the sex movie scene in Europe, making *Therese and Isabelle* (1968) in Germany, *The Lickerish Quartet* (1970) in Italy, and *Camille 2000* (1973) and *The Image/The Punishment of Anne* (1976) in France. Like Vadim's films and those of David Hamilton, Metzger's work belongs to what the French term *sophistiqué soft*. Connoisseurs of the harder stuff found them disappointing. Reviewing *Camille 2000*, Metzger's modernised version of the Dumas novel with Danièlle Gaubert as Marguerite, Robert Rimmer fretted that "the sad story of Marguerite has the twists and turns of a soap opera, but it is exquisitely photographed, and the acting and dialogue are believable. If the sex scenes had been more sharply focused, instead of choreographed, Metzger would have produced the first classic porn film worth owning."

Therese and Isabelle is technically German, though the script of this schoolgirl lesbian story is French, adapted from Violette Leduc's novel, and the principals French (Anna Gael) and Swedish (Essy Persson). As in Bergman's *Persona*, where Bibi Anderson describes in forensic detail a four-way sexual encounter on a beach, the most erotic element is its dialogue, a fact which helped Metzger and distributor Francis Mishkind of Alpha-France to win wide distribution for the film. Mishkind showed it to Jacques Duhamel, then the Minister for Cultural affairs, and amended it in line with his comments. Metzger made a similar accommodation with the British censor, allowing substantial cuts and some tampering with the text. Reviewing the film on its 1970 British release, critic Alexander Walker pointed out that, at two points, the English subtitles disappeared for more than a minute "while Miss Persson indulges in some overripe French prose about her sensations. The theory here is that if you don't know French, you won't be depraved or corrupted by it. It follows, I assume, that if your French is up to standard, you'll have the wit and intelligence to resist depravity and corruption."

Metzger was no more forthright in his 1976 *The Punishment of Anne*, an up-market S&M film adapted from *L'Image*, a flimsy 1956 novel by "Jean de Berg," alias Catherine Robbe-Grillet. The ex-lover of a jaded Parisienne is recruited into helping her torment her beautiful young sex slave. These indignities escalate from the trivial (forced to visit restaurants without underwear; urinating in a semi-public garden) through the piquant (a lesbian changing-room encounter with a sexy *vendeuse*) to a perverse conclusion involving whips, chains and red-hot needles. *The Punishment of Anne* abandons the Whorehouse Gothic design of other S&M films for a soft-focus modern Paris reminiscent of *Emmanuelle*. The effect is to trivialise the film's material even more.

Metzger redeemed himself the same year with *The Opening of Misty Beethoven*, which he signed with his porn pseudonym "Henry Paris." The story, cribbed from *Pygmalion*, has wealthy sex writer Seymour Love (Jamie Gillis) meet Dolores Beethoven, alias "Misty" (Constance Money) in a Pigalle porn cinema. A hooker, she administers hand-jobs to punters watching Claude Mulot's bizarre *Le Sexe qui Parle/Pussy Talk* (1975), in which the vagina of Pénélope Lamour finds a voice, and uses it.

Melanie Griffith in *Body Double*.

Misty has an unglamorous attitude to paid sex, similar to that of Melanie Griffith's porn star Holly Body in *Body Double*. "I do a straight fuck," she tells Love. "I don't take it in the mouth. I don't take it in the ass. I don't take it in the bed." This both disconcerts and delights Love. When Misty says later, "I think men stink," he responds delightedly, "They think *you* stink. It's one of the most perfectly balanced equations in nature." Love recruits Misty, intending to turn her into the most desirable of all sexual partners. After high-tech training, and having been fitted with an earpiece through which Seymour can feed her directions, she's taken to Rome (on a plane that, *Emmanuelle*-like, offers "First Class with Sex" or 'First Class Non-Sex") and unleashed on Larry Layman, jaded and undersexed editor of *Golden Rod* magazine, obviously based on Hugh Hefner. Abandoning all Seymour's technique and strapping on a dildo, Misty subdues not only Layman but his mistress too, penetrating him anally while he in turn fucks the girl, the process known as *pegging*. She's chosen as *Golden Rod* Girl of the Year, by which time Seymour is totally enamoured.

The ultimate refinement of the international sex film of the Seventies, *The Opening of Misty Beethoven* is at once an illustration of how to make a successful hardcore porn film and proof that such films will always have a limited appeal. This is still genre cinema, pitched at a coterie audience who will not look too hard at its shortcomings of narrative and performance. It is also, like most of Metzger's films, solipsistically self-referential. Metzger shared *Playboy*'s error of solemnly quoting his rhetoric back at himself, as if his taking it seriously would influence the audience to do the same. Both *Misty Beethoven* and *The Lickerish Quartet*, in which a family is encouraged to sexual experiment by watching an erotic film, use porn cinema as a central metaphor. The latter also features a technically impressive but unintentionally hilarious sequence in which a couple fuck on giant pages of a dictionary, humping vigorously across definitions of "masturbate" and "fornicate" – Hugh Hefner's "*Playboy* Philosophy" writ literally large.

All the same, Jaeckin's and Metzger's success did alert European filmmakers to the possibilities of softcore EuroProds, and French, German and Danish performers were seldom out of work in the Seventies. Harry Reems was even imported to appear in the German *Young Butterflies* and a 1975 Swedish update by "Bert Torn" (Mac Ahlberg) of De Maupassant's *Bel Ami* (released in Britain as *For Men Only*). As the priapic poet and journalist in the latter, trying to fuck his way into a connection with *Playhouse* magazine, Reems was less than convincing.

Some serious European directors were also tempted to try softcore. Jacques Baratier, who had directed *Goha* and *Dragées au Poivre*, was chided by critics for his *Vous Interessez-Vous a la Chose?* (*First Time with Feeling*). Joe McGrath, English director of *The Magic Christian*, hid from the inevitable drubbing after *Girls Come First* (1975) by signing it "Croisette Meubles." Even great directors were approached to make porn. François Truffaut joked about it in *Day for Night* (1973). A sleazy producer and two hideous German girls visit him on his set with the suggestion that he make a hardcore film. Federico Fellini put himself out of the running by declaring that his "customary symbolic values would transform the work in a way that probably would not please either the producer nor that kind of public." To further muddy the water, he went on, "I have never found anyone who said, 'Ah, I have seen a beautiful porno film.' I have always understood that there were hideous women in them who make you feel you're in the morgue or the stockyards. You breathe the atmosphere of a whorehouse there, which means a porn film makes you feel you know less than before and are participating in a degrading collective ceremony." This is ironic, given his later revelation that, after being introduced to porn by Groucho Marx, he became an enthusiastic collector.

Changes in social attitudes almost always start at the grass roots, to burst on policy-makers later as a total surprise. All over Europe, a revisionist movement was growing as the rebels of 1968 drifted towards middle age. In 1974, Denmark moved to ban the live sex shows from which Lord Longford had fled. Sweden also slowed the speed of its liberalisation as community groups won more power. A year later, the same wave of religious and family protest brought French porn cinema to grief.

The pretext in France was *L'Essayeuse* (1975) by "John Thomas" – actually actor/director Serge Korber. The story of a lingerie *vendeuse* who discovers the depths of human depravity on a visit to a homosexual sauna, the film opened in October 1975 at ten cinemas owned by the giant UGC chain. *L'Essayeuse* had been viewed by the censor and classed X, but a number of right-wing groups, including the powerful *Associations Familiales Catholiques*, decided to make the film a test case. In November 1975, allied by now with everyone from the French Boy Scouts to the Associations of the Deaf and Dumb, the militants held a noisy public meeting demanding that Korber, his writer, editor and the film's star, Emmanuelle Arsan, be charged with "outrages against good behaviour."

Panicked, the government caved in. Later the same month, Korber and Arianas were fined, and a print of *L'Essayeuse* symbolically burned. A year later, Paris' four last live sex shows were shut down. Since there was no longer any censorship of theatrical performances, the police had to invoke a law dating from 1789 against activities likely to lead to a breach of the peace. By then, a new system of film censorship was in place. Hardcore films were limited to a few cinemas and their profits heavily taxed.

The first French hardcore film to be given a censor certificate after the events of 1975 might almost have been chosen by the Élysée as a warning of the state of things to come. Jean-François Davy's documentary *Exhibition* followed porn star Claudine Beccarie in what turned out to be the last year of her career. Beccarie, a tiny brunette with flashing dark eyes and a manner that verged on the bossy – at one point in *Exhibition*, Davy chides her on camera, and is snapped at – spent time in a French reform school and worked in a Spanish brothel. She returned to France in 1972 and pursued a busy career doing nude "bits" in mainstream films, as well as doubling stars who preferred not to reveal their bodies. By the time she appeared in *Exhibition*, Beccarie, who, unlike many porn stars, was highly proprietorial about her work and her body, had soured on porn, and especially on *doublage*. "I'm certainly putting up my prices [for that kind of job]," she told Davy. "Because there are the girls on the poster and people say 'Oh, they're nicely built' and it's my ass that's used, I'm bored with that."

A precursor of the American porn actresses who would form support groups such as the Pink Ladies fifteen years later, Beccaire was fearless in defence of her beliefs, and of her business. After *Exhibition* had been seen by 600,000 people in Paris alone, a producer released, as *Inhibition,* a film she had made in Italy years before. Beccarie, who was getting a percentage of *Exhibition*'s income, went on hunger strike outside the cinema where *Inhibition* was showing.

Mostly because of Davy's failure to ask searching questions, *Exhibition* is a celebration of erotic cinema and an apology for its excess. Beccarie echoes the ritual enthusiasm for sex in almost all its manifestations, hymning fellatio but disapproving of *Deep Throat* ("I don't make films for sick people"), confessing "I'm not homosexual. I'm bisexual," then adding quickly, for fear punters will be scared off, "I like masculine love... that's very important."

Beccarie shares some of Sylvia Kristel's primness about her private life. Like the prostitute who won't kiss a customer, reserving that privilege for her lover, she is cautious about getting too involved. "I keep a cool head," she says. "But, you see, you can run into people who are really nice." Beccarie has just been shown coaxing/bullying a 16-year-old actor to whom public sex is new and a little frightening. "Like this last scene, for instance," she tells us afterwards. "I would have let it go with my partner. I could really have gone very, very far. But I didn't want to let things go, because I don't want to be unfaithful to my boyfriend."

This apparent reticence contrasts with an extended and convincing solo masturbation that became *Exhibition*'s major selling point. Eschewing the moans, writhing and Molly Bloom-like interior monologue of most such scenes, Beccarie masturbates in near silence and at considerable length, and seems genuinely to be gratifying herself. After the performance, she confesses she did in fact achieve orgasm. Critics at the time were impressed by her frankness. Only a few noticed that her busy fingers wear nail varnish for the first few minutes and none thereafter, signifying that the scene was shot over at least two days.

The film originally ended with Beccarie reminiscing about her days in reform school, an experience so fearful that all her companions turned to lesbianism. She collapses in tears and her fellow performers gather around to console her. Scenes such as this attracted enormous audiences of both sexes and *Exhibition* was in porn terms a major international success. On the profits Beccarie retired to the country to grow asparagus with her husband, photographer Didier Faya – "the only man capable," she confessed later, "of giving me a vaginal orgasm."

Davy later re-edited the film as *Exhibition '79*, adding new footage of a sadder, wiser Beccarie no longer living with Faya but sharing her farmhouse with a female lover. Broke, she performs as a stripper in a country tent show for an audience of bumpkins and their dogs, a depressing sequence which Beccarie's cheeriness only renders more pathetic. In 1983, a further update offered a more cheerful picture. Now living alone but with two children, Beccarie seems content to have put porn behind her. Davy, who went on to make other X-rated documentaries on *Prostitution* (1975), *Les Pornocrates* (1975) and *Exhibition* II (1976), about sadomasochism, promised in its end title to revisit Beccarie in four more years. In the world of the flesh, however, memories are short and after that she sank totally from sight.

18
Dirty Business

With *Deep Throat*, *Behind the Green Door* and *Emmanuelle* now accepted features of cultural history, porn stars felt able to come out of the closet and, more important, speak up for the business. Harry Reems, after his conviction in the 1976 *Deep Throat* trial, embarked on a lecture tour to highlight anomalies in the obscenity laws. Following his appearance at the Harvard Law School, the president of its Forum wrote patronisingly, "To be honest, you were not at all what we had been expecting, and we were pleasantly surprised not only at your general articulateness, but especially at your knowledge of the legal issues involved in your case and their ramifications."

Porn producers, too, no longer skulked in the shadows. In 1974, Toby Ross, America's only black porn producer, spent $5000 to launch *Not Just Another Woman* at the English Pub on 7th Avenue, opposite Carnegie Hall. Six hundred people attended the champagne event, including Tina Russell and Darby Lloyd Rains, the stars of the film, Georgina Spelvin, Harry Reems, Bob Guccione, publisher of *Penthouse*, composer Burt Bacharach, and newsmen from all three networks.

Playboy published one of the less hyped and more analytical studies of how a porn feature was made in the mid-Seventies. Ronan O'Casey's March 1977 *Getting It Up For a Porn Movie* describes in some detail how *The Double Exposure of Holly*, directed by Bob Gill and starring Catherine Earnshaw, Don Peterson, Terri Hall and Jamie Gillis, was written, produced and, hardest of all, financed for $100,000 by an *ad hoc* consortium of two New York investment bankers and some doctors looking for a tax shelter.

O'Casey, who scripted *Double Exposure*, was unprepared for the variety of sexual skills available for rent in New York. Marc Stevens, hired as both performer and technical adviser, demonstrated how he had won his nickname, "5-Cum," and an actor who called himself "Doctor Infinity" arrived with pictures showing he was capable of sucking his own cock. He was immediately cast. The pleasure, physical and professional, that many porn performers found in their work obviously surprised O'Casey. Describing a scene between Hall and Gillis, he writes, "Terri rose flushed from the bed and, with a seraphic smile and a tremulous voice, announced 'That was the best fuck I ever had on-camera.'"

Despite the general elevation of porn's image and budgets, however, it was still far from a paradise for its performers. In 1974, one of the more reputable paperback companies, Dell, published an account by John Warren Wells of how he wrote, directed and appeared in the porn feature *Different Strokes*. The book reproduced the full screenplay and Wells' jaded memoir of the problems of filming a porn feature: a director who couldn't direct, backers who demanded they be given a role as the price of investment, and a dog that refused to perform cunnilingus on the heroine. At least this last problem was solved – the dog liked peppermints, so she stuffed her vagina with them.

There was so little profit in the work that one had to take any job offered. Stars such as Marc Stevens couldn't stop hustling simply because *Playboy* reviewed them. They had only youth and enthusiasm to sell, and the sell-by date came quickly. Men could hope for ten or even fifteen years' work, but an actress had about five good years in front of the camera. Seven was exceptional, ten almost unknown. When most actors are just perfecting their trade, porn actresses had to leave it.

In the summer of 1968, Georgina Spelvin had been working as a captain of the dancers on the Barbra Streisand musical *Hello, Dolly* at Garrison, in upstate New York. About 10 p.m. she would leave the set, get the train to Manhattan, shoot two porno quickies, catch the 5 a.m. train and be back ready to work when director Gene Kelly called "action." She got $1500 for her work on the musical and $100 for each fuck film. Asked why she bothered for $200 a night, Graham said, "I did it because I was a star in those films, and in *Hello, Dolly* I was just in the background."

Harry Reems boasted of earning $30,000 a week at the height of his fame. "I made little on *Deep Throat*," he says, "but subsequently I was paid thousands of dollars a day just to have my name on the title credits. At the time I thought this was the greatest thing on earth. I'd end up with three teenage girls in a bed and get paid a thousand dollars to do it. Every week the number of women grew and the number of dollars grew."

For most performers, however, the figures were less impressive. Stevens, who, despite what he told Dennis Altman, wasn't in *Deep Throat*, said that Damiano offered him $700 for five days' work on the film, but that he accepted twice that for two weeks in Atlantic City on *The Hooker Convention* with Tina Russell. For *The Devil in Miss Jones* Spelvin got $500; five days at the standard $100 a day. For *Memories Within Miss Aggie*, newcomer Darby Lloyd Raines was paid $250. Rates were consistent from country to country in what was by then an international industry. Claudine Beccarie said in 1975, "If I'm asked to do something very interesting, I would work for 300 or 500 FF (US$60 to $100). For sex scenes I ask at least 2000 FF ($400) per day." Other actors in French porn at the time were getting 1000 FF (US$200) a day.

When "Mayflower Madam" Sydney Biddle Barrows launched her up-market Manhattan call girl service Cachet in 1979, sex with her girls cost $125 an hour, half of it paid back to Cachet as commission. By the time the New York Vice Squad closed Cachet in 1984 the rate was $175. A four-hour "date" cost $500 and six hours $750. Top girls cleared $1000 a week. In short, call girls and porn actresses earned roughly the same amount. The parallels went further. Manhattan in 1975 supported about fifty porn cinemas. In 1979, Barrows estimated it had exactly the same number of brothels. Ironically, Barrows fired one of her girls after discovering she had done porn loops. Cachet boasted of employing only amateurs: students and professional girls, supposedly earning a little on the side to keep themselves solvent in the Big Apple. "We couldn't risk anyone finding out that we weren't as sterling and as pure as we promised – and as we wanted to be," said Barrows. "Here we were telling our clients, and believing ourselves, that our girls were practically virgins, and now we had a porno queen on our hands!"

Barrows could afford to scorn porn films, but to many women and some men films and prostitution were both sex for pay. The more successful a performer, however, the more they disdained the connection, though their logic was generally murky. Ginger Lynn, one of the Eighties' most successful porn stars, tossed out two or three arguments, hoping one would fit. "A prostitute takes money from the man she's having sex with. She's there to turn him on. I don't care if I turn on the person I'm working with. I'm turning on my audience. I'm selling the same thing any actress is – a performance. I am not a porno star. Porno is animals, children. I am an erotic film actress. I'm there for a good purpose, not for sick people."

It is not surprising that many porn performers, like some prostitutes, claim therapeutic value for their work, since they are drawn from the same slice of show business; the girls with eyes a little too close together or noses a little too long for photo modelling; whose teeth need work; who don't have the carriage or co-ordination to model clothes; who can't sing or dance or read lines. Girls, in short, such as Bree, played by Jane Fonda in Alan Pakula's *Klute* (1971). She turns up stubbornly for modelling auditions even though she's rejected, after one glance, with the comment, "Funny hands." Or Michelle Pfeiffer in *The Fabulous Baker Boys* (1989). When her prospective employers ask if she has any entertainment experience, she stops chewing gum long enough to say, "Well, for the last coupla years I've been on call for the Triple A Escort Service."

Casting his "naked lady movies" in the Sixties, Bill Rotsler was under no illusions about the talent a porn project could command. "When I started making films in 1965, I would cast personalities. Because when you're working at this level, you're not working with actors. You're lucky if you get someone who can act. But if you can get them in a certain state of mind, where it's just their personality, they love it. They're not working. They're just having fun."

At the premiere of *Not Just Another Woman,* porn star Marc Stevens, accompanied by his mother, worked the crowd, distributing "Join the 10½ inch Club" buttons. His business card had no name on it – simply a drawing of an enormous dick, the figures "10½" (26.6cm) and a phone number, a further earnest that the length of one's penis was the new measure of manhood.

According to show business legend, comedian Milton Berle, famously well endowed, was once challenged to a comparison by a drunk in a bar. "Go on, Miltie," said a friend impatiently. "Just take out enough to win." Berle could have named his figure in the post-*Deep Throat* porn world. In *Hardcore,* George C. Scott, hoping to find his runaway daughter who's drifted into porn, poses as a promoter auditioning talent. After having answered his questions, Big Dick Blaque (Hal Williams) enquires in surprise, "Don't you want to see the equipment?" and drops his trousers.

It is indeed a solecism on Scott's part. An outsize penis was the absolute minimum requirement for a male porn star. Many reports of the Seventies comment on "Harry Reems' 12 inches" as if no other qualification counted. (Most people agree it is an exaggeration.) Though any stud with less than eight inches was almost certainly wasting his time, a performer earned points for his ability to "delay and deliver" or for being a "Woodsman," able to retain an erection for long periods. As "Jerry Butler," the conventionally hung Paul Siederman built a career on his ability to come (he claims) fifteen times a day.

Stevens, who can be seen in *It Happened in Hollywood*, Radley Metzger's *The Private Afternoons of Pamela Mann* and *The Devil in Miss Jones*, proudly called himself a "stunt cock," and boasted of his ability to achieve erections at will. Directors such as Damiano hired him by the day as insurance, in case a performer couldn't perform. "I did him a favour," Stevens said of his appearance in *The Devil in Miss Jones*, "because Georgina Spelvin was in it. I love watching Georgina act. She's the only actress in pornos. She made a nothing film into something good. He didn't direct her in those scenes. She created them herself.."

The biggest male porn performer of the Seventies (in every sense of the word) was John Holmes. By the time his career ended in 1985, he claimed to have had sex with 14,000 women and appeared in 2274 hardcore films. In *Around the World With Johnny Wadd* (1975) he brags, "I'm one of the wonders of the world. I have the biggest cock in the world, and I've been using it since I was seven years old. It's been inside 10,000 women at least, and none of them has been unsatisfied." Even allowing for hype, Holmes was a phenomenon. His uncircumcised penis was measured (by him) at 13½ inches and by others as only three-quarters of that, but nobody seriously challenged him as the best-endowed stud in the business. To Eighties groups such as the Hung Jury, a New York coterie of the gay enthusiasts for large penises known as "size queens," his status is that of a legend.

Stories of how Holmes got into porn are legion. His favourite, which is the basis of a script developed by the actor Christopher Walken, who was eager to play Holmes, claimed that he graduated from UCLA with a Physical Education degree and got into porn when a girlfriend introduced him to a hardcore filmmaker. As Abel Ferrara, Walken's director on *King of the City*, tells it, "John Holmes was an awesome actor. Made Willem Dafoe look like a choirboy! His story is incredible. He was an ambulance man, his wife was a nurse. A normal guy from the Midwest, who didn't know he had this enormous dick, gets discovered in some urinal by a film producer who just sees the dick."

Hard as it is to credit such a tale, if only because the chances of a man being unaware of a 13½-inch penis are remote, it is substantially true. Born in Pickaway County, Ohio, Holmes was the son of an alcoholic carpenter and a devout Baptist mother. A friend of his mother seduced him when he was twelve. He moved to Los Angeles and became an ambulance driver. At USC County General he met and married a nurse named Sharon Gebinini. After drifting from jobs as salesman and security guard until 1968, he was "discovered" again in the men's room of a poker club in Gardena, a Los Angeles suburb, by a professional photographer who recruited him for porn stills and stripping.

John Holmes.

Holmes initially hid this after-hours work from his wife, who described to Mike Sager of *Rolling Stone* how she came home one day to find him measuring his penis. "It goes from five inches to ten," he told her. "Ten inches long! Four inches around!" When she queried his excitement, he "fixed her with a long stare" and said, "I've got to tell you I've been doing something else, and I think I want to make it my life's work."

Holmes' first loops date from around 1971. They show a tall, slim, classically handsome young man with the sort of wavy hair style a new actor is likely to think attractive. With his first money he bought the large diamond solitaire ring that he wore in all his films, and designed a giant belt buckle showing a mother whale and her baby; like the Mitchell Brothers, Holmes saw himself as environmentally friendly, devoted to saving the whales and celebrating the joy of living.

Holmes is said to have made a thousand loops before he met producer/directors Bob Chinn and Richard Aldrich. They transformed his image. As a vehicle for his good looks and commanding presence, they invented "Johnny Wadd," a private detective and adventurer, forever seeking some jewel or curio, all as a pretext for sex with a variety of young women. Holmes' performances in, among other Johnny Wadd films, *Tell Them Johnny Wadd Is Here* and *Liquid Lips* (1976), *Jade Pussycat* (1977), *China Cat* (1978) and *Blonde Fire* (1979) established the persona so indelibly that producers often dropped his real name entirely.

Rare in porn films, Holmes had the bearing, the height and the looks to carry off costume parts. He is in the Mitchell Brothers' *Autobiography of a Flea* (1976) opposite Annette Haven. In *The Spirit of '76*, he plays John Smith, telling Pocahontas, "Boy! You've got great tits!" *The New Erotic Adventures of Casanova* (1979) featured him as the eighteenth-century lover, at least for two reels, apparently all the time its producers could afford to rent the costumes. After that, the action reverts to contemporary California.

Women found Holmes' easy insolence both infuriating and attractive. One critic rightly called him "everyman's gigolo, a polyester smoothy with a sparse moustache, a flying collar and lots of buttons undone." His height gave him an aristocratic command. Never moving faster than a stroll, he cruised into situations, settled back, put his arms along the back of the couch and let himself be pleasured. Like most porn stars, he improvised many of his moves, some of them hilariously arrogant. He was quite capable, after sliding his penis into a girl busy fellating another stud on her hands and knees, of reaching over her back and shaking hands with his companion. Such arrogance could only lead to a fall, and John Holmes was to fall further and more catastrophically than most.

19
Media Woman, Media Man

In 1975, Jean-François Davy, director of the documentary *Exhibition*, took Claudine Beccarie to the Paris cinema playing one of her films. In what turned out to be its funniest scene, she engaged nervous patrons in conversation as they left:

> Beccarie: Don't I look like the one in the movie?
> Punter 1 (*dubiously*): Well, I don't know… I'm not sure one looks very much at the faces.
> Beccarie (*to a second punter*): If I asked you to make a movie with me, would you do it? Would you go all the way?
> Punter 2: (*gamely*) Well, why not? It would be very nice.
> Beccarie: You think you would be able to go all the way in front of the cameras?
> Punter 2: Maybe. It's not impossible.
> Beccarie: (*professionalism offended*) Well, you have never thought about it. I can tell you it's very difficult!

Ten years later, the same scene would never have taken place. We can see, in fact, what would have happened by watching newsreels of the Italian porn actress Ilona Staller, aka La Cicciolina, when she appeared in the Piazza Navona on 14 June 1987. There was no risk that she would not be instantly recognised. She had just won a seat in the Italian parliament after running for the Radical Party on a platform of relaxed censorship, nudism and sexual rights for prison inmates. Budapest-born Staller campaigned vigorously, showing a flair for the political stunt. To protest against apathy towards the Chernobyl disaster she rode round Rome and Milan wearing nothing but a radioactive carnation. In the election, she accumulated a respectable 20,000 votes. In Piazza Navona, hugging her trademark pink teddy bear, Staller triumphantly pulled down her dress to show her breasts and the Roman crowd surged around her, shouting, grabbing and fondling. The fact that a porn star was part of the political and social establishment delighted them as much as it did her.

Ilona Staller.

In 1990, Staller married flamboyant American NeoPop artist Jeff Koons. It was a bizarre relationship, conducted from the start in the glare of publicity. The couple met in a Milanese nightclub in 1989, but Koons left for New York almost immediately. Their courtship continued by fax and phone, and mostly through interpreters, since Staller spoke little English and Koons no Italian. But the artist was unfazed. "Ilona and I were born for each other," he announced. "She's a media woman. I'm a media man. We are the contemporary Adam and Eve." To emphasise the comparison, his exhibit at the 1991 Venice Biennale consisted of a number of life-sized images – photomurals and wooden figures – of he and Staller naked and making love.

At the end of 1991, Staller announced her retirement from politics and also her pregnancy. She had also agreed with Koons that she would give up porn. Then, unexpectedly, at the start of a 1992 London showing of Koons' Venice work, titled "Made in Heaven," the couple decided to divorce, Koons citing "differences between our cultural and social standing." Insiders on the art scene, such as British artist Peter Blake, who had been cynical about the union, seeing it "a pretty ludicrous wedding by any standards" and "a marriage for publicity and exhibitionism," were unsurprised, simply suspecting another marketing ploy in the competitive international art business.

For La Cicciolina and for her profession, the liaison had also been profitable, representing a significant social advance. Like scores of *grandes horizontales* before her, she had risen above sex and above her trade to become a possession of history and art. What had once been a secret cinema was becoming thoroughly public. Renegades no longer, some of its performers, like certain sportsmen, had begun to emerge as individuals, and, in some cases, archetypes. As El Cordobes and Muhammad Ali were significant even to people who had never attended a *corrida* or a boxing match, so La Cicciolina and Linda Lovelace had entered the consciousness of people who had never seen a porn film.

Jeff Stryker modelling clothes for Gaultier, Ilona Staller running for office and Claudine Beccarie discussing the reality of porn performance were all aspects of the same process. One might have expected this deconstruction of their image to neutralise the effectiveness of porn performers, but the effect was, if anything, the opposite. In the apotheosis of that process whereby stag film audiences had tried to discern familiar faces or personalities behind the anonymous film performers, the porn stars, like sexual partners who enter into a consensual fantasy, became, by revealing their private selves, even more erotically stimulating to their audience.

Staller played on the new frankness with a bizarre stage act. Stalking near-nude round a set featuring Gothic lighting effects and giant diabolic images, she alternated four-square songs in her little-girl voice (they sound like Calvinist hymns fed through an electronic beat box) with homilies on politics and sex. Men were invited on stage to examine her body, fondle her, even fuck her – not, as in the standard sex show, for erotic effect, but to emphasise that she was as human as they.

In the US, Ellen Steinberg, aka Annie Sprinkle, independently presented a similar show. With her partner Veronica Vera, Steinberg/Sprinkle, Gerald Damiano's longtime girlfriend and star, left porn in the Eighties to re-launch herself as a performance artist. Initially the process was therapeutic, "to heal and transform my life." For a piece called "A Hundred Blow Jobs," she mimed fellatio with a dozen dildoes. "I played a tape of all the abusive remarks I'd heard, like 'Suck it, you bitch!' and I sucked on all these different dildoes. I'd cry and gag and really get in touch with the pain each time. After a dozen times I would no longer cry or gag – because I had *transformed* and *exorcised* that demon."

These pieces metamorphosed into a stage show in which Sprinkle talked about her porn life. Like Staller, she spread her legs on the edge of the stage and invited the audience to come forward to examine her vagina and cervix, a way of "demystifying" the female body. The show included slides that quantified the total length of the penises she had sucked in her career (approximately equivalent, she estimated, to the height of the Empire State Building) and broke down her motives for entering porn into a "pie chart" graphic. Money occupied a third, followed by "Didn't Know What Else I Wanted To Do" and "Love and Attention." The wedge given to 'Sex' was almost invisible. In 1993, a respected artist, she was still presenting the show, though only to audiences of women or men dressed as women.

When Marilyn Chambers made *Insatiable II* in 1980, she could have expected it to play in most of what producer David Friedman, chairman of the Adult Film Association of America, claimed were the 894 adult cinemas across the United States. In 1981, sex films accounted for $500 million in admissions, 17% of the income of the entire American motion picture industry. An estimated 2.5 million people each week paid about $5 to see an X-rated film. But in 1983, attendances at adult cinemas began to slide. Between 1984 and 1988, four hundred closed. Many of those that survived switched to a softer art house policy. If he had owned any X-rated cinemas, Al Goldstein told *Screw* readers succinctly, he would sell them for parking lots.

Reasons for the slump were varied. Gay Talese nailed one of them: "If there was a legitimate grievance against [sex movies] it was that the box office's admission fee of five dollars per customer was too high a cost to pay for the inferior quality of the films, the sophomoric scenarios, the unconvincing acting even in the bedroom scenes in which the actors were constantly losing their erections and futilely trying to simulate intercourse."

Films were also costing more, driving producers into other businesses. In 1975, the five-week production of *Not Just Another Woman*, the Tina Russell film launched with a $5000 New York champagne party, cost $350,000. By 1985, the five-day shoot of *A Coming of Angels: The Sequel*, with Annette Haven, cost $720,000. The old luxuries, of being able to shoot on location or in costume, to spend hours on lighting, or to employ ambitious young girls as "fluffs" simply to hang around the set and keep the studs pleasured and eager, were no longer economical.

The 1980 Miporn raids had also chilled East Coast porn production, persuading the Mafia its money would be better invested in less obviously illegal enterprises, like restaurant linen supplies.

The intelligentsia that had supported sex films through the Seventies was also losing interest. The next wave of American cultural enthusiasm, the "Me Decade" of the Eighties, had no room for porn. What excited the yuppies was not sex but money. Sensing a waning of porn's economic power and social cachet, its long-time opponents, militant feminists, the church and the police also bore down harder. Instead of mounting federal obscenity prosecutions like those that attacked *Deep Throat*, the police concentrated on individuals, destroying them with more prosaic powers. It was a technique that had worked in the Thirties, when J. Edgar Hoover, unwilling to take on organised crime, had instead targeted lone bandits such as "Pretty Boy" Floyd and John Dillinger and hunted them down in the full glare of publicity.

The producers of *Deep Throat* and its star Harry Reems were the first and most visible of these victims. His 1974 arrest and 1976 conviction blighted his career. Even though Reems' sentence was later overturned, Federal prosecutor Larry Parrish attempted to extract from the defendants in the *Deep Throat* case some of its $4 million costs, so enmeshing the actor in legal fees that he was unable to work. He retained Alan Dershowitz, who rallied a glittering array of showbiz greats in defence, including Jack Nicholson, Mike Nichols, Stephen Sondheim and Gregory Peck. Reems' conviction was reversed on appeal but he made no films for six years, accumulating massive tax debts and a dependency on cocaine and alcohol. In 1980, he appeared as "Bruce Gilchrist" in a low-budget rape revenge thriller with no sex scenes called *Demented* (Arthur Jeffreys). Resurfacing in porn in 1982 with *Society Affair*, he made several brief pseudonymous or anonymous appearances, becoming an increasingly disagreeable member of the LA porn fraternity. Jerry Butler, working on *Marilyn Chambers' Private Fantasies #6* in 1985 was distracted from his work in part by Chuck Traynor's gun-toting presence on the set but more by a furious Reems interrupting the shoot to demand his pay from the director. Mainstream director Harley Cokeliss, visiting an LA police station around the same time, encountered Reems there. He was manacled to a steel bench in a holding cell, raging, "Don't you know who I *am*?"

After spells in prison and mental institutions, Reems drifted to Utah, where he was arrested a number of times for assault and battery. Finding himself drunk in Park City, Utah, a tiny ex-silver mining town of five thousand people mainly known as the site of Robert Redford's Sundance Film Festival, and unable to remember how he got there, he entered an alcohol dependency programme.

Linda Lovelace, in part with her books, shrewdly distanced herself from the film, and avoided prosecution. After abandoning porn, she tried various projects, including the dismal comedy *Linda Lovelace for President* (Claudio Guzman, 1975) and a play called *My Daughter's Rated X*, which closed in Las Vegas during try-outs. A starring role in the 1975 film, *Laure*, shot in the Philippines, fell through when (Lovelace claims) sex scenes were gratuitously inserted into the script. The role was taken over by Emmanuelle Arsan, the actress/writer whose book *Emmanuelle* was the basis of Just Jaeckin's 1974 film. Recovered from a liver transplant and breast surgery (which she blamed on silicone augmentation), Lovelace married a New Jersey salesman named Marchiano and retired into suburban seclusion.

John Holmes engineered his own destruction, subtly aided by the forces of the new repression. In 1980 and 1981, he featured in Marilyn Chambers' lavish *Insatiable* and *Insatiable II*, playing her publicist and, inevitably, lover. He was at the top of the porn heap. He was also freebasing cocaine, an expensive habit he shared with a number of Hollywood fast-laners richer than himself. Julia Phillips, producer of *Close Encounters of the Third Kind*, who was also into freebase at the time, and who would lose her entire income from the film to the drug, noted, "From November [1979] until the end of January [1980] I spent $120,000 on cocaine."

Holmes didn't have that sort of money. To service his habit, he became involved with a ring of Los Angeles drug dealers and burglars known as the Wonderland Gang. Holmes hung out with them and ran errands in return for coke. Early in 1981, the gang robbed dealer Eddie Nash after Holmes helped them evade the house's security. In retaliation, on 1 July, in Laurel Canyon, Nash and his bodyguards murdered four of the gang, forcing Holmes to witness them beaten to death with an iron pipe. Arrested, Holmes refused to testify against Nash, fearing revenge, and was jailed. When Nash was himself imprisoned on drug charges, however, Holmes changed his mind, gave evidence, and was released.

According to the legend, Holmes, after prison, had to play in gay porn to raise money, and this hastened his physical decline. He was certainly furiously active in the last few years of his life. In 1985 alone, in addition to a quickie video called *Coming Holmes/Hung Like a Horse*, made to cash in on his reappearance, and the compilation *John Holmes and the All Star Sex Queens*, he appeared with Harry Reems in *The Grafenberg Spot* and *Rub Down*, played in *Lust in America* and *Stormy*, and two Miles Kidder films, *WPINK-TV* and *Those Young Girls*, the latter with the up-and-coming Ginger Lynn and Traci Lords. That same year, Holmes tested HIV positive. "My cock is my responsibility," he boasted in *Around the World with Johnny Wadd*. "I must use it. Fortunately I can fuck four or five hours a day, but I'm still looking for that special woman who can make my cock disappear in her mouth, cunt and ass." He died in 1988, of colon cancer, presumed to be AIDS-related, still looking. He asked to be cremated, but only after friends had inspected his body and confirmed it was intact. "He didn't want any part of him ending up in a jar," said one. His ashes were scattered over the Pacific.

But the Holmes legend thrives, driven by people such as Christopher Walken, who was eager to play Holmes. "Holmes ends up," says his potential director Abel Ferrara, "he's fucked 10,000 people, still married to the same girl, wanted for murder, a junkie, AIDS victim, king of the porn industry... Walken *relates* to this. That's what Hollywood does to you, man. Thirty-five years in show business does that to you. Walken's obsessed with him! Of all the characters he wants to play, he wants to play John Holmes the most. It's really bizarre."

When Ronald Reagan's Meese Commission on Pornography urged local and state police to move against porn, the law found it easier to act against individuals rather than organisations, and to find pretexts outside the hazy obscenity laws to do so. New York's S&M clubs such as The Mine Shaft were closed for offences against the health and liquor regulations. The owner of Plato's Retreat was jailed for tax evasion. Porn cinemas and sex shops all over America suddenly found themselves facing problems with fire regulations, or accusations that prostitutes solicited on or near their premises.

Since it was not illegal to sell or rent porn in California, merely to produce it, police harried filmmakers by targeting performers. If they recognised someone they had arrested for a dope or prostitution offence as a porn actor, they would offer immunity in return for testimony against their producers. In 1985, in such a case, producer Harold Freedman was given a three-year jail sentence by a Californian court. The charge wasn't obscene publishing, notoriously difficult to prove, but "pandering" – procuring a woman for an immoral act, i.e., making a porn film.

"It's a grey area," says Bill Rotsler.

> Not black and not white. Is [porn] illegal? It depends how you interpret the law. So what they do is, they harass you. They arrest you, cost you a lot of lawyers' fees, and then you're never convicted. They go for pandering. They try a lot of things they know are not going to work. And they know it's not going to work. But what they're trying to do is make it so difficult for you, and so costly to stay in operation,

that a lot of people – actors and producers
– go out of business.

Whatever the legality of the system, it was effective. In 1987, *Time* reported that "porn theatres and other sex emporiums – bookstores, peep shows and strip joints – have fallen on hard times. Manhattan had 121 such outlets a decade ago. Now there are only 42 in all of New York City. There are now about fewer than 300 porn theatres in the US, half the number of a decade ago."

Hollywood also played its part in destroying X-rated cinema by co-opting some of its more desirable features. As censorship became more liberal, the mainstream producers who had lost their nerve in the early Seventies when prestigious porn projects such as *Blue Movie* were on offer, invested, albeit gingerly, in films that would a decade before have earned the sobriquet of *sophistiqué soft*. The doyen of this field was Zalman King, who began as an actor in low-budget alternative films in the Sixties, including *You've Got To Walk It Like You Talk It or You'll Lose the Beat*, a softcore porn comedy by Peter Locke that also featured Allen Garfield, Robert Downey and Richard Pryor. King graduated to production on the films of Alan Rudolph while trying to crack the majors as writer/director.

With his wife Patricia Knop he wrote a script from the controversial novel *9½ Weeks* about the brief sadomasochistic relationship of a rootless New York art gallery manager and a decadent millionaire. Unable to raise money on his name, King sold the screenplay to MGM/UA and British director Adrian Lyne, then hot after the success of *Flashdance*. Lyne attracted Kim Basinger and Mickey Rourke to the film, and turned *9½ Weeks* into a sort of New York *Emmanuelle*, an approach King was to adopt with the films that he wrote and directed himself.

Moving from Rourke's minimalist all-black apartment to the clutter of SoHo, the film played on the exoticism of New York life and the imagined corruption just under its surface. Some scenes were imaginatively erotic, such as Basinger masturbating while watching slides of classic paintings in her empty gallery or stripping to Joe Cocker's grating performance of Randy Newman's fetishist hymn *You Can Leave Your Hat On*. Others were amusing, such as her blindfold force-feeding by Rourke to the frantic rock tune *I Like Bread and Butter*, though some, especially Basinger's unconvincing attempt to play a man, complete with false moustache, and a sex scene in an alley during a rainstorm, with photogenic rats in the shadows watching with Hollywood aplomb, tipped into the absurd.

Two Moon Junction.

Two Moon Junction, King's first directorial credit, was a piece of rural erotica. High born southern belle Sherilyn Fenn runs off with the randy carnival man (Richard Tyson) who breaks into her house to take a shower. A similar erotic shower scene turned up in King's *Wild Orchid* in 1990, where an innocent girl from the US observes a black couple making love under a broken water pipe in a ruined Rio building. King's greatest success, *Wild Orchid* resuscitated Mickey Rourke as another shadowy money man, this time operating in Brazil and sporting flamboyant outfits and a fashionable two-day beard. The production dramatised the nervousness with which Hollywood, and especially its stars, still viewed erotic films. Brooke Shields had been tested for Emily, the innocent who is sexually educated by Rourke while on a visit to Rio, but refused to strip for the camera. Anne Archer, who was to have played her hustling boss (and rival for Rourke's body) left the film over its sex scenes, to be replaced by Jacqueline Bisset.

Rourke, who had casting approval, pushed hard to have his mistress, model Carré Otis, play Emily. Though he had just had his cheekbones enhanced by plastic surgery and was obviously in pain, Rourke co-operated so vigorously in the sex scenes with Otis that it was generally assumed they were actually fucking. Pirated footage and illicit stills circulated to magazines such as *Playboy*, leading to lawsuits but also to useful publicity. Rourke says today that the film was "not artistically satisfying." King went on to make *Blue*, about another innocent in the steamy south, this time an apprentice whore in a brothel who, improbably, escapes to enter high school, only to fall in love with a fellow student who was one of her clients. The film flopped, a signal that Hollywood felt it had exhausted the vein.

Boosting his 1984 film *Body Double*, Brian de Palma bragged it would be Hollywood's first genuinely erotic film. On the basis of *Dressed to Kill* (1980) and *Blow Out* (1981), De Palma appeared to have all the credentials to make such a breakthrough. The erotic scenes in the former, of Angie Dickinson enjoying masturbatory rape fantasies in her shower, then being picked up at the Museum of Modern Art by a handsome stranger and seduced in the back of a cab, and of Nancy Allen as the slick call girl materialising in black lingerie in the office of psychopathic shrink Michael Caine and driving him over the brink into total mania, set benchmarks.

With *Blow Out* De Palma edged closer to the moist underside of eroticism. Allen is a dumb part-time hooker involved in a blackmail plot with the seedy Dennis Franz, and John Travolta a sound recordist for horror films. De Palma evokes brilliantly the funky milieux of both trades; Travolta assembling the track for college girl sex/splatter pictures, and Franz's office littered with curling stills of a flashlit Allen caught *in flagrante* with various paunchy punters.

Inspired by the opening scenes of *Dressed to Kill*, where Angie Dickinson was replaced in the shower close-ups by someone younger and more voluptuous, a "body double," *Body Double* tried to combine the themes of both earlier films by making one of the main characters a porn star and imposing on the porn world a glamour it never possessed in real life. Trapped in a Hitchcockian murder plot, horror film actor Craig Wasson tracks down an unwitting accomplice in the killing, porn actress Holly Body, by impersonating first a porn stud, then an apprentice producer. The ease of Wasson's acceptance for a role in the porn film is unconvincing, as is the film itself, which looks more like a rock clip, with Frankie Goes to Hollywood's hit *Relax* bawling on the sound track as Wasson is used up by a slinky female performer and ejected with the sneering comment that he "didn't know what a cum shot was."

De Palma, who wanted Annette Haven to play Holly Body, had gone to the Consumer Electronics Show in Las Vegas, where porn producers and stars, having been refused space on the main floor, were meeting people and showing their films in hotel rooms, and seen Haven in a tape. Hearing that she had retired from porn to improve her education, he tracked her down in her home in Oregon City, Oregon, and offered her the role.

Haven was bitter at the direction taken by what she, in common with many in the trade, preferred to call "adult movies" rather than "porn." Hoping to elevate its tone, she had tried becoming a producer, but her sole effort, a softcore prehistoric tale, *Once Upon a Time/Cave Women* (1977), flopped. She was cynical about the films being made in the Eighties. "For the most part I think they are crap... but unfortunately I must say that it seems to be what the public wants. For years I thought that if you gave the public quality, they would respond, but the box offices have proved me wrong. What people want to see is a stiff dick or a wet vagina. If they want to see superb acting or production values or clever dialogue, they go to Hollywood. We supply sex. Story, plot, lighting, acting are just incidental to scenes of people fucking."

Haven agreed to try out for the part of Holly. She took acting lessons but never achieved the facility to convince a studio. Holly Body was eventually played, with insinuating skill, by Melanie Griffith, who brings a business-like reality to her scenes, not to mention the real-life tattoo of a sprig of holly on her left buttock. When Wasson proposes starring her in his spurious film, she coolly lists her requirements: $500 a day, no "water sports" (i.e., enemas or "golden showers"), no S&M or anything like it, and no coming in her face. The more highly regarded appearance by Victoria Abril as a porn star in Pedro Almódovar's *Tie Me Up, Tie Me Down*, pales by comparison, though we can only guess how much more impressive Haven would have been in the sex scenes, which the film, in the great Hollywood tradition, fakes. Haven was scornful of such cop-outs. "Hollywood sex is getting harder and harder," she said. "They're trying to compete with us. Well, they'll never be able to compete with us. There is no way you can compete with actual sex."

Not all porn people who left the business in the Eighties did so under duress. Many who had entered in the post-*Deep Throat* boom of 1972/4 simply retired. Leslie Bovee, Amber Hunt, Mike Ranger, Marc Stevens, Abigail Clayton and hard-boiled Streisand-lookalike C.J. Laing all stopped filming. Jack Wrangler, who had already made the switch from gay porn to straight, left the field altogether to marry his long-time companion, singer Margaret Whiting. Marilyn Chambers announced her retirement, repeatedly. Jessie St James moved to Aspen, Col, where she had the ill fortune to become a neighbour of journalist Hunter S. Thompson. They were soon embroiled in litigation.

A few performers died. Tina Russell succumbed to cancer in 1981. She was 31. Her passing was little noted by comparison with the scandal surrounding the 1984 death of Colleen Applegate. Cheerleader Applegate ran away with her boyfriend from Farmington, Minn. to Los Angeles in 1982. She appeared over the next two years in thirty porn films, as "Callie Aimes" in *The Young Like It Hot* and *Feels Like Silk*, then as "Shauna Grant" in, among others, *Summer Camp Girls, Valley Vixen, Suzie Superstar* and *Virginia*, her last film. She earned, she claimed, $100,000 in her two-year career. Most of it, however, went on cocaine. When her lover was arrested in March 1984, Colleen, then living with her mother in Palm Springs, died from a shotgun blast in the head. She was twenty.

Jerry Butler has given a harsh picture of Grant, a humourless collaborator and joyless performer who often appeared on the set with her nose dripping blood from her membranes eroded by cocaine. She had, he said, already attempted suicide with pills before leaving home, but Butler subscribes to her mother's theory that Grant was murdered because of her involvement with a coke dealer. PBS told her story in the documentary *Death of a Porn Queen*. Her own producers weighed in, for less noble motives, with *Shauna Grant, Superstar* (1984), a compilation which, despite a sympathetic commentary, manages to avoid being too specific about her death. Finally Sandor Stern covered the story fictionally for CBS in his 1988 feature *Shattered Innocence*. The fascination, it seems, never fades.

Some porn actresses, such as Annie Sprinkle, embraced alternative lifestyles. A number of them came out of the closet as lesbians and, in one case, set up a north Californian company to produce only lesbian films. Dorothy Hundley Patton, the archetypal hard blonde of Seventies porn, better known as "Seka," relocated in Chicago and went into production.

Production values of feature film quality were no longer in fashion in the Eighties, but in 1983, in an attempt to restore them, along with the softer, more loving style of two decades before, Candida Royalle, in collaboration with her husband, director/cameraman Per Sjostedt and veteran performers Gloria Leonard, Veronica Hart, Annie Sprinkle and Veronica Vera, launched Femme Productions to create video porn for the female audience.

"Candida Royalle dares to bring to the screen the fantasies that women have been dreaming about all these years," promised Femme's publicity. "I wanted to throw out the whole formula of mainstream porn," Royalle said in an interview. Into the dustbin went the money shots, the "pink" shots, i.e, female genital close-ups, the obligatory lesbian scenes, and in general the emphasis on male sexual supremacy. Royalle rejected most porn as "entertainment aimed at satisfying the fantasies of a certain group of heterosexual men who feel the need to dominate. Our culture is in desperate need of positive sexual material. Typically, films such as *Body Heat* link sexuality and criminality. They imply that women who are highly sexual are either victims or whores, the message is that highly sexual people are bad. I want to give women back dignity."

Supporters of Femme who expected strongly-structured narratives with a feminist subtext were puzzled by the company's first productions. In a calculated appeal to the same audience that had taken Nancy Friday's 1973 collection of female masturbatory fantasies *My Secret Garden* through twenty-nine impressions, *Femme, Urban Heat* and *Christine's Secret* (all 1983/4) were largely plotless successions of sexual episodes.

Royalle's couples, in classic demonstrations of Erica Jong's ideal "zipless fuck," meet and, without preliminary conversation, make love in art galleries, discos, at photo sessions and in their own homes, with everyone from a fantasy stranger to the Avon lady, a popular figure of erotic fantasy. The episodes of *Urban Heat* share only the setting of summer in the city. Lovers lather each other with suntan oil, get carried away in a disco, and fuck in an elevator after a chance meeting. In *Christine's Secret,* the setting is rural, focusing on a country house, once the home of Christine (Carol Cross) but now managed as a hotel by Chelsea Blake.

Often the studs in Femme's films are directed to remain limp throughout foreplay, putting their partners' pleasure before their own. Disrupting the conventional order of fellatio/cunnilingus/entry/ejaculation, Femme's males withdraw and satisfy the woman before coming themselves, or occasionally ejaculate inside their partner, such as Jerry

Butler and Rhonda Jo Petty in *Femme*; startling variations on an act that often seems to have the ritual inevitability of the Mass. Royalle also insists that all performers not lovers off the set wear condoms; the only producer in the business, according to Butler, to do so.

The industry applauded *Femme's* courage but renters were not so sure. Briefly intrigued, they quickly demonstrated their preference for stories whose characters occupied familiar fetishised roles. Butler articulated the common response: "I understand the approach but I don't think romantic sex will sell. Like it or not, most men enjoy seeing raunchy, animalistic sex. A lot of women are probably the same way, even if they are afraid to admit it." The message got through to Royalle and Sjostedt. Their fourth film, *Three Daughters,* while retaining the emphasis on love over performance and foreplay rather than penetration, has a complex plot revolving around three girls, one a virgin, another going through a career decision with her prospective husband. The result, however, while marginally more tender in its sex numbers, appeared to most viewers a lethargic version of the standard porn feature. A *Time* magazine report dismissed it as "a cross between *Debbie Does Dallas* and *The Waltons,*" and summarised the plot as "three college-age sisters groping their way toward adult life, surrounded by randy and caring males, a warm emotional family and a good deal of expensive lingerie." The same report quoted X-rated distributor Steffani Martin's view of Femme and its films that 'sensitivity is wonderful, but it's not grounds for arousal'. The industry shares her scepticism.

Unlike their female colleagues, most male porn performers of the Seventies soldiered on into the Eighties, though sometimes in new guises. The "Joey Nassivera" of *Finishing School* (1976) became "Joey Civera" for *Christine's Secret* (1984) before metamorphosing into the "Joey Silvera" of *The Cat Woman* (1989). Eric Edwards, Jamie Gillis, Randy West and Paul Thomas continued to get work simply because they were better at it than younger men. With John Holmes gone, John Leslie had a corner on tall, commanding leading man roles. He preferred, however, to spend more of his time directing, a craft that also preoccupied Paul Thomas.

Another stud who moved into direction was Ron Jeremy. Squat, overweight, balding, olive-skinned, hairy as a hearth-rug, Jeremy, famously insatiable, always an improbable stunt cock, was even less impressive behind the camera. "He does as many as two [videos] in two days," said Bill Rotsler. "He's done *three* in two days. It's nothing but people on a couch. There's no plot, and usually they're not even well written. The only question you ask with these films is, 'How many times can a man have an orgasm in a day?' And that's how they time it." Jeremy was to reach the pinnacle of his career in 1994 with *John Wayne Bobbit Uncut*.

Many older male porn performers, such as Harry Reems and John Leslie, had some experience in drama or music theatre. The new generation of studs, including Tom Byron, Randy West, Marc Wallice and Jeff Stryker, emerged from modelling, TV commercials and male strip shows such as the LA club Chippendale's. These men, especially Stryker, are less actors than movers. In *The Switch Is On* (1988), first and most successful of the crossover bisexual films, Stryker performed an extended nude dance in a shower room that established him overnight as a major new star. Sex shops began selling neoprene facsimiles of Stryker's genitals, Lifelike and Guaranteed Authentically Proportioned. There was a considerable demand. His popularity was undercut, however, by the circulation of an out-takes reel which offered a glimpse of the reality of the New Porn. In the clips, Stryker is seen arrogantly refusing to acknowledge the boy he's sodomising over a dustbin, but complaining to the director that he lacks the muscle tone to give him the traction he requires. "Jeffy, Jeffy, we'll re-do it, ok?" the director wheedles from off camera.

20
New Kids on the Block

What changed porn more than any other development in its history was the video cassette.

The decline of cinema made the neighbourhood video store into a fixture of the American suburban mini-mall, along with the 7-Eleven, the dry cleaner's, the office supply shop and the frozen yoghourt bar. With cardboard "standees' ' outside and Hollywood posters stuck against the windows, these stores became scaled-down goosed-up versions of the old neighbourhood cinemas, long since razed or turned into furniture emporia. Except on special occasions when they visit a multiscreen in one of the satellite shopping centres, most American kids will never know the excitement of that transit from light to dark, from public world to private that used to be an essential part of the cinema experience. For them, watching a movie will always mean choosing from ceiling-high racks filled with glossy videotapes.

The arrival of the VCR solved at a stroke many of the porn film industry's problems with censorship and the law. Video shops offered producers a new marketing structure that by-passed cinemas. Reformers who'd felt confident at picketing an X-rated theatre were powerless to enter the living rooms of Middle America. Production costs plunged, so output could increase. The resulting technological shift caused seismic changes in the video world. "Sex not only sells technology, it promotes it," noted Gavin Hills of the London *Observer*. "In the great Betamax versus VHS war of the early Eighties, VHS triumphed over Sony's superior Betamax video recording format. There are various ideas about why this happened, but one of the more intriguing is the nipple theory. It proposes that since one of the most popular uses of the video recorder was in showing porn, and the bulk of video porn available was on VHS, then it was inevitable that VHS would triumph over Betamax."

Video radically changed the demographics of porn. Despite Annette Haven's hopes for a family audience, the female turnout for adult movies in the cinema had been negligible, and couples equally so. However, 33% of adult video borrowers were male/female couples. After that came men alone (26%), women alone (21%), male couples (12%) and female couples (8%). By the early Nineties, about 300 video porn cassettes were being issued every year in the United States. Distribution ranged from 10,000 copies to 50,000 for a big hit. Budgets hovered between $70,000 and $200,000, though companies such as Video-X-Pix produced films for as little as $15,000, merchandising them to shops for $20 and $25 a copy, as against the more standard $40 and $50. Even conservative estimates put the total annual value of the industry at around $3 billion. 70% of that was generated from the San Fernando Valley.

If video was a bonanza for the audience, it was a disaster for some producers and performers, in particular those who adhered to the old-fashioned cottage industry values of porn. "[Video] wouldn't be bad for the industry," Annette Haven said in 1984, "if you could make your money off video. But you really can't because most of the tape stores buy one tape and they rent it until the stupid thing is in ribbons, and everyone copies it, so your actual sales of video tapes as opposed to rentals aren't that high."

Throughout the Sixties and Seventies, small producers such as Bill Rotsler who worked on film rather than video had adjusted to each change in the trade, but with increasing difficulty. "In those days the labs were very edgy about that sort of thing," Rotsler says.

> And what they would do is make an inter-negative, then give you back your original. And the inter-negatives were kept, in this particular lab, at the home of one of the employees, so the cops could never find anything. One morning, this guy, who had scores of these inter-negatives at home in a closet, didn't show up for work. Come

> Tuesday, they needed some negatives. So someone went over there, and found he hadn't been seen for several days. And there were something like three hundred films that had disappeared, along with him. I knew that I was going to be out there trying to sell my picture in competition with someone who hadn't paid any more for his than the cost of a print. So I quit.

He wasn't the only one. Bill Osco, once LA's golden boy of porn, also drifted out of a business increasingly dominated by newer and more ruthless elements. In 1976 he produced a porno version of *Alice in Wonderland*, after which he sank into the ooze of exploitation filmmaking, producing the low-budget horror film, *The Being* (1980, released 1983) in which he co-starred, as "Rexx Coltrane," with his then-wife Jackie Kong, and *Night Patrol*, yet another spoof of the popular *Police Academy* series, this time directed by Kong, and with puzzled appearances by Linda Blair of *The Exorcist* and famous midget actor Billy Barty.

The Mitchells Brothers were no less jaded than Rotsler and Osco by the new shape of the business. "What's the point?" Artie demanded in 1987 when asked about production plans. "You make a video movie and the Koreans take it in the back room and dub ten copies." There was talk of breaking up a business empire already fraying at the edges. Artie, a heavy drinker and drug user, became increasingly unstable. "I always thought the Mitchell brothers were immortal," Marilyn Chambers said, "but Artie lived on the screaming edge of insanity, and that can never last forever."

Throughout the Eighties, the Mitchells had continued to act as if the Sixties were still going on. Old loyalties survived. When Harry Reems, almost destroyed by vice charges, tax problems and dependency on cocaine and alcohol, was reduced to anonymous guest shots, usually wearing heavy make-up and in a clearly unresponsive state, the Mitchells starred him in 1985 with the equally discredited John Holmes in *The Grafenberg Spot* and gave their appearance wide publicity.

They were also the first porn producers to campaign against AIDS and encourage safe sex. In their 1986 *Behind the Green Door: The Sequel*, a near-carbon copy of the first film in its second half, everyone wears condoms and there are frequent and visible displays of pro-Safe Sex propaganda. Gloria is played this time by Artie's mistress of the time, Elisa Florez, aka 'Missy Manners', billed in some films as 'The Republican Porn Star' because she had once worked as an aide to California politician Orrin Hatch. Florez is seen rolling condoms onto the penises of her trapeze lovers. When the satyr appears, complete with Pan pipe, horns and hairy haunches, his erect penis is also very visibly covered with a condom. Aubrey Beardsley must have been spinning in his grave.

The Mitchells were one of the last of the porn pioneers to survive into the Nineties. When their destruction came, however, it was not from outside but within the family. In May 1991, Artie was shot dead at his home in the town of Corte Madera, north of San Francisco. Jim Mitchell, found nearby with a .22 rifle, was charged with his murder. With both a bang and a whimper, the summer of love had come decisively to a close.

Video made Los Angeles the capital of a new centralised porn industry Some producers were established names, such as Anthony Spinelli, Bruce Seven and Ron Sullivan, aka 'Henry Pachard'. Spinelli produced and distributed his own films, but most preferred to sell their tapes to distributor/producers such as VCA, Vivid Video, Caballero Control Corporation and X-Citement. Low budgets and high potential profits attracted a mixed group to the porn world. Many self-styled producers were ignorant first-timers out to make a quick buck. "Most of them hadn't a clue as to what they were doing," says Bill Rotsler. "These kind of guys – they'd never made a porn film before. The fact that a woman will take off her clothes turns him on. They were producing junk." Cost-cutting on these starvation productions often led to almost entirely male casts. In one such masterpiece, three men screw three women on all fours facing the camera while three surplus studs sit naked on the couch behind them, mechanically masturbating in unison, like victims of galloping satyriasis waiting their turn in a doctor's office.

Cheap video porn also became a showcase for the stranger fetishes: giant breast and obesity compilations, the golden shower and enema films, the dwarf performers, transitional transexuals with artificial breasts but male genitalia which hormone injections have rendered incapable of erection, and amputees like Long Jeanne Silver, who penetrated women and sodomised men with a stump of a leg from which the foot was removed during childhood.

The first modern porn actresses such as Marilyn Chambers and Annette Haven were products of the late Sixties sexual revolution. Mostly models and strippers, they never shook off the residual prudery of a more repressive society. The performances of more elegant actresses such as Haven are invested with a visible disdain. There was little of that among performers of the late Eighties and early Nineties such as Traci Lords, Hyapatia Lee and Ginger Lynn. Schoolgirls in the Sixties, raised with TV, rock and the pill, they brought to their performances an edge and a danger their mothers could never match. There was a calculation about them. They stretched the envelope of what was permissible to say and do, how it was desirable to look, to behave. Old-timers found their eccentric style disconcerting. "Their nails are so long," growled Bill Rotsler.

> And their make-up is so elaborate. And they spend so damn much time shaving their pubic hair. Now I understand why a girl wearing a bikini would kinda trim it up around the edges, but they shave it into Band-Aid strips and heart shapes. There's one woman, Laurel Canyon, who's shaved it up, square, about halfway to her navel!

> It doesn't look like the top part of her pubic
> hair at all. It looks like Hitler's moustache.

Hyapatia Lee made her first film, *The Young Like It Hot*, in 1983. Strikingly beautiful, with night-black hair flowing to her waist, she brought a sort of savagery to porn cinema. Except for black performers such as Angel Kelly and the grotesquely trashy Cuban Vanessa del Rio, racial minorities feature little in American porn. Lee, who co-wrote and produced most of her own films, played up to the rarity of her darker skin and exotic features by casting herself in tough, assertive roles. Typically she's a businesswoman who employs sexual gymnastics to save a telephone switching office (*The Young Like It Hot*), dance studio (*Let's Get Physical*), night club or model agency; roles rare in a field where the standard female is usually a grovelling submissive. "Hyapatia Lee?" said one Los Angeles video shop operator. "She has a stronger woman quality than a lot of the stars. She's very popular. She's definitely one of the top ones."

Hyapatia Lee.

Hyapatia's collaborator and, in the early days, co-performer, was her husband Bud, an ex-dinner theatre actor from the same town, whose mother was in business with Bud's mother. Hyapatia started on the striptease and beauty contest circuit, was twice "Miss Nude Galaxy," then went into movies in 1983 with Bud as her manager, promoter and producer.

Unlike most porn performers, Lee didn't live in Hollywood but in her native Indiana. She and Bud also had two children. Jerry Butler, however, has revealed a different side of the Lee relationship: "She and [...] Bud invited me up to their hotel room. We talked as she sat there crocheting. I knew they were swingers and was getting tense because Bud kept suggesting that I fuck his wife – with him watching. Lying on the bed, Bud finally told me very bluntly. 'Maybe you'd like to screw my wife, but I normally like to eat the guy's ass out while he fucks her.'"

The danger and strangeness of Hyapatia's films emerge in *Saddle Tramp* (1988), the porn Western that was her first film after giving birth to her son Cochise. Still with clothing draped over her waist to hide the post-partum slackness, she's about to be fucked by Randy West. As his erection grows, she smilingly squeezes her breast. Milk spurts startlingly over his erection, and she takes it in her mouth. Lee also, like many parents, had the birth of her children videotaped. Robert H. Rimmer, noting this is *The X-Rated Video Guide III*, wondered aloud if these too would find its way into one of her releases.

If there's an emblem of the Eighties porn world comparable to Marilyn Chambers in the Seventies, it's Traci Lords. Lords, however, had none of Chambers' humour or personality. A parody sex queen, she embodied mindless carnality. Her expressionless, unblinking stare, toneless voice and heavily lipsticked mouth, lower lip swollen as if repeatedly bitten, suggested the beady-eyed, infantile greed of a baby for the teat.

In September 1984, *Penthouse*, in an issue that also offered a layout of Hyapatia Lee, plus nude shots of the recently elected Miss America, Vanessa Williams, featured

Lords as its centrefold Pet of the Month. Its caption claimed that "Traci Lords has spent her 22 formative years in Nevada, Florida, South Caroline, and now Redondo Beach, California." In fact, Lords was only sixteen and had been born Nora Kuzma in Steubenville, Ohio. She ran away from home at thirteen, appeared in her first porn film a year later and was freebasing cocaine so lavishly that, as she says, "I lost three years of my life."

For a decade, Lords was one of the most active and popular of porn stars. Her mother, Patricia Briceland, later testified that she saw little of her daughter once she became a star. "She started getting very hard, very tough after she started making movies." Briceland claimed she threatened to blow the whistle on Traci because of her age. "She told me if I did that, the people she was involved with would kill her. She told me to keep my mouth shut, or I would get her in terrible trouble."

Arrested in 1989 as part of the FBI crackdown on porn (and the illegal copying of and distribution of feature films on video, a lucrative sideline of the porn business), Traci made a deal. What followed was a shock to a porn industry accustomed to a shared solidarity, and, for outsiders, a window onto the ruthlessly competitive distribution end of porn. Rubin Gottesman, head of X-Citement Video, was convicted on three charges of distributing child pornography, i.e. Traci Lords films. US District Judge David Kenyon was in no doubt that Gottesman knew or at least strongly suspected that her birth certificate was faked. It was equally clear, claimed Gottesman's lawyer Stanley Fleishman, that Lords was sophisticated beyond her age, and that the case had little to do with morality. Instead, it was, he said, 'a studied, successful coup' by Lords intended to make her a lot of money. Not only did the Internal Revenue Service and the FBI agree to reduce charges against her in return for testimony against her associates. Since the conviction rendered every film she made before she was eighteen illegal, she had also, charged Fleishman, "at one stroke eliminated from the marketplace all the films where she had no royalty interest, leaving on the market only one of her films; a film on which she received a royalty of $10 per tape which yielded her a cool million dollars, with the royalties still rolling in."

Traci Lords.

Traci, rich on the profits of her own productions such as the first, *Traci I Love You*, and *Traci Takes Tokyo*, left porn for a straight career, playing in the horror film *Out of This World* and minor roles in TV. The *Hollywood Reporter* led its review with, "The answer is yes. She *can* act." In John Waters' spoof Sixties teen musical *Cry Baby* (1990) with Johnny Depp, she played a supporting role alongside another headline figure, kidnap heiress Patty Hearst. In 1995, she was making guest appearances in the TV soap opera *Melrose Place*. *Vanity Fair* published a charitable estimate of her chances in the mainstream. "No actress," it said, "has successfully crossed over from hardcore to Hollywood films before, but in Lords' favour are her age and the fact that the stigmata aren't quite what they used to be."

Lords also diversified into pop, recording an album called *A Thousand and One Fires*. Taking a leaf from Linda Lovelace's book, she tweaked her image towards that of the abused child and victim of the crime-ridden world of porn, telling journalists she had been raised as a near-hillbilly in the mountains of Appalachia, and to have been brought to California by a "timid cowering mother" who finally had the nerve to escape a drunken father. A song on her album, *Father's Field*, purports to describe him raping her when she was ten. A columnist in *Hot Times*, the porn trade paper, could barely suppress his indignation at her new career. "Can you believe it? There I am at the MTV Music Awards and who gets up to accept an award for Guns and Roses? It was none other than the little Hussy known as Traci Lords! *Traci Lords*! Gimme a break. She's pumped us and now she's pumpin' the music world."

21
Candid Ginger

An 8 a.m. call in the rundown Los Angeles suburb of Venice isn't everyone's idea of movie glamour – but then producer Roger Corman has never been much concerned with people's expectations. It might have been a converted lumber yard to everyone else, and the weathered "Miracle Pictures" sign over the gate a prop left over from *Hollywood Boulevard*, made here thirteen years before. But to Corman, Hollywood's king of starvation cinema, it was his current studio, Concorde, and let nobody forget it.

Tall, impassive and composed, Corman stalked through the chaos of preparations for *Hollywood Boulevard* 2. He looked as close as he ever does to content. And why not? The bleary-eyed group in the shed that passed for a hospitality suite, dunking doughnuts in polystyrene coffee cups, was in fact a cross-section of Hollywood's second-string glitterati.

They had turned out to play extras in a party scene in *Hollywood Boulevard II* as a tribute to the man who, if he didn't give them their start, at least booted their waxing or waning careers when they needed it. Actor Bradford Dillman drifted by. He nodded to two guys who graduated with honours from this Termite Terrace more than a decade ago. Once Corman's Head of Publicity, Jon Davison has since produced *Airplane* and two *Robocop* films. His companion, Joe Dante, who co-directed the first *Hollywood Boulevard* here in 1976, with Allan Arkush, went on to *The Howling*, *Explorers*, *Innerspace*, two *Gremlins* films and *Matinee*.

The yard fills up quickly. Since everyone is some sort of celebrity, everyone covertly eyed new arrivals, looking for that other reality behind the face. A dark-eyed teenage siren turns out to be Sidney Greenbush who, from three years old to eight or so, tumbled down the hill at the start of *The Little House on the Prairie*. But what about the tiny girl with dirty-blonde hair who was actually starring in *Hollywood Boulevard II*? In her tight white dress and too-large white shoes, she looked oddly familiar, but out of context. Belatedly I consulted the press release, to find she was porn star Ginger Lynn, going straight as "Ginger Lynn Allen." I just didn't recognise her with her clothes on.

If you're meeting an X-rated movie queen, the logical venue is the kind of house where adult movies are usually shot. Tucked back in the Hollywood Hills in wooded Nichols Canyon, the home of veteran agent Ruth Webb is that sort of place: roomy, old-fashioned, secluded. These days, Webb mostly represents Hollywood's geriatric semi-retired performers. The much-recycled Mickey Rooney is a client. So is singing star Anne Blyth. However, Webb, a lady Of A Certain Age and, to judge from a tightness in the skin about the cheekbones, somewhat recycled herself, has only one client who has risen from the louche world of pornography.

Waiting for Ginger, who is fashionably late, Webb offers a guided tour of the house. Unexpectedly it is filled with raccoons. Toy ones, mostly, though two live specimens lurk out by the pool. There's a coon loo, with the furry rascals painted on the seat, and a living room with coon cushions. In a coon bedroom, carpeted in polar bear white, drifts of stuffed coons lap the vast white bed. One even has a head wrapped in white bandages. "A gift from a friend," rasps Webb coquettishly, "after my last face-lift."

Ginger whines up in her Porsche, flushed, but only, she assures everyone, from her karate class. Pert in a green and black spandex mini, but with unaccountably bare legs that look bony and unprotected below the short skirt, she is articulate, funny, self-assured, yet with a flinty glint behind the Barbie doll bouffant and automatic smile.

Most porn stars come from related fields – stripping, modelling, dancing. Many share a physical type: tall, slim, languid, with a stripper's haughty stare. In this company, Ginger stands out. She's tiny. She was never a stripper and, before her X-rated career, never even appeared professionally on stage. By temperament, however, she seems made for the X-rated movie trade. Yet in February 1986, she finished her last erotic movie. Today, she's "straight," with non-sex performances in almost a score of mainstream pictures, sufficiently sanitised to be invited as a guest to the 1993 London Film Festival to introduce her newest film, *Bound and Gagged*.

Why, at only twenty-six, abandon a promising career? And what brought her to it in the first place? Had she show business ambitions?

"I'd always put on plays in my garage," Ginger admits. "I'd sing and I'd dance for the neighbourhood children. And I'd charge them ten cents to get in. But I'd never thought of being an actress. I liked being in front of people. I liked entertaining, being the life of the party." She seems a little wistful. "I liked the recognition." And the money too, presumably.

Ginger managed a record shop in Rockford, and the owners offered her a job running their Los Angeles branch. Once she was in Los Angeles, however, the smallness of her salary convinced her she had to change jobs. "I found out quickly that I couldn't live at the beach on that kind of money," she says and, looking for quick cash, answered a newspaper advertisement for figure models.

Such ads still appear in LA's lifestyle weeklies, inserted mainly by the two major agents of this field, Jim South of World Model Agency or Reb Sawitz, who operates as Pretty Girl International. *GIRLS! Earn $50 a Day as a Figure Model. No exp. Needed!* Most are come-ons for adult video. But in Ginger's case, the agency, South's World Model, also handled magazine work.

Ginger says she had never posed nude before. "But my parents had raised me in a very open environment. *Penthouse* and the nicer men's magazines were around the house, and nudity was never something bad or taboo." In fact this, like most accounts of her childhood, is dubious. Her parents divorced when she was 13. She grew up with her grandfather. There is no doubting, however, her instant success as a model. The day she visited World Model, she had some shots accepted for *Penthouse*. She worked for the next seventeen days straight, and was soon earning (she says) $1500 a day. The experience could have been sleazy, but she fell into quality company. "[Photographers] Suze Randall and Stephen Hicks and Ed Holzman were good-looking and friendly and intelligent. I mean, Suze has three children!"

The next step into porn was doing stills for Larry Flynt's *Hustler*, editorially committed to "pink" and "split beaver" layouts, bondage and hardcore. "They took me to this leather store," Ginger recalls, "and were buying ropes and spikes and things to pinch. I went home and broke down in tears and called my agent hysterically and said 'I can't do this.' But the money keeps coming and you get pulled into it a little more, and things you thought were bad at the beginning seem a little less bad. I did a layout with another girl, just a simulation. I did a simulation with a boy one day. People were asking me to do hardcore stills, and I asked my boyfriend what he thought and he said 'Well, let's do it together.' So we did. And that was the first time."

So how did Ginger migrate from the relatively chaste world of men's magazines to X-rated videos? She claimed a semantic misunderstanding began it. She had been modelling for some months when an agent asked if she was interested in doing "commercials." Not realising that "commercial" is X-rated movie shorthand for a hardcore sex scene, Ginger enthusiastically agreed. "I'm from Illinois," she grinned, "and I'm going, 'Toothpaste. Yeah!' When I found out what they really meant, I said, 'I'll *never* do that. I'm not that kind of girl.'"

And she kept refusing – for six months. She might, she said, have continued to do so had she not walked into the agency and seen a beautiful auburn-haired girl in a Victorian gown, reading a script. "She had the big white hat, the umbrella, the cigarette, the whole thing," Ginger says, awed to this day. "And she was an X-rated actress! I thought, 'This girl is beautiful. She's intelligent. She's not wearing a mini-skirt and fishnets.' So I took her to lunch and picked her brain for everything I could find out about 'commercials.'" The most significant thing she learned was how profitable they could be. Performers of stamina, by hiring out for single days, or even individual scenes, can earn six figures annually. At her peak, Ginger made around $1500 a day, and $1000 for personal appearances.

But the girl warned Ginger not to sell herself cheap. "She said, 'Go in there, tell them how much you want, and stick to it. Once you back away from what you think you're worth, that's what people will think you're worth. You can pick and choose your path in this business if you're intelligent and pretty enough.'"

Ginger told South she would appear in X-movies, but at a higher price than even her stills modelling. Initially, producers laughed. But producers David and Svetlana Marsh of Collector's Video saw her potential. "OK," Ginger claims they told her. "We'll pay your price. You're the lead in the film. You choose your leading man. You're working for two weeks in Hawaii."

Faced with the reality of an X-rated career, Ginger briefly lost her nerve. She had never stripped in public before, let alone on film. "I started to think 'What am I doing? I have to take off my clothes and have sex in front of people. I can't do this.' I was crying, and I was all upset. I said, 'I don't want to get to Hawaii and realise I can't do it.' So I did a short film."

Ginger's debut took place in 1984 in a Santa Monica flat owned by a woman called Cookie. The director was Suze Randall. There was something cosy, almost domestic about the experience. Cookie bustled around, tidying up, as Ginger's nails and hair were done. She was introduced to her co-star, Tom Byron, and immediately felt better.

"Tom's my age, and he's sweet and young and healthy. He said 'Well, where're you from?', like it was a date. And he *made* it like a date. At the back of my mind, I *knew* what was supposed to happen at the end of it, but he was so nice and sweet and charming it made it a very natural thing, and it just happened. It was a very warm experience for me, my first time." Warm enough, anyway, for the producers to take Ginger to Hawaii fully confident of her abilities.

Flown out at the same time were veteran studs Jerry Butler and Ron Jeremy, who would star with Ginger in the three films made on the trip – *Surrender in Paradise*, *A Little Bit of Hanky Panky* and *Pink Lagoon*. Butler later described this Hawaiian location shoot. In his version, Ginger, far from being in control, was a "beautiful, raw gem of a woman... ready to be cut into something even more beautiful," and easy meat for the assertive studs. In their first scene, he says, "she screamed louder than any girl I've ever been with and came three times in fifteen minutes." Butler was immediately in love with her – and thus all the more disgusted to see her, in a break from shooting, fellating for fun the hairy, horny Ron Jeremy, one of porn's least prepossessing performers, known in the trade, because of his mass of body hair, as The Hedgehog. Their intimacy added to the impact of their first filmed scene together, with the tiny blonde Ginger being fucked from behind on a beach by the frankly sinister Jeremy, Beauty and the Beast brought grotesquely up to date. Butler's hopes of a long-term relationship with Ginger survived the Hawaiian shoot but not the return to LA. Turning up at LAX with an engagement ring ostentatiously wrapped in a two-metre box, he found she wasn't even on the plane.

Ron Jeremy.

Within three months of her debut, Ginger was voted Best Actress, Best Female Performer of the Year and Best New Star in the X-Rated Film Critics' Awards. When she quit porn, she had earned 24 nominations, and won six more Best Actress Awards, one of them for a sex scene between her and Jerry Butler in *Beverley Hills Cox*, conducted mainly in and on top of a red Porsche. Lit and shot as skilfully as any TV episode, it is a benchmark in the technical sophistication of porn.

"Most people would hire me for one day," Ginger says. "That was all they could afford. Sometimes for a single scene. I had a good time. I liked it." The sex remained good, but she was less happy with the dialogue scenes, which directors usually skimped. During her first year in porn, Ginger enrolled with acting coach Alan Landers at the Studio of Performing Arts. It was, she says, a revelation. "I was up on the stage, doing plays. Then I'd go to the movie set and they would hand me my script and I'd just talk. I needed more."

Ginger indulges in the usual rationalisations about porn. For the audience, it's harmless – "You want to laugh, you see a comedy. If you want to cry, you see a drama. If you want to get turned on, you see an adult movie." It may even be therapeutic. "I saved a lot of marriages," she says, with apparent sincerity. "I have tons of fan mail. Guys who are out on a ship in the Navy, doing things for our country for months and months and months. One guy wrote me he raised the flag for me every day. I inspired people. I made them get up in the morning." She laughs. "A bit early, sometimes, maybe. I made them do good things. And I *liked* doing it." Occasionally, however, there was a backlash, as with the fan who besieged her with letters and gifts, left his family and even bought her a wedding dress. In response, Ginger bought two Rottweilers.

Did she worry that her family and friends would see her on screen, and be shocked? Ginger simply dismisses that possibility. "I never thought anyone would know I did it," she says ingenuously. "I thought, 'I'm blonde now. Nobody's going to know it's me. This is Ginger Lynn, not Ginger Allen.' It was stupid. I never looked ahead. I never imagined that I would become so well known so quickly – or at all." In fact, when her father did see her in a video, he disowned her, a blow that, it is evident, still smarts.

All the best porn performers have a flair for the work. Ginger was no exception. "It was quick money," she says tersely. "It was good sex. You could choose your hours." The key is an ability to separate person and performance. Like most actresses, Ginger sees herself as two people – her real self and her screen persona. The Naughty Little Girl isn't her, she insists. "Ginger Lynn is a *character* I created. I could never do the things in real life I do on film. Never."

"There are very few people who should really be in the adult industry. It takes a certain frame of mind. You have to like yourself, like what you're doing – otherwise it's the biggest mind-fuck in the world. You have to defend yourself all the time. You have to fight for yourself. You have to believe in yourself."

By the end of her first year in adult video, the acting lessons were starting to take. Ginger by then was, like most top performers, in effect directing almost all her own scenes. Only in that way could she retain the spontaneity that was the core of her appeal.

As her ability to control her work increased, she hired her own writer, Penny Antine aka 'Raven Touchstone'. She also found a director she liked, Bruce Seven. And she favoured the same leading men; Jerry Butler, Tom Byron and the semi-retired Harry Reems. And the women? About female X-rated stars, Ginger is guarded, even bitchy. "A lot do it for the money or because their boyfriends do drugs. They do it for the wrong reasons." The contrast was evident at the first presentation ceremony she attended of the Heart-Ons. "Most of the girls spend their money on clothes. The women look on themselves as starlets. They really want to be at the Academy Awards, not the Adult Film Critics' Awards."

She did respect some pioneers of the trade, many now semi-retired and working as producers. "The only one I was really intimidated by was Seka. She's a very intelligent, very powerful woman. I didn't do a film with her. I was too intimidated." A narrowing of the eyes shows a familiar subject about to surface. "Also, she was producing it, and she couldn't match my price – that was the second reason." And, one suspects, the more important one.

What about the dark side of the X-rated world? Self-evidently, it's no picnic. "I had a lot of wonderful times and I had a lot of…" – her voice shades into a more cynical tone – "…growing experiences, which weren't always the best experiences in the world. There were times when I laughed and times when I cried."

Almost two years into her career, Ginger felt burned out. X-rated film "wasn't fun any more. I had gone to the furthest point in that segment of the industry. I'd played every character and done so many films: there just wasn't any place else to go. I felt stifled. I needed to grow. I wanted to be a character for more than two days. I wanted to create something and be involved in all the little details, and there aren't any [in adult videos]. Your creativity is instantaneous. It happens *now*. You don't go home and think about it."

The trigger for change was her romance with photographer Ed Holzman. In 1983, they moved in together. "I can be in love and play any character," says Ginger, "but to be in love and play a character who's physically making love to someone else messed with my mind."

Ginger could give Traci Lords some lessons in the problems of getting into straight films. The hurdle first was finding an agent. Ginger imitated the thousands of hopefuls who mail out glossy portraits and neat resumes to every agency in town. Most agents toss blind submissions into the wastebasket. But a house guest of Ruth Webb noticed Ginger's picture and pointed out that this ingenue at least had proved she could rivet an audience. Webb took her on, and a trickle of auditions began. 'In my first year out of adult films, curiosity brought me into a lot of places. People wanted to meet Ginger Lynn. I was offered a lot of things as the girl who had two or three lines and would take her top off. That wasn't what I wanted to do. So I turned down everything the first year.'

"The first film where I got to read for a lead role was called *Wild Man*. I walked in and there's one of my favourite directors of adult films. I'd never worked for him but I'd always liked him. His name's Freddy Lincoln. I said, 'What are you doing here?' and he said, 'What are *you* doing here?' Freddy cast me as one of the three leading ladies in the film. And since then, the roles haven't stopped."

Ginger Lynn Allen and Elizabeth Kaitan in *Vice Academy 3*.

She had a brief scene in Blake Edwards' *Skin Deep* but it ended up on the cutting room floor. Her low-budget comedy *Vice Busters* was a modest success. "Three weeks between films is a long time now," she says proudly. "And the roles are getting bigger and better and more colourful, and the budgets are getting bigger."

For some actors, the moment of total acceptance as an artist is when they step onto the stage at Stratford as Hamlet, or stand, Oscar in hand, conscious for the first time, like Sally Field, that the industry really loves them. Ginger's moment was in a lower key, but no less significant for that. "The first time I realised I was really an actress was when I did a movie called *Buried Alive*," she confesses. "In the last twenty minutes of the film my hair's dead-looking, I've got circles under my eyes, I've got parched lips, I've been beat up. I look trashed. And I'm saying 'Wow, look at that. I'm ugly!'"

"If I had to do it over again," Ginger said, "I wouldn't. Say there's ten men who're right for you. Mine's narrowed down to one, because of what I've done. It's ruined... it's made my life really difficult. I'm going to have to tell my kids. No matter where I go, there'll be people who recognise me. If I get a job as a real-estate agent, there's going to be some Joe Schmo sitting next to me who's watched all my films. Only the strong survive, and I've learned from my mistakes. I guess this has been a mistake. I've made a lot of money at it. It turned out with a happy ending. Once I get out of the business I'll be a lot happier."

Ginger's relationship with Holzman didn't last. In 1990, she was "with" actor Charlie Sheen, with whom she had a small role in *Young Guns II*. She played bits bit parts in the TV series *Superforce* and Ken Russell's *Whore*, featured in *Buried Alive, Leather Jackets* and three incarnations of the *Vice Academy* series, but has yet to produce a performance that earns more than a passing mention in reviews, or fails to mention her porn past. The same appetite that drew her into sex movies continues to put her in the headlines. In December 1990, the tabloid *Globe* headlined her as Sheen's "Bisexual Gal Pal," and quoted her about her taste for swinging both ways. She had seduced her masseuse, she said. "Now she wants me to herself. I like to get girls who've never been with another woman. They enjoy it so much, they never go back to men again."

A happy ending? Maybe not so much.

www.ingramcontent.com/pod-product-compliance
Lightning Source LLC
Chambersburg PA
CBHW070131080526
44586CB00015B/1640